ABOUT THE AUTHOR

Robert Phillips quit his job as President and CEO, EMEA of Edelman, the world's largest Public Relations firm, for reasons that will become apparent as you read this book. He is the co-founder of Jericho Chambers, a progressive strategy consultancy and thinktank, and advises companies at senior level on strategy, policy, communications and trust. Robert is a Visiting Professor at Cass Business School and co-founded Jackie Cooper PR.

Robert set up his first business at the age of 21, while still at university. It marketed Italian bridalwear (don't ask). *Trust Me, PR is Dead* is his second book, but the first one his mother thinks he has published "properly".

Robert is on Twitter @citizenrobert

TRUST ME, PR IS DEAD

TRUST ME,
PR IS DEAD

ROBERT PHILLIPS

unbound

This edition first published in 2015

9 8 7 6 5 4 3 2 1

Unbound
4–7 Manchester Street, Marylebone, London, W1U 2AE
www.unbound.co.uk

Typeset by PressBooks
Cover design and illustration by Jamie Keenan

A CIP record for this book is available from the British Library

978-1-78352-084-8 (limited special edition)
978-1-78352-083-1 (trade edition)
978-1-78352-154-8 (ebook)

Printed and bound by CPI Group (UK) Ltd, Croydon, CR0 4YY

For Venetia, Gabriel and Gideon

CONTENTS

LETTER FROM UNBOUND

Dear Reader,

The book you are holding came about in a rather different way to most others. It was funded directly by readers through a new website: **Unbound**.

Unbound is the creation of three writers. We started the company because we believed there had to be a better deal for both writers and readers. On the Unbound website, authors share the ideas for the books they want to write directly with readers. If enough of you support the book by pledging for it in advance, we produce a beautifully bound special subscribers' edition and distribute a regular edition and e-book wherever books are sold, in shops and online.

This new way of publishing is actually a very old idea (Samuel Johnson funded his dictionary this way). We're just using the internet to build each writer a network of patrons. Here, at the back of this book, you'll find the names of all the people who made it happen.

Publishing in this way means readers are no longer just passive consumers of the books they buy, and authors are free to write the books they really want. They get a much fairer return too – half the profits their books generate, rather than a tiny percentage of the cover price.

If you're not yet a subscriber, we hope that you'll want to join our publishing revolution and have your name listed in one of our books in the future. To get you started, here is a £5 discount on your first pledge. Just visit unbound.com, make your pledge and type `trustm3` in the promo code box when you check out.

Thank you for your support,

Dan, Justin and John
   Founders, Unbound

DISCLAIMER

The views stated in this book are mine and mine alone. Often they are strongly expressed as I feel passionately about the issues I discuss. But that is the beauty of free speech. Where necessary, I have altered names and identifying details. Occasionally, I have used redactions (those big black block things) to ensure that the person or event is not identifiable. This is because I do not want the personal to detract from the political. The points I want to make are not based on who or what did something, but on why it was done in the first place. Hopefully this will enhance, rather than hinder, your reading experience.

CENSOR'S NOTE

"You cannot write that."

"Why not? It's the truth."

"It may well be the truth, but that doesn't mean you won't get sued."

"Isn't there a certain irony in a book about the end of PR not being able to tell the truth?"

"Yes."

Such are the perils of having a libel lawyer for a sister.

Be careful what you ask for (in this case an advance read of this book).

I owe a lot to my younger sister. For a start, she laughs at my jokes. We share the same dark sense of humour. We inadvertently provoked a giggling outbreak at our father's funeral 30 years ago. The truth is, had he been alive and not in the coffin, John would have laughed with us. But the majority of mourners, who knew us less well, were shocked. They wanted to see the truth their way. Funerals were only for sadness and tears.

Truth somehow seems to hurt, and people struggle to see and tell it as it is.

Jane and I were 19 and 21 years old at the time. Our sense of truth then would serve as an anchor for both our future careers.

Jane emailed me after reading an early draft.

"*You can't say that.*"

"Why not?"

"*Because* ▮▮▮▮▮ *is notoriously litigious.*"

"But that's exactly what happens. He always either arrives late or leaves early. Despite his success and his wealth, he is obviously desperate to get noticed."

"*It's not going in. Trust me.*"

PREFACE

Trust is a funny word. It has been used and abused to the point of exhaustion. I would gladly ban the "t-word" forever – or at least campaign for its suspension from the English language for a decade or two. CEOs and politicians have become notoriously serial offenders – living proof that trust often spoken is trust rarely earned.

And over the past ten years or so, "trust" has somehow been kidnapped by the Public Relations industry. My *alma mater*, the world's largest Public Relations firm, has placed its Trust Barometer (an annual "exploration of trust," which it unveils at the World Economic Forum at Davos every year) front-and-centre of its intellectual argument. Others sell to endless promises of trust. A quick Google search will reveal the headlines, as so-and-so or such-and-such is hired by a bank/energy firm/oil major (insert an industry of choice) to restore their particular trust deficit. But trust is not a message. It is an outcome. We must beware the PR firm that suggests otherwise.

Excited by the calamitous state of world business, many opportunists in the Public Relations industry see trust as a vital lifeline for an otherwise moribund "profession" (*please note the use of inverted commas; no pro-*

fessional qualifications are in fact required). But PR has run out of options and has missed its moment to lead. It is in terminal decline. About to be overrun and overwhelmed by the age of data, PR today is to communications what analogue was to digital at the turn of the century. I am afraid PR is dead, even though the body may still twitch for a while.

Few will mourn its passing.

* * *

CHAPTER ONE: THE DEATH OF PR
THE ONLY AGENCY WE NEED IS CHANGE

The Only Agency We Need is Change

Dan was dying.

It was October 2012 and I had come to pay my respects to one of the genuine legends – for many, the godfather – of the global Public Relations industry.

Dan Edelman, founder of the eponymous firm, had undergone major surgery only a few days before. I feared that this would be my last chance to say goodbye. I held deep affection for Dan and for his son Richard, now CEO of Edelman, my boss and a good friend.

I had flown to Chicago to pay respect and to celebrate the 60th anniversary of the firm for which I had worked for over eight years, since selling the company I had co-founded with Jackie Cooper to Edelman in 2004.

My business report was pretty straightforward. "Revenue growth is 15% year-on-year. Margin is improving. We have installed new, stellar management teams in Germany and France and headed off a major labour dispute in Russia. We continue to win awards across the region – especially in the UK and the Middle East. Spain and Italy are defying their economies and showing robust growth."

Despite Dan's frailty, and the pall that cast across us all, these were good times. We were on top of the world.

Walking through the quads and avenues of Kellogg University on that Sunday evening, I shared with Richard my deep concerns about the future of the Public Relations industry his father had helped create and shape: its failure to embrace data; its insistence on championing generalists in an age of mastery; its focus on physical expansion rather than developing the skillsets and intelligences needed to better serve clients' needs; the way it obsesses about advertising and the dreadfully-named "C-suite" (PR-speak for board-level executives), rather than focusing on groundbreaking ideas rooted in citizen truths; the building of bureaucracies rather than centres of excellence; and more. It was quite a long list. It was quite a long walk.

Richard listened intently. "Of course you're right," he said. "But we cannot change our model. It would take six years and too much disruption."

He was right, too, and I told him so. Richard's was the dilemma of many large professional services firms, who have to prioritise their own interests. Our relationship has always been an honest one. But it was there and then I decided to quit. I could not be a hypocrite. I felt like an imposter. I had fallen out of love with the industry I had spent the best part of 25 years obsessing about. I needed to call bullshit on what had become the bullshit industry. And to figure out what came next.

* * *

The modern Public Relations profession owes as much to the likes of Dan Edelman and his generation as it does to the supreme commander of the consumption fetish, Edward Bernays.

Emerging from the debris of Europe in 1945, Dan Edelman and Harold Burson returned to their native USA to found the legendary companies that bore their names, and which would sit at the vanguard of the modern PR industry for the next 50 years. They defined PR, in a slightly sub-*Mad Men* kind of way. From humble beginnings in regional US cities, they headed first to New York and DC, then to London and beyond. They span before spinning had entered the vernacular as a PR misnomer. And, in so doing, they accidentally accelerated the obsession about buying (and selling) stuff that eventually led the entire system to the brink of collapse. From its US base, the web of subtle persuasion spread both east and west.

The world had, however, gone wrong. Unchecked consumerism was turning out to be the great philosophical cul-de-sac of the 20th century – and PR signposted the way. Marketing, advertising, communications (call it what you will) had been a huge part of the problem. As the writer Vance Packard had predicted in *The Hidden Persuaders* as far back as 1957, marketers "had invaded the privacy of our minds." Worryingly, everyone was still in denial.

Professor Tom Watson sees two distinct forms of PR emerging from the 1950s onwards, the time during which consumer marketing rocketed and "publicity" effectively hijacked the title of PR and became a mainstream practice, confining Public Relations, as practised by governments and corporations, to a minority role. "PR" thus became seen as short-term, sales-led and opportunistic. "This is at the heart of the constant bickering," writes Watson, "over definitions, professional standards, measurement and evaluation."

What is clear, however, as Professor Lynda Gratton has pointed out in *The Shift*, is that we now live in exciting, revolutionary times. "There are forces at work," she writes, "that over the coming decades will destroy forever many of the old assumptions of a traditional job and career. Around the world, outdated hierarchies will crumble ... our world is changing at an extraordinary pace."

* * *

In 2012 and 2013, two terrible accidents befell garment workers in Dhaka, Bangladesh. The first involved a fire in which over 100 people were killed; the second a building collapse which claimed over 1,000 lives. Most of these were working women. Building standards, notoriously sub-standard, were inevitably to blame. Regulations were non-existent. Doors had been locked and prevented escape. Human beings were burned alive.

Many of the developed world's famous brands use the factories of Bangladesh as production hubs to minimise costs and maximise profits. One day after the 2012 fire, I received a call from ███████ ███████ the CEO of a global corporation. I had spoken with him before, but we had never met. He was after crisis counsel. In previous conversations, he had always seemed a decent bloke.

"I need some help with my chairman," he started. "He is giving me grief."

"Go on," I said, unsure about what was coming next.

"He thinks we are failing to get our message across. We are not emphasising our CSR credentials well enough." CSR: Corporate Social Responsibility, the programmes companies run to demonstrate their commitment to people, planet and society. He paused, almost embarrassed at what he had to say next.

"He wants us to go on the offensive and play up how we have been investing in local CSR initiatives. He says our communications are failing us."

"While 100 women's bodies are still smouldering?" I asked. I was struggling to contain both incredulity and temper.

"I know," he said. "Please help."

"You start with actions, not words," I said. "You do not try and spin the message and you certainly don't trumpet your CSR credentials as some kind of distraction. You get company officials out there on the ground with resources and a chequebook. These people are our responsibility. Nothing else matters right now."

"I know," he said. "But I am just not sure he gets it."

In the wake of deep human tragedy such stories were told elsewhere. Some companies rushed to flaunt their CSR credentials. They would have been better advised to tackle the substantive issues: low wages, illegal working conditions, and the artificially and "unfair trade" low prices offered to customers. The smart organisation would have been the one that immediately addressed these issues and then chose to communicate with customers and stakeholders around real and important transformational change.

The future relationship between corporation and customer needs to be more open, honest and explicit.

* * *

Jackie Cooper and I had very little of substance to report since our last meeting with the Managing Director and Sales Director of Playtex (our client, once famous for its Living Bra's "lift and separate" strapline). It was 1989.

We feared being fired – something that, in very real terms, we could ill afford. So, in the long-held tradition of PR, we began to type, and to, well, be creative.

The headline came to us in an instant: *"Eight Out of Ten Women Wear The Wrong Size Bra."* And the sub-header underlined the point: *"You Wouldn't Wear The Wrong Size Pair of Shoes."*

It may be something of an over-claim to say that this flash of inspiration set our careers on an upward trajectory – but it didn't hurt. The client loved it, a campaign was launched, further research found that eight out of ten women were in fact not fitted with the correct back or cup size – and a memorable marketing statistic was happily born.

Several years later, sitting in the office of ██████████ ████████ a legendary Fleet Street editor, we were discussing a joint promotion for a client. Underwear was again involved (it was a tabloid after all), but this time only indirectly. Said client did not manufacture knickers.

"We could do some research to launch the promotion," I offered. "Our client will happily fund it."

"Fuck the research," he said, "just make it up. Say whatever you want to say. We will print it anyway."

* * *

I had been a proud member of the PR conspiracy – conceiving strategies, ideas and campaigns that captured the popular imagination and helped fuel the hedonistic treadmill of consumption. Having proudly told the world that "eight out of ten women wear the wrong size bra" in that epiphany moment, Jackie and I later brought the infamous "Hello Boys" advertising to life for Wonderbra. Twenty years ago, there was not very much that I didn't know about women's underwear.

Other campaigns followed: some trivial, others less so. A colleague once commented that PR people knew about so many things but in such little depth, and he was probably right. From the UK launches of Snapple ("made from the best stuff on earth") and "That'll Be The Daewoo" cars, through to the creation of Britain's leading mobile phone brand, O2, out of the dreadful dullness of its BT Cellnet predecessor, we loved every bit of what we did. We went on crazy escapades to the Arctic Circle for the government of Finland and did photo-shoots on Mexican beaches with supermodels and the legendary photographer Herb Ritts, all in search of column inches and the money shot. We even managed to secure what we believed to be the first-ever branded Page 3 in *The Sun*, "Fozzies in their Cozzies" on Bondi Beach, in a week-long special courtesy of Foster's lager.

In the old world of media, relationships were pretty straightforward and linear. Have good idea; will travel. It was less about the truth and more about the story. The brand with the best story wins.

In our own golden age of security nothing much else seemed to matter.

* * *

I rarely wore a suit to work until about 2004. The shift was partly because, at 40, I no longer looked much good in jeans, but mostly because that was the year that Jackie and I sold the company that we had founded to the global Public Relations giant Edelman. People at Edelman mostly wore suits.

The Edelman adventure brought with it many things (not least my own career trajectory, which I had neither planned nor anticipated) but, above all, it re-connected me to my first love: social democracy.

As I moved from consumer brands "guru" (their word, not mine) to suit-wearing CEO, so I became increasingly fascinated with the PR industry itself. On reflection, I think I was already struggling with an inner voice that told me it was over.

When I published my first book *Citizen Renaissance* in 2008, with its call for a citizen revolution to help address huge issues of well-being and climate change, many saw it as a cry for help – or at least a dig at the world in which I professionally existed. It was probably both. We had, I believed, to start thinking of ourselves as citizens again, not as consumers, and to recognise that the power to change things for the better lay in our (increasingly digital) hands. Old structures were crumbling.

Writing *Citizen Renaissance* and subsequent essays crystallised what I know now to be true. Revolution is on its way. Our communications world is now *social* – of and between the people – and *democratic*, because it gives voice to all. Joined together, this provides a unique opportunity for communications to be transformative – the need for which should be apparent to anyone interested in the current state of business, politics and society. We cannot continue spouting flimsy research statistics, empty slogans, and crass diversionary tactics. Put simply – there is a better way.

* * *

Towards the end of 2013, as the core argument of this book began to take shape, I took to the pages of the ad industry bible *Campaign* to signal my first death knells for the PR industry.

Shortly afterwards, I met a senior PR industry figure at a reception.

"Traitor."

"I'm sorry?"

"Why did you give that to *Campaign*?"

"Because I wanted to. I have spent years arguing that PR is a higher evolved discipline than advertising; that the future is ours. And now I want to say I was wrong."

"You are shitting on your own doorstep."

"No. I am telling it as it is."

And here is roughly what I said...

* * *

I had proudly spent the best part of 25 years arguing that advertising is over and that PR's time had come. Now, I no longer believe that to be true.

I remain deeply sceptical about the relevance and core purpose of advertising, but I am also increasingly convinced that PR will never take its long-coveted seat at the boardroom table, where it will be recognised as an essential component of strategic business rather than a bolt-on.

As for so many brands and organisations before it, the reason is simple: a failure to modernise. The PR industry spent much of the past two decades talking about "its rightful place" and, for the most part, failing to earn it. PR did not take the medicine it should give to clients: *it's what you do that counts, not what you say*. Amid all the verbose excitement of the late 90s and early millennium, PR did not appreciate that its business model, especially as it related to the large consultancy networks, was broken.

Opportunities to lead peaked and passed. Take Corporate Social Responsibility – a trend spotted early by PR folk. In the frenzy to monetise, the industry failed to think. Rather than lead a progressive agenda based on co-created, citizen-centric actions, it defaulted to selling stuff. What emerged was mostly "greenwash" and, thereafter, an ill-formed CSR industry that today is more about bureaucratic, tick-box compliance and reporting than it is about social movement and societal change. (Thankfully, as one recently re-branded CSR practitioner recently informed me, a "reform movement" has started within the CSR sector.)

Had the PR industry seized the moment 15 or 20 years ago, not only would it now hold a legitimate position in the boardroom, but the boardroom itself would also be a more enlightened place.

The same pattern emerged with social media. Technology platforms aside, PR recognised the "conversation economy" early on. The ad industry was surprisingly slow to get going in this space. As some of us warned at the time, however, early-mover advantage was quickly eroded by those with bigger budgets, if not brains. The true long-term decline of many of today's global PR networks is now masked by social media work.

Arguments over "who leads in social media?" have been transcended by the world of data. The PR industry's inability to properly embrace data is the first – and possibly the greatest – of five major threats to the sector's relevance.

Threat One: Data and Insight

The big network chiefs are clearly not putting their multi-millions in data investment dollars behind the PR companies in their empires. This is also an issue of substance. Publicis chief executive Maurice Levy, even before the 2013 (subsequently failed) merger with US giant Omnicom was announced, kicked-off a $4 billion (£2.5 billion), five year digital spending spree in September 2012 – and it was not to support PR.

Other sectors simply offer greater insight and more measurable success. There is now a purer evidential base on which to build relationships. PR is nowhere near fully understanding or embracing it.

Threat Two: Outcomes, not Outputs

Seventy-five years after Edward Bernays germinated the modern PR industry, there is bizarrely still no consistent application of proper measurement criteria. Show me one board-level executive who is prepared to sign off a significant budget against loose promises of increased awareness or engagement. The evolved form of measurement shifts away from measuring "stuff" towards accountability to a wise crowd and to society at large. The sterile measurement of absolutes is, in any event, a busted flush.

Without proper measurement, though, there can be no accountability. And without accountability, PR will only become further marginalised. The Barcelona Principles (a set of guidelines established by the PR industry to measure campaign efficacy) have yet to be universally adopted, some five years since first being raised.

For too long, many of us happily emphasised the storytelling art – the clever words, smart positioning and opaque layering – over any kind of science of PR. We paid lip service to the challenge of measurement. Today, other residual issues notwithstanding, art without science will simply not cut it. PR can no longer be Creationist in its thinking.

Threat Three: Networks, not Hierarchies
There remains a perverse determination within PR to defend top-down behaviour in a flatter world. PR currently speaks to hierarchies in a world of networks. It is therefore starting in the wrong place, both for its own domain and the wider universe of citizens, companies and brands. PR can no longer dictate on its own terms

It is not about loudhailer broadcasting or "managing the message" any more. Shrill press releases are irrelevant in a world that sees through obfuscation and deceit. Building advocacy and activism from within networks is the way forward. The voices of regular people need to be heard.

Moreover, PR people have for too long ignored the

importance of organisational design and the implications of its evolution. Deeper structural issues are frequently overlooked in the rush to communicate.

Threat Four: Scale

Creative PR ideas mostly remain tactical and without scale. They rarely establish organising principles that genuinely transform businesses and brands. When was the last time a really big idea (not an amplifying one) could be credited to PR? Perhaps the Dove "Real Beauty" campaign – but the advertising agencies might dispute that this was ever a PR idea in the first place. I was there when a few of them made their case.

Increasingly, numerous ad agencies look to their PR brethren only for added spin – an ugly and anachronistic need that too many PR practitioners happily fuel – but the PR industry has a responsibility to think and deliver big and accountably if it is to be taken seriously.

Threat Five: Talent

Ultimately, it may be the lack of talent in PR that finally kills it: too few big brains to do the big thinking required in a world of Progressive Communication. Lord Chadlington, the outgoing chief executive of global PR group Huntsworth, has voiced concern that it may be that not enough PR people are bright enough to engineer change. The talent pool is too shallow, the future-facing part of the industry is insufficiently enlightened, and the big industry players (dominated by multinational companies) are trapped by business models that force them to sell arms and legs rather than investing in whole new areas of talent.

The overwhelming majority of Multinational Corporations (MNCs) urgently need to re-evaluate their communications talent at a global level and reorganise to ensure that they have best-in-class practitioners in each of the identified expert areas: from employee engagement to brand marketing; crisis and risk management to content, social media and data.

This is not the current reality. An overhaul of outdated managerial constructs is necessary and the war for talent will soon become acute.

Barclays' Global Comms Director Stephen Doherty sees "a great schism" ahead as the war for talent intensifies. His shift is from external to internal agency, with professional communications advisors working within the corporation of the future.

* * *

These five existential threats are exacerbated by significant global trends.

Public trust in major institutions in Western economies – finance, business, media and government – has collapsed, not least because of the rise of individual empowerment, which sees power shifting from state to citizen; employer to employee; corporation to consumer. Activism is everywhere – including institutional shareholder activism, which was, according to a *Financial Times* report in late 2013, up five percentage points in the previous 12 months alone. Society is atomised and authority is now a rented space. Trust is understandably complex and fragile. There are no silver bullets. PR is not prepared, or even fit for purpose, in this age of activism, nor does it properly understand the restoration of trust.

This new world is a long way from the early, optimistic days of Bernays, Dan Edelman and Harold Burson. Transparency is the default position. Spin is dead and ethics, values and behaviours, not mission statements, provide the framework for future communications. Institutions are being asked to demonstrate leadership through actions not words. Yet PR is still too busy talking, not doing, and frequently advising its clients to do likewise. Talk is cheap and control is over. Message massaging and media management, once the mainstay of corporate PR folk, are no longer possible; reputation and issues management are easily broken open. The pages of most national and international newspapers are littered with such corporate victims.

Advertising agency VCCP co-founder Charles Vallance, with whom I helped launch the O2 brand in 2002, emphasises this point: "You cannot control your customer. Empowerers thrive."

"Brands," says Vallance, "have to organise themselves to be free. Really good communications concedes that not everything works."

* * *

The "philosophy" (again, PR is *not* a profession) may be moribund, but just because PR is dead doesn't mean that the industry will actually vanish overnight. This is, after all, where people make money.

As the entrepreneur Luke Johnson said to me at a drinks reception (I paraphrase): "You may think that PR is dead. But that doesn't mean the *industry* will disappear. Where there's a market, there will be buyers. Where there are buyers, there will be business."

Luke may be right, but the PR consultancy model is increasingly redundant. Its demise is only a matter of time. Global PR firms – though not all offenders in equal measure – continue to build the same tired bureaucracies to service client hierarchies, rather than addressing core issues of purpose, products and services.

They have an entrenched addiction to sales and revenues (selling stuff to clients), and many have lost focus on solving strategic problems. They are obsessed about their competitors, less so their clients. "Value" evaporates from the relationship, like steam off a kettle. One friend resigned from a consultancy when, returning to the office after winning a new client, the chief executive asked not what the issues were or about the work involved, but when and what the client would pay. I have, myself, been guilty of asking exactly this question in the past. This is what the system does to all of us.

Another friend, the Chief Marketing Officer of ██████████████ a FTSE 100 company, summed up the sentiments of many: "I am so sick of my agency fobbing me off with junior teams when what I need is a couple of hours with the guy I hired who, incidentally, I never see." It is a familiar refrain.

Vodafone's Group Communications Director, Matt Peacock, puts it this way: "When I find an adviser who I like and trust and whose judgment and skills are proven, I don't give a toss what logo he or she has above their door: my money follows the person, not their employer.

"Selling a PR agency full-service proposition to a client," he continues, "is like trying to sell the merits of a general hospital (Great X-ray department! Great catering!) when all I want is the name of the world's best cardiovascular surgeon."

Clients, therefore, need to challenge the perceived orthodoxy of their consultancies. Too many consultancies get away with it because so many organisations see business problems as *communications* problems, when they are not. PR and communications firms cannot transform a bad product or business plan into a good one, through any amount of spin or anything else. It is time to recognise this and to change not the way we communicate but the way we act.

* * *

"You are essentially a financial shop," I said to one of the directors of ██████. "You take a 40% margin and a massive win-fee in the good times and re-position yourselves as corporate experts and squeeze a 25% margin when the deal-flow goes slow. As soon as the economy picks up, you return to your specialism."

"How come you know this?"

"One of your fellow directors told me."

I have long been fascinated about how the big ████████ communications firms make their money and, to be frank, how they get away with offering strategic corporate advice when they rarely themselves believe in a world beyond shareholder value. Their world and the real world essentially do not connect.

"What do you do when someone comes to see you with an employee engagement issue?" I asked.

The pinstripe-suited smoothie smiled in that knowingly patronising way, as perfected by so many in City firms.

"We send him down the corridor."

His words had Orwellian overtones.

"And what happens there?"

"Well, he just meets one of us, wearing a different hat. And we sell him the programme."

"So, you don't have the expertise?"

"We don't need the expertise. The clients buy us anyway."

Never buy a man with a different hat.

* * *

It was Go Ahead Group's comms strategist Simon Craven who shared with me the story of Blockbuster and Netflix. It is a sweet parable.

"In 2000," he recounted, "Netflix had only 300,000 subscribers for DVD rental by online order and was losing money. Blockbuster, based on physical stores, had been valued at $4.8 billion in its IPO the previous year.

"Netflix had a vision of distributing films over the internet, but fast internet for the mass market wasn't ready. Netflix offered Blockbuster 49 per cent of itself, suggesting it become Blockbuster's online video division. Blockbuster didn't see internet video as a threat, and turned Netflix down.

"In 2002, Blockbuster reported a $1.6 billion loss for the year. In 2003, Netflix made its first annual profit. In 2004, Blockbuster launched an online service, but it was too late. By 2006, Blockbuster was valued at a mere $500 million. In 2010, it went bust."

Today, in 2014, Netflix is valued at anything between $19 billion and $30 billion.

The choice is now straightforward and immediate. PR, like all businesses and indeed politics, can embrace the progressive revolution. Or, like Blockbuster, arrogantly swagger forth ... and sleepwalk over the cliff.

* * *

Wise Crowd Contributor:

The (Final) Death of Spin

George Pitcher

It's a little over a decade since I published a book predicting that our "spin-culture" was coming to an end. I've just taken *The Death of Spin* (Wiley, 2003) down from my top shelf and I'm pleasantly surprised – or perhaps smugly reassured – by my prescience.

It was written in the shadow of 9/11, not long after the dot-com bubble burst, when Tony Blair had only just embarked on his Iraq misadventure, but before 7/7, Gordon Brown, the 2008 financial crisis, MPs' expenses, phone-hacking and the Coalition. It was, with all the implications of the old Chinese curse, an interesting time.

I noted of "traditional" financial PR that, "it knew of no existence other than the equities up-trend" and, "was left with one of two options before it – deny the existence of change or find something new to do." More broadly, when the Big Society was but a twinkle in the eyes of David Cameron's focus group, I asserted that the "responsibility for social provision lies as much with business as it does with government."

I wrote that a necessary change could be forced on us by "a prolonged reversion of the economic growth cycle," which has come to pass; that the re-invention of the Tories was solely about image and that they would have to confront their demons in Europe (ditto); that honesty was "the new brand value" and that its outcomes could only be about "how you behave, rather than what you claim." We're still waiting on that last bit.

"We have covered politics and business with the tarmac of a spin-culture and then wonder why the grass isn't growing," I wrote. "There is more to life than what we think about it. We have to *do* too. That means being brave enough to use communications as a means of action, not positioning; of joining the debate, not evading it... It is for the mass of people to alter the culture in which they live."

This isn't an exercise in I-told-you-so, nor a grubby attempt to get a two-for-one deal with Robert. I was unwittingly addressing a symptom of PR's terminal disease in 2003. That symptom was "spin," which was an over-developed talent for posturing and positioning one's political or business interests in relation to critical issues, rather than tackling the issues themselves.

At the start of the new millennium, I believed (I was in a minority, but I wasn't alone) that this tendency towards spin, which had its roots in American politics and was imported into the City of London, could be corrected by imaginative communications professionals.

But I was treating the symptom rather than curing the disease. The patient, in the shape of British business and politics, had presented with "spin", but the underlying condition was far more serious.

While much has changed since then, much has stayed the same. Freeloading MPs, thieving bankers, lying police officers, gangster utilities, treacherous journalists and fraudulent retailers have collectively demonstrated that spin was an effect, not the cause, of our malaise.

As it happens, I believe that my conclusions from 2003 mostly hold good. PR, as it had developed as a parasite on the body corporate, had a Hobson's Choice before it: denying the existence of change was not a long-term solution, while finding something new to do required it to be something it was not.

But the problem isn't PR. How could it be? The prosperity of public relations has only been enabled by its paymasters. The be-suited PR flaks are but the suppurating buboes on the plagued bodies of our national institutions. Nor will shooting the rats which carry the plague help very much – banging up bankers, or simply rescinding their knighthoods, may provide temporary satisfactions, but they hardly address the disease.

Back in 2003, I wrote that there was time to win back trust, but "you cannot trust someone who is not honest with you. Honesty doesn't have a moral genesis in this context – it is a practical demand." And we can't recreate an honesty that our forebears took for granted – a capitalist free market in which my word is my bond, in which asset-ownership depends on a mutuality of interests, in which the buyer need only beware of his or her poor judgment rather than the deceits of marketers – unless we know what sort of domestic society we believe in and what sort of world we want to build.

I recall a conversation I had in 2002 with Richard Addis. He had just returned from Toronto and could compare the business and media cultures of the UK and North America. In Britain, he said, it's usually sufficient to offer a clever-clogs view gleaned from the media. Across the Atlantic, this is likely to be listened to politely before you are asked: "Yes, but what do *you* believe?"

After Lehman Brothers, Enron and WorldCom, that kind of demand on our credibility may be harder to accept from that source. But we can aspire to make business and politics better once more. And we should. Because without belief there can be no remediation of our social sickness, only quack cures offered by the mountebanks of PR. Which is perhaps, when I wrote *The Death of Spin*, why they were called spin doctors.

* * *

CHAPTER TWO: TALKING ABOUT TRUST
THERE IS NO SILVER BULLET

There is No Silver Bullet

Politicians and business leaders have abused trust to the point of exhaustion. Think about how many times you have heard them use the "t" word in an entirely insincere context. In very simple terms, this is because they fail to understand that trust is not a message, it is an outcome. And it is not a right. Trust has to be earned.

Recent history is peppered with abuses of trust, from Fred Goodwin to Bernie Madoff; from illegal horsemeat in the food chain in Europe to poisonous melamine in infant milk formula in China. But we are now expected, once again, to trust our banks, our regulators, our supermarkets and our broadcast institutions simply because they say we should.

* * *

The story of Vincent de Rivaz might be seen as a parable for our times.

Vincent, CEO of energy giant EDF, gave what was, I think, one of the worst speeches on trust that I have ever heard. He perfectly encapsulated everything that I believe is wrong about those who talk trust but, in my view, rarely earn it; those who seem to use PR to try and spin their way out of trouble.

Few of us need reminding that the energy companies, of which EDF is a member, are just about the least trusted organisations in Britain, accused by politicians of forcing millions, especially the elderly, to choose between heating and eating in the winter months of 2013/14.

It was an already bleak January evening and Vincent was addressing a sustainability forum. Trust was again uppermost in people's minds, courtesy of recent scandals surrounding supermarkets and horsemeat, paedophiles and the BBC.

Just before the event, I bumped into ███████████ ██████, who told me that he had helped Vincent with the speech and that the key theme was, of course, trust.

When Vincent appeared on the stage, stuttering as if he was reading directly from someone else's script, it seemed to me that, in a very literal sense, he did not know what he was talking about.

"It is very important that our customers trust us," he said, as though this was a unique insight. Such words have been spoken by so many in his position, so many times before, in equally vacuous ways.

Vincent made the classic mistake of the many. In his tone, content and delivery, he spoke as though there was a magic wand that could quickly restore trust in his company, in his sector and in society.

He was wrong. Trust does not reside with leaders like Vincent, but with citizens like you and me. Trust can only be built through actions, not words. It needs to be hard fought for, hard earned and hard won every day. This is usually where today's leaders are getting it wrong. They often think that PR can protect them or save them, and it can't. Their legacy will be based on what they do, not what they say.

If the crisis of trust is a crisis of leadership, then it is also a crisis of legitimacy. This runs to the heart of this debate: who has the *legitimate* right to govern – whether in nation states, city-states or business states? What, in fact, is the real purpose of trusted leadership? Is it the promotion and preservation of power among traditional elites? Or is it to support the common good – the flourishing and well-being of we, the citizens? Legitimate leadership is most certainly *not* a function of communications, still less of PR. PR has become the ugly spawn of the consumer society. It has encouraged wants over needs and jeopardised the planet; has celebrated spin over honesty; and has sought to manage the message *to* the people rather than let the people speak for themselves.

* * *

As we learned from Vincent, the "t" word has been abused and exhausted. The Global Financial Crisis has contributed to this, as companies and brands suddenly feel they all need to be in the trust business.

Look around: so many are at it. "We trust our customers." "Our customers and our employees trust us." Except they don't. Everyone ends up sounding like Vincent.

In today's world of constant chaos and disruption, trust is more fragile and more complex than ever before. It is tougher to win and much, much easier to lose. Anthony Jenkins, CEO of Barclays, said exactly this in his 2014 New Year's message – admitting that it may take a generation before trust in banks is properly (if ever) restored. And given the disruptions of networks and technology, a return to "old" trust is not even possible. Trust is now forever fragile.

Since the turn of the millennium, trust has moved from a culture of "me" to one of "we". The Edelman Trust Barometer, the bedrock of global trust surveys, confirms this shift. We trust fellow employees and "someone like me" more than we trust CEOs or established authority figures and institutions. Companies now need to consider the interests of their employees and those of their customers ahead of the interests of the shareholder – proof-positive of the shift from a singular shareholder to a multiple stakeholder focus for businesses and business leaders today.

"They" are no longer in control, in their boardroom bunkers. "We" are – in the workplace, in the shopping centres and at the till points, even in the media and with institutional shareholders. We are all activists now, and the future of business and government is safer in our hands. If only we all recognised and embraced this, and had the confidence to use our collective citizen-power to better effect.

The smart, trusted organisations of tomorrow are therefore those who recognise the implications of the mega-trend of individual empowerment: to behave like activists themselves; to love and involve the citizen crowd; to mutualise thinking, if not business models; to gain co-operative or collaborative, rather than competitive, edge; to re-balance profit and purpose; to put society first. When it comes to trust, PR has been part of the problem. It is certainly not part of the solution. Beware the PR firm that tells or sells you otherwise.

* * *

Just as we must divorce trust from communications and PR, we should never separate trust from profit. Profit optimisation is acceptable. Profit maximisation, to the detriment of the greater good, is not.

A cautionary, real-life tale from the front line:

"This is really a vital piece of work."

"Thank you."

"But we probably won't use it."

"Oh, why not?"

"Because we have to make money."

"I know. I am not arguing *against* making money. I am arguing for making a reasonable profit over an excessive one. You cannot build trust if you are constantly seen to exploit your customers and under-reward your employees."

"It will put too much pressure on our business model."

"Have you considered re-thinking the model?"

"Why would we do that?"

"Because if you don't, trust and profit may become incompatible."

"We would rather sacrifice trust."

"Then please stop banging on about how you want to be trusted."

* * *

It was about minus 25 degrees outside and I had come dressed for the Moscow cold. I was wrapped in thermal layers – not really thinking that, bar the short journey from hotel reception to car and out again, the whole day would be spent indoors. I had not bargained for the staging or TV lights.

The occasion was the annual meeting of the Russian Association of Industrialists and Entrepreneurs. The setting was the plush Ritz Carlton in Moscow. The whole place was drowning in gilts, yellows and golds. Security was tight. A special guest was expected – and it wasn't me.

I had prepared my 20-minute talk more thoroughly than usual. Vladimir Putin was not, at that moment, actually President of Russia. He had temporarily swapped posts with Dmitry Medvedev and was merely Prime Minister. Either way, presenting the data on "Trust in Government" in Russia was always going to be a challenge, but even more so in front of *him*.

It was spring 2012 and there had been mass protests on the streets of Moscow. Global news channels were buzzing with the coverage. I had decided to play it safe. Trust in government was on the decline everywhere, I mused. What was happening in Russia was merely symptomatic of a global trend.

Except I do not think it was.

The conference was a funny affair. I was swept into the green room to be greeted by someone introduced to me as, I think, the Mayor of Moscow. He immediately asked about my expert area. "Trust," I stammered. He looked at me quizzically. His eyes said it all: *"Trust? Here? You crazy?"*

I was scheduled to speak at noon. It was just before 9am. We were ushered into the main conference room to be met with a sea of suits (50 shades of grey) and a wall of lights. I went to take my place somewhere near the back, seeking anonymity.

"Where are you going?" one of my hosts asked. "You are expected on the platform."

That was to be my spotlight for the next three hours, before my 20-minute slot.

The lights were blazing, the on-stage temperature soaring. And, beneath my suit, I was still cocooned in thermals. I began to melt.

I quickly discovered that you hallucinate when you are melting.

I fantasised about leaving the stage, removing my underwear in the bathroom (maybe depositing a mystery pile for the next visitor) and returning to the stage so much cooler. But I never managed it. I was mesmerised and paralysed. It became a battle of mind over matter.

The conference itself was a funny affair. The VIP guests (and that included me) were sat behind a long, Politburo-style trestle on an elevated stage. Speeches were divided into two categories: of the 20- or the 10-minute variety, depending on status.

Introductions were to a formula: "My name is xyz and I am responsible for the waste removal policy in the district of wherever." (For waste removal, read road construction or sewerage maintenance – it does not really matter which.)

To this day, I remain unsure where the entrepreneurial bit came in. One of Putin's likely opponents in the forthcoming Presidential elections spoke. He was unnaturally tall, imposing and charismatic in equal measure. Applause, for him and for others, was rhythmic, as though it had been choreographed. Shorter speeches got shorter applause, in line with the status of the speaker. Listening through my translating headphones, no one seemed to say anything important. These were the set pieces of the predictably safe.

Obviously trust in government in Russia was down.

My slides were self-censored, so as not to offend. Applause for me was polite rather than enthusiastic. The audience probably wondered why I was there. I was beginning to wonder too.

Despite my deliberately anodyne delivery, I stepped off stage to be engulfed by cameras and interviewers. I was thankfully shepherded by the brilliant Ekaterina, my colleague and interpreter, though I would have felt better served by Kevin Costner.

"They want to know whether you think the fall of trust in Russia is the fault of Prime Minister Putin?" she said, rather too deadpan for my liking.

And we all knew the answer to that.

The same question was put to me an hour or so later, as I was interviewed live in the studios of "Russia Today". The segment still exists somewhere on YouTube. I used my very best bridging techniques.

"I don't think it's a question of Russians losing trust in their government – this is a worldwide trend," I began. "Edelman has been doing the Trust Barometer for 12 years and this is the steepest decline we've seen in the trust in governments worldwide in that period. So Russia is simply mirroring what is happening elsewhere. It's just as dramatic in the United States and it's very dramatic in the Eurozone."

All this was, I argued, evidence of a much wider shift away from the institutions of government and towards networks of everyday citizens (which it absolutely is). But I was deliberately obscuring the point. If the old adage runs that you cannot spin your way out of a crisis, that is exactly what I was doing.

* * *

"So how was the trip?"

"Great. But not what I expected."

"What did you expect?"

"Camels."

"Camels?"

"Yes."

"You mean you wanted to go camel riding in the desert?"

"Well, I thought I would see camels waiting at the airport. You know, like tethered to posts."

"Instead of taxis?"

"Yes – exactly!"

I wish this had been a fictitious conversation. But it

happened in 2012, with someone who held a big, fancy global title.

Just as we can't view trust through a Western lens, we can ill-afford to take an American tourist view of global business. Or of trust. Or of the global PR industry, for that matter.

* * *

CHAPTER THREE: PUBLIC LEADERSHIP
PROGRESSIVE ALTERNATIVES FOR PR, CSR AND TRUST

Progressive Alternatives for PR, CSR and Trust

It is no longer good enough to speak simplistically, as I did while at Edelman, of the transition from Public Relations to Public Engagement, which was the PR solution for the stakeholder society. This thinking is now outdated. And we must stop lazily mistaking "being trusted" for "being trustworthy". It is the latter that counts.

The future belongs to Public Leadership and, within this, trust based on reciprocal vulnerability, progressive business behaviour and a new accountability to Public Value.

* * *

Philosopher Baroness Onora O'Neill, who delivered the important Reith Lectures on Trust for the BBC in 2002 and with whom I shared a Roundtable in spring 2014, is very clear about the different dimensions to trust: the *claim*, the *aim* and the *task*.

Dealing first with the *claim* that trust is in decline, O'Neill points out that certain sectors (media, politicians and, I suppose, estate agents and PR people for that matter) have always demonstrated a significant trust deficit. The claim of "trust in decline" therefore rests somewhere between being irrelevant and being misleading, although it sells well at Davos.

The *aim* to have "more trust" is a "stupid aim," argues O'Neill in her 2013 TEDx talk, poignantly delivered in the British Houses of Parliament. "Intelligently placed and intelligently refused trust" should be the proper aim.

What matters in fact is not trust but *trustworthiness* – and therefore judgement. Better judgement is based on a combination of competence, honesty and reliability. No one would seek "more trust" from the likes of Bernie Madoff – but neither would you trust a dear friend even to post a letter if you knew they were unreliable and had a history of forgetfulness, O'Neill points out.

Calling the *task* "re-building trust," moreover, gets things back-to-front. Trust is personal and distinctive. It is given by other people. It is reciprocal. It is not "ours" to own or rebuild. (Vincent, please note.)

When I met O'Neill in early 2014, the idea of "reciprocal vulnerability" dominated the trust conversation – although that was focused more on the public sector. Reciprocal vulnerability makes accountability mutual: organisations are rightly as exposed – and therefore vulnerable – to their employees and customers as their employees and customers have traditionally been to them.

"Reciprocal vulnerability," wrote Geoff Colvin, "is the beginning of trust."

This holds important implications for those seeking a progressive alternative. Just as we are vulnerable to our friends – and they to us – so a trusted company should admit and accept raw vulnerability to its employees and its customers.

In the frenetic world of Twitter, Instagram and Snapchat, a world of instantaneous news and views and multiple channels and networks, this is the reality anyway. In this context, *trustworthiness* is a more relevant consideration than trust, evidence is more important than promises, transparency is fundamental, and accountability is more powerful than all-encompassing sound bites resulting from endless tracking studies, polls and focus groups and marketing spends.

Vulnerability to the crowd – standing naked, if you like – is the best and most honest way to demonstrate reciprocal vulnerability in the corporate and brand worlds, and therefore to engender trust.

Baroness O'Neill's thinking speaks to the idea of Public Value and also to false notions of control:

"We will need to give up childish fantasies that we can have total guarantees of others' performance. We will need to free professionals and the public service to serve the public. We will need to work towards more intelligent forms of accountability. We will need to rethink a media culture in which spreading suspicion has become a routine activity, and to move towards a robust configuration of press freedom that is appropriate to twenty first century communications technology."

That was written in April 2002.

* * *

My proposed new model of Public Leadership reflects the thinking of O'Neill and social business expert Philip Sheldrake.   It   is *activist*, *co-produced*, *citizen-centric* and *society-first*.

1. First principle of Public Leadership: *Activist*

Individual empowerment sees power continue to shift from state to citizen; from employer to employee; from corporation to consumer. Society is becoming more atomised and more activist as a result. Power and influence are increasingly asymmetrical, both in politics and in business.

Traditional theories of leadership are simply not appropriate in this complex and chaotic context. We are seeing a dying breed of charismatic leaders being replaced by the new generation of "horizontal" leaders, who understand that participation and freedom is more important than control.

The message of Occupy, "we are the 99%", continues to reverberate, even though the movement itself has faded. Public Leadership is the logical answer to Occupy's calling – which is why I also suggest it is co-produced, citizen-centric and society-first.

2. Second principle of Public Leadership: *Co-Produced*

To the point of reciprocal vulnerability, Public Leadership is *co-produced* with regular people.

In companies, this means giving greater voice to employees, customers, regulators and even the supply chain. It is an argument for increasing collaboration, mutualisation and co-operative ownership. It means more than simply co-creating ideas via extended focus groups. Co-production runs to the heart of how a business is organised and how it behaves. Co-production extends to communications, too.

When mutualised business models are not viable, then it is at least possible to mutualise the thinking. A wise citizen-crowd can better shape both policies and products. Put simply, the Public Leader embraces and loves the crowd and becomes accountable to them. Decisions are no longer made in boardroom bunkers or the splendid isolation of ad agencies, nor is communications (or messaging) dictated from the top.

The UK's John Lewis Partnership and Spain's Mondragon are good examples of co-produced leadership.

Business planning itself can also be co-produced from within. Will McInnes, in his book *Culture Shock*, offers the great example of India's HCL Technologies: better solutions, more belief, higher levels of engagement and, yes, exponential revenue growth often results from a co-produced approach.

3. Third principle of Public Leadership: *Citizen-Centric*.

This demands an intimate relationship between an organisation's leaders and the needs and aspirations of everyday people. This in turn helps re-connect the purpose of business with the needs of civil society. It also leads to an important re-think of the balance between profit and purpose, challenging the prevailing business orthodoxy of profit maximisation.

Public Relations has persistently sold to consumer *wants*, rather than working within the bounds of citizen *needs* – encouraging a consumption fetish over the longer-term sustainability of people and planet.

This is why enlightened Public Leadership in this, what Barack Obama identified at his 2008 inauguration as the "Age of Citizenship and Responsibility," is also *society-first*.

4. Fourth principle of Public Leadership: *Society-First*

The US clothing company Patagonia is a celebrated example of *society-first* thinking. Social Enterprises like Grameen Bank offer equally good examples. And despite those who accuse them of "greenwashing," large commercial organisations such as Walmart, GE, Unilever and the UK's Marks & Spencer are re-thinking their business models, moving towards citizen-centric and society-first thinking.

Sweden's Handelsbanken is establishing best practice leadership on de-centralised decision-making and localism. Denmark's Novo Nordisk is determining to "solve" global problems of diabetes, even though it may eventually undermine its own business model and existence. They, too, are demonstrating Public Leadership.

The role of the CEO within organisations such as these

is crystal clear, as Darcy Willson-Rymer, Chief Executive of Costcutter Supermarkets Group (and a former UK CEO of Starbucks) observes simply:

"The leader's values and behaviours are a proxy for the rest of the company's values and behaviours."

* * *

The author Philip Sheldrake, writing on the death of hierarchy and the need for asymmetrical leadership, says that even military command is not immune from tectonic changes.

"The military has attacked its traditional hierarchy, much to the surprise of many who consider the armed forces synonymous with command and control. The prior strong association makes the lessons all the more palpable. The Joint Special Operations Command recognised during the Iraq War (2003–2011) that 'if we're going to win, we need to become a network.' According to its commander, 'we had brought an industrial age force to an information-age conflict. … We became an organisation that could move and adapt just as rapidly as the environment around us, while maintaining a disciplined focus on our strategic goals.'"

* * *

Corporate Social Responsibility is an ugly discipline. It is also a perfect example of a secondary market created through the failures of leadership and the shortcomings of the market society.

"If we really believe in putting our employees and our customers first, then we must put ethical behaviours at the heart of everything we do," I said to ▋▋▋▋ ▋▋▋▋, a serial Board Director at ▋▋▋ and one of Britain's foremost Non- Executive Directors.

"Oh, that's not my problem. We have a sub-committee that handles that," she said.

* * *

Ethical behaviour – what Aristotle would have called virtuous leadership – should never be sub-contracted to working committees or remote departments. Like ethics, behavioural trust has to sit at the heart of everything and be embedded into every business action. It cannot be either side-channelled or sub-contracted. Trust is built through the honest behaviours of all real people from within, not by rules and words commanded from above.

Neither advertising nor over-spun PR will work in building a trusted brand or company. Empowering employees and customers to build a shared future with shared values will. This co-produced approach makes trust more rooted, more credible, more authentic and more powerful – and reinforces the relationship between trust and the Public Leadership model, between the leader and the institution, and everyone else.

Since its emergence towards the end of the last century, CSR has supplanted a market of virtue with one of compliance. Instead of asking: "what's the right thing to do?", an industry of production and conformity has been created. Companies continue to outsource their consciences to those whose own barometers of success are often the self-preservation of influence or budget, rather than the transformation and betterment of society. A business case must be made for making money, while "doing good" is relegated to those running CSR. A noble cause – ethical leadership – has been reduced to another commercial machine. Intellectually, it is an odd divorce.

The irony is that CSR was invented to help engineer a better and more responsible world. Instead, it begat a global behemoth with unreported but undoubtedly huge monetary value, and a bureaucracy that enshrined rules and reporting mechanisms over ideas for transformational change. The very reason for CSR's existence became the opposite of what CSR could ultimately achieve. Compliance beat values, hands-down.

Dagmara Wojciechowicz studied CSR as part of her Master's Degree, and her work led her tutor to subsequently rethink the CSR course content. "I analysed ▇▇▇▇ ▇▇▇▇▇ ▇▇▇▇▇ ▇▇▇▇," she told me, "and it was clear to me that it was …. little more than a colourful way of excusing bad practice … and full of misleading terms. It was little more than questionable storytelling."

* * *

This book has been funded via Unbound, one of the next generation of crowd-funding platforms which, like Kickstarter, is bringing radical democracy to the creative world. *Trust Me, PR is Dead* was originally going to be published by one of the traditional houses. Their arcane systems and painfully slow processes made the switch to Unbound a no-brainer – trust in a peer network to get the right thing done and for the creator to be better informed in the process.

Zopa is the UK's largest peer-to-peer lending company and social platform that offers an alternative source of financial services to banks. Understandably, its profile was raised after the financial crash, as trust in traditional banks dropped dramatically, and as savers continued looking for alternate investment options in the face of pathetic saving rates. In a closed world of institutional sterility and consumer apathy, Zopa is at the forefront of a rare trend of innovation in retail finance.

By July 2013, the company had lent £327 million (£105 million of which had been offered in the previous six months). Zopa's loan book and revenues were growing by more than 55% a year and boasted over 500,000 total members. There had been 200% uplift in savers signing up in 2013 alone. A 2012-13 Which? survey identified that, while 2% of those surveyed had invested in peer-to-peer platforms in 2012, by 2013 the figure had risen to 9%.

Zopa's corporate aim is clear: to develop as a mainstream alternative to the high street banks, offering both a fairer financial deal to customers and operating more transparently and ethically. Its web platform enables competitive rates because it cuts out the middleman by connecting lenders and borrowers directly. It has lower overhead costs than a bank and online technology further reduces transaction costs.

Whether it is with PR, publishing or even finance, there is no real need to intermediate in today's world. Zopa relies on a critical mass of website visitors to access capital for lending and so securing trust in the security and viability of its services is crucial. Trust is at its most exposed when it comes to capital transactions, but trust vested among peers is more robust.

The rise of peer-to-peer lending (which the bigger banks are now attempting to emulate) was mostly born of crisis. "We are witnessing the growth of the non-banking lending market," Lord Rothschild commented in December 2012. "Following the 2008 crisis many of the banks remain under-capitalised. In these circumstances alternate forms of credit will be developed on a significant scale. This is happening."

The Bank of England's Andrew Haldane also understands the shift: "the mono-banking culture we have had since the 1990s is on its way out. Instead we are seeing a much more diverse eco-system emerging with the growth of new non-bank groups offering peer-to-peer lending and crowd-funding which are operating directly with a wider public." Interestingly, as *The Economist* also noted, institutional money is now flowing onto these platforms as well.

In summer 2013, I tried to initiate a campaign that saw a major retailer and one of the banks develop a shared crowd-funding platform for business enterprise – allowing those Small and Medium Enterprises denied access to capital to expand local stores using community funding. The idea was to create a virtuous circle: the retailers would be able to grow, and that growth would be financed by community members who had a vested interest in their success. The bank, however, whose sector's own failings had led to the credit crunch in the first place, refused to play ball. Financially, it could not see what was in it for the bank.

* * *

A PR industry in self-declared evolution has continued to treat trust as a message, not as an outcome or, more importantly, as something deeply behavioural. It is almost as though, every time PR folk are faced with writing a keynote speech or making an announcement on products or people, trust tumbles to the fore and out spills so many vacuous words. Perhaps that's how Vincent and his peers ended up where they did. (A recent low point: the CEO of a world-famous luggage brand speaking on the BBC Radio 4 *Today* programme and proclaiming that trust is absolutely integral to his brand. You do have to trust your luggage, I suppose...)

In January 2013, having left Edelman weeks previously,

I sat down to try and focus my thinking on what it takes to be a trusted leader. The great and the good of the world's business elite were about to gather at Davos. Their annual pre-mountaintop murmurings were again rich in trust messaging, but low in trust actions. I was struck at the time by the words of the Reuters commentator Lucy Marcus:

"Actions speak louder than words, and trust must be earned through acts of integrity. Those sectors, organisations and individuals who have broken our trust will have real work ahead of them to regain our trust. The next time you are tempted to use the phrase 'trust me,' remember: trust must be earned."

Acts of integrity had a rather nice ring to it. It is almost as though Davos has become an annual healing moment – a group apologia for the previous year's abuses of trust and integrity.

The American columnist and polemicist Michael Wolff, writing in *USA Today*, had become as weary as I had of the constant flagellation of the t-word. He called for trust's reinvention as a form of social media – a sort of glassdoor.com ratings system that would essentially halt the continued trivialisation of trust. There is without doubt an inversely proportional relationship between the frequency with which leaders speak the trust word and how trusted they really are – hence my assertion that trust often spoken is trust rarely earned. Wolff's observation is acute: trust is about perpetual accountability, not sterile measurement.

It is difficult to actually quantify something as deeply personal and behavioural as trust (as the Barometer methodology has shown, excusing some odd statistical variations, it *is* possible to track rises, falls and "no changes" in sentiment). Nonetheless, we must attempt to make trust properly meaningful, rather than full of bullshit platitudes. This means establishing a new accountability framework when it comes to trust.

Acts of integrity would be a good start, but they must surely be consistent and ingrained, not occasional or opportunistic. And what role for honesty? Surely telling the truth is the most obvious starting point?

It *is* possible to combine the base thinking of the Edelman Trust Barometer (much loved by Davos-man) with a dash of Ms. Marcus, a hint of Professor Kotter (more on him to come) and some Wolff, too – to ask *questions* about actions and leadership and thereby to build a framework within which to consider a leader's legitimate trusted (or not) status.

By better understanding the characteristics of spin-free, non-PRed, trusted leaders, it is possible to ask questions of them to see how they might be rated. In fact, it would send a powerful signal if all the leaders who want to be trusted – or, still worse, insist that they already are – effectively expose themselves to a universal rating system – a framework, if you like, based on the following five questions. Now that would make an interesting trust barometer for Davos, especially if the scorers were employees and customers, regulators and suppliers.

I am suggesting five questions that could create this framework and accurately measure trust. Crucially, each question that follows here can only be answered through actions, not words. In other words, PR will never save you.

1. Vision?

The Public Leader's vision should be credible, deliverable, sustainable and consistent with what they have demonstrated before. It should lead the organisation (and indeed society) to a significantly better place – it cannot reinforce the malignant status quo. The trusted leader must have the courage to ask bigger questions and be prepared to have bigger questions asked of them.

Barack Obama had the vision and the courage to ask these questions. But his Congress would not allow him to deliver the answers, and the system ultimately strangled him.

2. Honesty, Transparency, Accountability?

The trusted leader should be open and honest. They must be fully accountable for their actions – not just to a boardroom or cabinet, but to a wider universe of employees, customers, suppliers, citizens: a true majority. They should be often and openly measured against benchmarks of success and the manifestos that they have co-produced. They should quickly admit failure when failure strikes. Their reward must be proportionate to society and not just to the 1%.

The John Lewis Partnership model of employee councils and fairer profit distribution meets many of these criteria, although it fails to pay its (contracted) cleaners a living wage.

3. Empowerment and Democracy?

The trusted leader empowers and enfranchises those around them. They are committed to citizen democracy – listening from the bottom-up and within and not just dictating from the top down. They are a participant in social democracy – that is, the new leveller of social media, social value, social impact and social business. Every stakeholder (an ugly word) enjoys an equal share of voice. Trusted leaders know when, to quote HSBC's Global Head of Communications Pierre Goad, "to shut up and listen."

4. Transformation and Transition?

The trusted Public Leader understands that the status quo is not sustainable. They viscerally comprehend the key challenges for citizens and society today – around climate change, inequality, social justice and re-calibrating the relationship between wants and needs. Their programmes extend beyond shareholder value (or political capital, for that matter), actually facilitating the change business and society needs. Their programmes also have measurable and accountable outcomes. They are, above all, committed to the concepts of common good and Public Value – placing purpose alongside profit. They have a transition plan in place. They are committed to constant change and are even prepared to disrupt themselves. As my publisher Dan Kieran has noted: "I wake up every day and ask, *how can I disrupt my own business model?*"

Unilever's Paul Polman speaks openly about common good, about the need for capitalism to reform itself, and the fact that "the Unilever Sustainable Living Plan is our business plan." I am not what one correspondent called "a Polman groupie," but the Unilever CEO is very much leading the way here.

5. Proof?

The trusted Public Leader walks the walk and does not just talk the talk. They use tangible evidence to underline this. This evidence is independent and socially sourced through a crowd to whom the leader becomes ultimately accountable.

If a leader is to be truly trusted, then they must be held to account against these five questions. On this basis alone, if trust is alive, then PR is surely dead.

This five-question approach, which, in collaboration with others, I am continuing to refine, crosses a deep political fault-line. That is, for me, the defining and dividing principle of social democracy – interpreted in both the political and non-political senses of the term. The forces of conservatism, sometimes operationally cautious but mostly defending profit and power, remain averse to change or can see change only in increments. But a post-Crisis, less trusting world deserves better. It deserves progressive change: among and of the people, giving voice to all.

* * *

There is good news in all of this, though. Rather than be verbally used and abused at the whim of the CEO and his PR team, trust *can* be re-positioned as a legitimate, effective, systemic and powerful strategic concept, as well as a central principle and cultural value for any organisation.

This is an important pivot.

To achieve this, leaders need simply to ask themselves (and answer honestly and be accountable to) the five questions listed above – and then build an operational system that enshrines, protects and advances the framework.

The case for "real trust" can be extended further still. All communications, internal and external, can be developed around trust-building behaviours. This demands rooting everything an organisation does in action, not words: in what it does, not what it says. This is a true function of Public Leadership, not Public Relations, and the hallmark of a progressive organisation: avoid the rush to communicate, change your behaviours before you unleash your words, and base everything you do in radical honesty and transparency. As Neal Lawson, Chair of think tank Compass and a fellow partner at my most recent consultancy venture, Jericho Chambers, sees it:

"do the right thing or they will get you." Every deceptive leader's own Tahrir Square moment now awaits.

Trust built on action provides companies with distinctive leadership positions that are real, have tangible commercial benefits and play well in the wider regulatory, political and investor environment – any CEO's holy grail. Trust, genuinely and honestly earned, provides the licence to lead, not merely the much-vaunted licence to operate. And once the crowd trusts you, you can use them to mutual advantage. There is simply no need to spin when you are honest and fully transparent from the start.

Finally, we need to get real. There is no return to "old" trust. By this, I mean there is no return to the kind of trust that existed in the age of empire and before the perpetual disruption of social technologies. Those were the days when we went to the doctor and trusted him (usually *him*) with both his diagnosis and prescription, before we could find out more about disease-states and likely remedies through websites that are sometimes thinly disguised, funded fronts for the major pharma companies. We were more trusting in the ingredients in our foods, the security of supply chains, the ethics of manufacturing and the authority of our teachers and the police. We would never have dreamed that MPs would be fiddling their expenses, that child abuse on the scale of the Jimmy Savile scandal would be revealed, or that the police would be so criticised in the wake of the 1989 Hillsborough tragedy or in the 2013 "Plebgate" affair. In Britain, we trusted that the *News of the World* would always provide a factual, if titillating, account of the weekly news. We trusted them not to hack phones, too.

We were comfortable in our ignorance but we were, in effect, being controlled, manipulated and led – and we did not really know how to answer back. We granted the establishment trust because we had little option except to believe what they said. Until 1989, Edward Bernays and chums were winning both the propaganda war and the trust battles also.

Those days have passed.

* * *

Jim Woods runs a brilliant organisation called The Crowd. At its heart lies a simple proposition effectively based on the insight of a TV show. In *Who Wants To Be A Millionaire?,* contestants who ask the audience have a 91% chance of getting the answer right.

Trusted companies of the future are not those built on PR or comms. They are those informed by regular people – their aims and their ambitions; what they love and what they loathe. They are fully participatory, embracing the crowd constantly and democratically as citizens, rather than targeting them as consumers. They are interested in their customers' well-being and not just in selling stuff. The actions of the trusted organisation are guided by the shared wisdom and shared values of regular people – not by the isolated and lonely opinions of falling and failing business elites.

The organisation and Public Leader of the future will need to stand naked before the crowd, and trust will have to come because they actually deserve it, not just because they say they do.

* * *

Wise Crowd Contributor:

The Death of the Focus Group... and the Rise of the Crowd

Jim Woods
The way that business makes decisions is changing fast, driven

by powerful disruptive influences. First came the internet and its disrespectful cousin, social media. Then the words "social purpose" entered the boardroom, accompanied by a new generation that asks prospective employers what the organisation creates beyond shareholder value.

It's not surprising that many executives call this the most challenging era for decision-making yet.

But decision-making becomes considerably easier when you recognise that the walls of an organisation, which have been carefully constructed over many decades, are now the obstacles to good decisions. They have become a barrier between you and the people who can help you. The value of your business depends, to an increasing amount, on your ability to dismantle these walls.

Let's remind ourselves why these walls were built in the first place. They were born out of a rational desire to keep intellectual property out of the hands of competitors, and to allow the image projected by an organisation to be managed. Big industries were born for people who could distil the incoming message (focus groups and market research), and control the outgoing message (advertising and PR).

And still today, many of the most valuable companies are the best wall builders. Why, then, are organisations such as Tesco and Apple starting to chip away at their carefully-constructed walls?

The internet bears the ultimate responsibility for the demise of the walled organisation, and also poses an existential threat to the industries (like PR) that operate outside the wall: as the walls become more porous, these industries become increasingly superfluous. The internet enables a new quality of conversation between companies and stakeholders, one that is efficient and two-way, turning stakeholders into co-creators. For the stakeholder, it is engaging and empowering.

At the bleeding edge, this dismantling of walls is resulting in some decisions which are unfathomable to those who have been schooled in the Milton Friedman era of business.

Tesla Motors, a ten-year-old car manufacturer with a $27 billion market cap, recently announced it will share its electric vehicle (EV) patents with competitors to accelerate the adoption of the EV market. Many of its customers care about environmental issues, and they applauded the boldness of the decision. Tesla's share price rose by 12% in the week following the announcement.

GlaxoSmithKline (GSK) is a FTSE 100 pharmaceutical company that recognises the power of using many minds to solve a problem. In 2013 it began a process of putting its clinical drug trial data in the public domain, allowing other research organisations to develop cures from its data, in the belief that it could halve the development times for drugs used to treat critical diseases such as malaria.

This decision to create an "open platform" puzzled the pharmaceutical industry, which is traditionally very guarded about sharing its IP. GSK argues, however, that they derive value from the process, not least because the move inspires valuable trust from governments and society – and indeed another global pharmaceutical company has since followed suit.

Whilst the internet has created a way of pulling down the walls, questions around the social usefulness of business is adding to the momentum. Online platforms allow companies to efficiently connect with large, diverse crowds that become a proxy for society, allowing business to treat society as a stakeholder in their decision-making.

Where are the tools for connected decision-making emerging? OpenIDEO has won many plaudits as an open innovation platform, using an online community to develop solutions to solve society's challenges. Coca Cola Enterprises, for example, recently used the platform to find a way to improve recycling rates within people's homes, something it had been unable to tackle by just asking experts.

The Hotspots movement helps organisations to host online conversations between thousands of employees at a time. When PricewaterhouseCoopers (PwC) wanted to understand why a high proportion of its millennial employees were leaving two years after joining, a 72-hour conversation with 1,000 employees in 29 countries established it was because they wanted global career paths. PwC was able to develop new career paths whilst showing it was listening.

At The Crowd, we've developed our "Going Naked" format, which allows one organisation to have its strategy peer-reviewed by over 200 experts from other organisations. Using a mixture of online and offline formats, it combines the wisdom of crowds and crowdsourcing, and gives an organisation a high degree of confidence in its decision-making.

In ten years time we'll look back at these emerging tools and marvel at how embryonic they were. But already a number of key principles for connected decision-making are emerging:

- *Diversity of opinion allows for better decision-making.*
- *"Group think" is valuable when introduced at the right stage in the process.*
- *Crowds should inform decisions, but not make them.*

In this more connected, more authentic era of business, focus groups are destined to go the same way as the PR industry. There will always be a handful of Steve Jobs in this world who have an instinctive understanding of where the world is heading. For everyone else, the crowd awaits.

* * *

The setting was the boardroom on the top floor of the London HQ of one of the world's leading companies. The table was populated with the great and the good of British industry. I was actually not quite sure how I'd got invited and, respecting the Chatham House Rule, I can only report back in the broadest of terms. Accordingly, all names have been removed as have any identifying features: *When a meeting, or part thereof, is held under the Chatham House Rule, participants are free to use the information received, but neither the identity nor the affiliation of the speaker(s), nor that of any other participant, may be revealed.*

I felt very much the kid in the corner. I had worked with the company for a number of years and should have expected it, but the meeting nonetheless got off to a surreal start as our host tapped his oversized wine glass and asked for silence.

It was autumn 2008 and Lehman's had already fallen. The Great Financial Crisis was upon us and the purpose of the meeting was for these business behemoths to discuss "what next?" I was the expert contributor on trust. I was eager to listen, learn, absorb and advance, and excited about what these guys had to say.

"My analysis is this," said the CEO host. "The situation is bad; it is going to get worse; and we should fear more regulation."

And that was pretty much it.

"But the banks are really at the centre of this storm," he finished, before resuming his seat. "So I would like to hand over to the Chairman of ████████, to offer his analysis."

████████ was to fall on his sword a few years later, but he was undoubtedly a major player. What he had to say surely mattered.

"My analysis is this," said the respondent. "The situation is bad; it is going to get worse; and we should fear more regulation."

And that, too, was pretty much it.

Part of me screamed "stay silent," while another part really wanted to jump in. So I went in.

"I think we are missing the point," I said. "What has happened is in fact a huge fracture in society. Business and government, together, will be blamed and held to account. There is no going back. People will not allow institutions to return to bad old ways once the crisis is over. We should not fear more regulation but think instead about a popular uprising against those who are not prepared to change their models. Government will not need to regulate heavily if businesses simply behave better. Society cannot afford to go on like this."

There was a momentary silence.

It was not because what I said was wrong but rather because such heresies are rarely spoken in public. They are the dirty secrets of business institutions, not really for airing. I was, after all, meant to be one of them.

"The young man has a point," said ████ █████████ ██████.

"He does," agreed ████ ██████. "The truth is we cannot come out of the crisis with the same business models as we entered it with. That is a recipe for disaster. We cannot go on like this."

Returning to the office, I called a good friend and advisor – a journalist of brilliant distinction – who was close to the board of one of the companies present. I expressed my dismay at what I had heard.

"Welcome to my world," she said. "Meetings are all like that. Comments are general and generally meaningless. They are all quite happy in their self-deception. And because they all dine with one another, shoot with one another, play golf with one another, and holiday with one another, nobody points out their madness."

And despite their momentary agreement, pretty much every leader gathered in that room has since returned to their own version of "business as usual".

* * *

CHAPTER FOUR: THE STATE OF POLITICS
THE PARTY IS OVER

The Party is Over

Somewhere between the mid-1960s and the turn of the millennium, (Western) society lost its sense of citizenship, as we were all engulfed in the rush towards consumerism. We failed to calibrate what we needed with what we wanted, swamped by the consumption obsession that Edward Bernays himself had always hoped to ignite. Giddy on debt, we could suddenly have it all. Politics became likewise infected – the brilliance of Thatcher and Reagan, Clinton and Blair, was to offer "hope" through unsustainable promises. Lower taxes and better public services were suddenly possible – two irreconcilable positions achieved through the craven addiction to focus groupthink. But then politicians, like CEOs, are there to win power for the short term. It is a mostly selfish journey. They talk of legacy – but that is *their* legacy, not ours.

* * *

I am occasionally asked by politicians to offer quiet counsel on how to restore trust in politics and government. They, like me, are often despondent that it is simply a lost cause.

Politics is rarely about long-term strategy. Just as CEOs see their tenure in five-year bursts, so politicians live in the moment, seizing opportunities for short-term, personal victories regardless of the longer-term, wider consequences. Self-interest invariably wins over societal interest. The parallels between politics and business are striking.

During the fated Gordon Brown Labour government, I was asked to address some senior civil servants in one of the departments. ████ ███████████ was then Secretary of State.

"It is so depressing," one mandarin confided. "Every day starts with the same refrain from the Minister: 'What's the headline in the *Daily Mail* this morning?'"

And then the policy follows the paper.

* * *

Some politicians are blessed with higher idealism. Others are touched by political madness. Two men called Douglas exemplify each type.

Douglas Alexander (at the time of writing, Shadow Secretary of State for Foreign Affairs) and Douglas Carswell (the author of *The End of Politics and the Birth of iDemocracy*) encapsulate what is right and wrong about politics today. Within this lies a fable of leadership, for the boardroom as well as for Parliament.

If Douglas (A) were not so nice, he would probably be leader of the Labour Party and the next Labour British Prime Minister. Softly spoken, deeply thoughtful and quietly charismatic, there is an intelligent authenticity in Douglas Alexander that so many other politicians simply lack.

I have spoken with Douglas about trusted leadership on a few occasions and we remain in broad agreement. "Politics," he has written, "is about much more than identity. It is about higher ideals."

Soon after David Miliband's decision to stand down from Parliament, Douglas wrote a piece for *The Independent*:

"[David and I] share a politics that is fiscally responsible, economically radical, socially liberal and globally aware. We share this because it's the only way for the centre left not only to win but to govern. But the years and this friendship have taught me something else. Decency matters in politics, as well as in life. Politics is about ideas and ideals ... but it also involves negotiation and compromise. So how you do your politics matters, as well as why you do it."

Douglas (A) is an enthusiast for participation – a democracy that is properly social. He often holds his constituency surgeries at Tesco till-points. The crisis of legitimacy has been provoked not by apathy but by disengagement and by the imposition of top-down elitism in an increasingly bottom-up world. The 1% cannot suppress the 99% for very much longer. Legitimacy can only properly be restored with the transfusion of power from state to people that will lead to a new era of participation.

The truth is that political or business systems built on hierarchies cannot survive in an age of networks. Yet most politicians – or indeed CEOs – remain blind to this fact, trapped in their own world of power and ambition, lacking the true humility that characterises great leaders. That is why I have long argued that the crisis of trust is in fact a crisis of leadership. The important shift is not just from state to citizen but from thinking about power to thinking about *people*.

The first time I discussed citizen democracy in the social-digital age with Douglas (A), I challenged him on the end of politics as we knew it and how, I argued, the future lay less in representative democracy and more in direct political accountability – from "they" the elected, to "we" the people. That was in 2009. This exact language would soon be used by the Occupy movement.

Douglas' response was singularly robust. Direct democracy could be a recipe for chaos, but it would at least inform and reform the representative system. He was right, but the transition remains painfully slow, even though the Occupy movement gave it an unexpected – though since exhausted – surge.

Peter Mair writes: "the age of party democracy has passed. Although the parties themselves remain, they have become so disconnected from the wider society, and pursue a form of competition that is so lacking in meaning, that they no longer seem capable of sustaining democracy in its current form."

* * *

Douglas Carswell achieved infamy in September 2014 when he resigned from the Conservative Party to seek re-election for the United Kingdom Independence Party (UKIP). In the early hours of Friday 10th October, Douglas (C) became UKIP's very first Member of Parliament.

If Douglas Alexander is the high idealist in this story, then Carswell is his arch-enemy. I know Carswell to be a thoroughly decent person, as well as a terrific sparring partner in political and academic debate. However, every time we come up against one another I have to ask myself: is this Friedrich Hayek, the ultimate market fundamentalist, in disguise?

Douglas (C)'s book on the birth of iDemocracy was published in 2012 to some critical acclaim (although John Rentoul's review in *The Independent* rather brilliantly demolished it). At first glance it is energising and exciting stuff: politics has failed us (true); digital technology enables disruptive change (true); open primaries can help reform politics (true); in time, we can all choose our own public services (maybe); there is no real need for the state (false).

It is on this last claim that Douglas (C) and I fundamentally parted company. If his diagnosis is 80% correct, his prognosis is 100% wrong. What he is really saying is something that Margaret Thatcher always wanted to and never quite managed: "there is no such thing as society."

We are all atomised – fragmented, individualistic – now. Carswell uses this to make his play for libertarian ascendancy, and I firmly believe he must be stopped.

The really worrying thing from my point of view is how plausible what Douglas (C) says sounds to his audience, as the voters of Clacton demonstrated *en masse*. During my first debate with him at the London School of Economics, he was applauded in all the wrong places – his antidote to a failed system and his call to the barricades somehow seemed fresh and invigorating

But at what cost does Douglas (C)'s technology-driven, stateless policy triumph over Douglas (A)'s citizen-orientated social democracy?

First, at the cost of disenfranchising those with no real access to technology (one example: 30% of the voting population in the Newcastle Central constituency do not have access to the internet).

Second, at the cost of those living in sink estates, or with failing schools and/or an over-burdened health service – those trapped below the poverty line.

Third, at the cost of those who have no sense of engagement in the first place, who choose not to participate, or whose own political illiteracy is in itself a failing of the post-war system.

* * *

By the time of debates two and three with Douglas (C), I was better prepared. I counted and recounted the number of direct references to Friedrich Hayek's free-market and libertarian theology. I quoted directly from Douglas' book and then the audiences understood. What was dressed up as a revolutionary pro-citizen text was in effect little more than a tired re-run of discredited 80s Thatcherism.

I have never voted for the Conservative Party and Carswell's book is a reminder of why I never will. The theory goes that we shift to the right as age encroaches, but I have always drifted leftwards instead. It is easy to blame the state for everything, as politicians often do. It is their quick-win enemy. But we should not mistake the bureaucratic state for the good state, or the state as an agent of change, just as we should not mistake the bureaucratic corporations for those who drive a progressive agenda and reformation through better practice.

* * *

As this book began to take shape in my mind in the spring of 2013, I found myself at a dinner with one of Tony Blair's closest political allies. The conversation, inevitably, turned to the former Prime Minister's Iraq legacy. As has become sadly fashionable, fellow dinner guests piled in with their version of why this was Tony's greatest mistake.

I argued otherwise.

Iraq was the third of his big mistakes, I suggested. The first was his failure to sack Gordon Brown after the 2001 election, when he had both the political capital and the popular support to do so. The second was his failure to initiate wholesale constitutional reform – of parliament, of the monarchy, of our bureaucracies and tired institutions of state, immediately after sweeping to power in '97.

"I think Tony would probably agree," said ██████ ██████, before waspishly suggesting that Tony might also be considering running for Pope.

* * *

Approaching two decades after Blair's May 1997 victory, Britain remains trapped in the Oxbridge Union gladiatorial adversarialism that the House of Commons represents – childish yelling across the despatch boxes, a tired relic of a previous age. Now is the time for the greatest act of political reform since 1832.

Many years ago, when asked what his first act would be on becoming Prime Minister, the SDP's Dr David Owen promised to rip out the seating arrangements of the Commons, replacing them instead with an altogether more civilised semi-circle, better suited to sensible debate. The clumsy first-past-the-post electoral system is not only hideously un-democratic, it is also the progenitor of Punch and Judy politics and an anachronism in an age of networks and coalitions.

A better system would be one that supports the formation of smaller, more focused parties (and even single issue campaigners) and calls an end to the cliché of "broad churches". The UK electoral system would need to be overhauled, just as political funding would need to be re-thought. Politics could re-embrace localism, ideas and ideals, while citizens could convene around issues that are felt to be personal and relevant. Citizens could reclaim the political agenda from the (party) machine broadcasters – and share and prosecute their values together. The 2014 pledge to increase devolved powers to Scotland and the implications this may yet have for more localised powers in England will inevitably accelerate the change.

In real terms, for example, the Labour Party would thus be freed from the yoke of the Trades Unions, while others on the left could organise themselves around a more (in their terms) "socialist" or "Blairite" agenda. We could have London Social Democrats and Rochdale Co-Operative Socialists. Libertarian liberals could split from old-leftie liberals ("bearded sandal-wearers, mending pavements" as one politico friend describes them) and, vitally, the Tories could divide themselves into pro- and anti-Europeans, pro- and anti-immigration. Some could coalesce with UKIP (and would be more honest doing so anyway), while others might find common ground with left-of-centre social democrats and/or the few remaining Liberals. The free-marketers would happily distinguish themselves from the softer, socially liberal conservatives, whom they clearly hold in contempt.

Space would also be provided for the emergence of new groups that could re-energise the doldrums of the current political landscape: single-issue campaigners; human rights activists; parties of business statesmen or health workers or prisoner reformers or faith groups or teenagers. In a truly democratic world, everyone deserves a voice.

None of this would preclude the formation of future partnerships or coalitions – even pre-election deals – but it would allow all groups to be refreshingly honest about their own agendas and ambitions. It would make the coalitions explicit and authentic, rather than opaque and often forged via questionable trade-offs.

Accepting that we live in an increasingly atomised yet connected, activist world, it makes little sense to ignore this atomisation as it plays out with politics or political parties. We should respect it instead. I am sure the likes of the liberal conservative Kenneth Clarke take little pleasure in (metaphorically) waking up in the same bed every morning next to a Norman Tebbit or a David Davis. Conservatives would therefore be as liberated as their Labour opponents, whom they have taken to calling "sham". It cuts all ways.

Future coalitions can be better built on honesty and clarity of belief. Public discourse would be richer for it and the electorate's choices would be clearer and more democratic. A more radical and progressive approach, therefore, would be to call time on party politics. This would demonstrate moral courage, political vision and real leadership from today's political class. It would out-think prevailing stagnant thinking. It would also be more truly representative of how today's world really works.

The Labour MP Jon Cruddas addressed the Royal Society for the Arts in early July 2014 on the subject of Radical Hope:

"The shift to a services economy is flattening out old, hierarchical command and control structures. Digital technology is unseating whole industries and workforces, and production is becoming more networked and disorganised. Our class system is being reconstructed.

"The institutions and solidarities workers created to defend themselves against the power of capital have disappeared or become outdated and ineffective. As such, social democracy has lost its anchorage in the coalitions built up around the skilled working class. Once-great ruling parties can appear hollowed out, in danger of shrinking into a professional, political class. Often in government they were not very social, nor very democratic.

"Top down and state driven. Compensating for the system not reforming it. A politics about structures and not about individuals. This model of social democracy built in the industrial era has come to the end of its useful life."

The same thinking can happily be applied to major corporations. A different world asks that we consider different practices.

* * *

In October 2013, *The Huffington Post* published an article dedicated to UKIP candidate Godfrey Bloom's best-ever quotes.

"Politicians," he is quoted as saying, "are smooth-talking sociopaths."

Bloom is often seen as an entertaining political fringe figure, a kind of rent-a-quote angry Colonel from Tunbridge Wells. I do not find him quite so amusing – his references to "bongo bongo land" (where Britain apparently sends its overseas aid) or to women as "sluts" who (in)famously "don't clean behind the fridge enough" are just offensive. Bloom is courted by the satirical TV shows and news channels, despite hitting one reporter, Michael Crick, over the head when challenged on the lack of diversity in UKIP party literature.

The atomisation of politics into more dynamic tribes is axiomatic. It is surely only a matter of when, not if. But this will likewise enable a thousand flowers, fragmented peoples and parties, to Godfrey Bloom – and we must guard against the perils of unintended consequences. Democracy can be messy, too.

* * *

I was in Rio de Janeiro for the Global Economic Symposium, with the opening paragraphs of this book swirling in my head. I had initially wanted to examine the rise of business states in the 21st century, just as city-states had originally blossomed in the 15th. With echoes of flourishing civic pride and citizen values in the quattrocento, the thesis would also explore the rise of the *new* city-states – of London, Frankfurt, Singapore, Luanda, Abu Dhabi and Shanghai – as the sun continues to set on nation states, and certainly on empire, elsewhere. It was the intersection of cities and business that particularly fascinated me.

The economics of cities were already clear, from established 30-year plans to the threatened erection of protectionist defences against perceived economic invaders. Moreover, in a hyper-networked world, citizens of these states were more likely to find commonality and shared interests trans-nationally than they are among those with whom they would otherwise sing their national anthem. It is no coincidence that Silvio Berlusconi chose *Forza Italia* as the name of his political movement, reflecting the thought that sometimes only football can unify, while truly local considerations divide and atomise, but ultimately identify, peoples. 2014 events in Ukraine and Crimea underline this.

"Business in the future," argued Dutch Premier Wim Kok, "will not be the same as business in the past." But then neither will our cities. "We need to move from more to better," he said. Shared societies – where city and business agendas will inevitably collide – also seem to make a lot of sense in the context of trust: here, the big estates of government, business, NGOs and media find confluence, each with issues of active citizenship at their centre. Where shared interests coalesce, so shared societies can advance. Convenor of the Global Economic Symposium Professor Dennis Snower's call for a "more caring, more compassionate world" finds resonance here.

The world can progress from its current position of advancing shared interests through tentative Public Engagement, to a future one of embracing shared society through real Public Leadership.

In *The State We're In*, Will Hutton identified, popularised, and championed the idea of the stakeholder society, helping give birth – in the UK at least – to the cornerstone philosophy of New Labour along the way. States of the future might now be considered three ways: as nations (great for sporting occasions and as an occasional excuse for monarchy); as cities (economic powerhouses); and as businesses. The latter two are perhaps best placed to drive societal transformation through active citizenship and Public Engagement. As Wim Kok pointed out while arguing against GDP growth as the ultimate end-goal: "global answers should be more than the sum of national answers." We need to think smarter and beyond reductive national solutions.

Kok's wider analysis of business may be little more than a simplistic, self-evident truth, not least because of the huge reforming power of the social-digital movement But, again and again over the two days of the Rio conference, themes of citizenship and society, empowerment and democracy, "caring" and responsibility, were inter-woven within an intricate tapestry of today's world condition (or at least the remedies for its recovery). In his conference summary, Booz & Co's Shurmeet Banerji – despite being a self-proclaimed social-digital sceptic – said that it all boiled down to "a real need for active citizenship." This active citizenship is most likely to flourish in the city-states and indeed the business states of the future. And this is where Public Leadership can find its defining moment.

The social power of business is not news. The Tata

family of India or the heirs to Lord Lever would argue that social responsibility – well beyond the tick-box compliance of CSR – is in their corporate DNA. Business States can become a reforming force for good. The modern world will only accelerate their role and this transformation. If the will is there, businesses can get shit done, and so can nations.

City-states of the future will construct themselves as businesses (maybe just like Singapore), and vice versa, with the active engagement of citizens (and employees), the determination to re-balance purpose and profit, diversification away from carbon-fuelled economies, the pursuit of well-being and not just GDP growth, and, as Bill Gates said in 2012, the use of "strategic philanthropy". It may be naive to see a world that is entirely bottom-up, but it would be equally anachronistic to believe in the continuity of a top-down structure ruled by controlling elites in this changed world.

"Shared societies," continued Kok, "[are] where all individuals share a common capacity to participate economically, politically and socially . . .[and] democracy is where diversity flourishes most. Democracy ensures accountability to citizens and supports collaboration across countries."

These words hold true both for the state of cities and the state of business. Democracy remains, for many, the axiomatic outcome of a properly digital society. Moreover, as John Stuart Mill wrote: "the idea is essentially repulsive, of a society held together only by the relations and feelings arising out of pecuniary interest."

The pecuniary interests of PR will secure its ultimate downfall. We have to think about citizens before we think about capital.

* * *

Wise Crowd Contributor:

The Death of Party Politics

Neal Lawson

It may be 14 years overdue but the 21st century is finally catching up, and fast overtaking, our 20th century party political system. A politics of two tribes is being replaced by a complexity not just of multi-party politics but with the added spice of politics beyond parties. Citizen-led forms of deliberative and direct democracy are increasingly being adopted, contesting the domination of representative democracy, with profound implications for the way our world is governed. But to understand this 'party-less' or at least 'party-lite' politics of the future, we need to understand the existential threat to the old political parties.

For over 200 years in Britain, democracy has primarily been the exchange of executive power between, mostly, two political parties of the right and the left. The system of party politics is built into the constitutional practice and structures of our government. The Commons is divided between Her Majesty's Government and Her Majesty's Opposition, who vie to keep or win power through a first-past-the-post electoral system designed to favour two-party politics.

All of this has its roots in the 19th century class system of an establishment (Tory/Conservative Party) and a liberal and later working-class set of beliefs and interests (Whigs, Liberal, Labour and more lately Liberal Democrats). So entrenched was the two-party system following the Second World War that in 1951 the parties won 97% of all the votes cast between them. And then it all went downhill.

The welfare and full employment settlement of this era lasted while the tectonic plates of geo-politics and class forces allowed it to. But gradually things began to unravel. Slowly, the dour culture of the 1950s gave way to the more individualistic culture of the 1960s. In the 1970s the Soviet Union declined as a cold war threat, and the working classes, based around mining and heavy industry, started to lose their salience as a political force. The unions were now a pale shadow of their former post-war selves, reined in by legislation and a workforce that no longer operated together in huge numbers and no longer shared a class consciousness based on collective production but increasingly belonged to an individualistic culture based on consumption. The oil shock of the 1970s led to a period of political and global decline in Britain that Thatcher and then Blair tried, in their own ways, to turn round with varying degrees of success. Neither was convincing, at least to a sustained majority within the country. The party system was beginning to disappoint.

But the process was about to be accelerated. The Big Bang in the 1980s saw finance capital liberated from national borders. Globalisation took off, and with it the power of national governments to be masters of their economy. A mixture of hot money and corporate blackmail, based on the threat of investment flight, ushered in the neo-liberal era of low taxes and even lower labour market regulations. All of a sudden, there was no alternative.

By 2005, the two main UK parties were getting only 67% of the vote between them and voter turnout had fallen from the mid-80% range to 61%. In part because of the toxicity of the expenses scandal, by 2010 neither could secure an overall majority. Today it's doubtful whether either will – ever again. This isn't just because power has escaped up to the global corporate and financial economy, but also because party politics is now fast being eroded from below as well.

The breakup of the bureaucratic systems of production and administration that dominated the 20th century (called Fordism, after the car plants of Henry Ford) was to have a profound effect on what we believed and how we behaved. In these vast factories, not only did everyone knew their place as parts in the production line process, but they also demonstrated the class settlement between labour and capital – disputes were not over whether we had a mixed economy, but over what this mixture was, as workers bargained to be able to buy the new cars they were producing more quickly. All of this large-scale production began to break down into what was being called Post-Fordism, an era of more dispersed, local and smaller units of production using techniques such as just-in-time production and increased automation. Over the last 20 years the internet has accelerated this process and production has become even more dispersed, niche and specialised.

It is not just the economy that was and is being revolutionised, but society, too. Access to the internet and the rise of smartphones meant we could know everything everywhere. Now the ubiquity of social media means that in a world dominated not by the factory but by Facebook, the old top-down, deferential, centralised, command-and-control model of politics of the last century can no longer hold. From the bottom up people are more demanding, curious and autonomous. They have found their voice and they like what they hear. On- and off-line they are organising, thinking and doing. They join a multitude of groups and enjoy a plethora of social, cultural and political identities. When you can "like" whatever you want, blind allegiance to a single party, over which you have no control whatsoever and that will do politics "to you" and not "with you," no longer works or fits.

In a networked world of peer-to-peer collaboration the number belonging to the political parties has plummeted from millions to less than 300,000 in total. Meanwhile over 2.5 million have joined the online campaigning organisation 38 Degrees. The splintering of the old system, seen through the rise and fall of the SDP in the early 1980s, then the upsurge in green votes, the growth of the SNP in Scotland, Respect on the left winning surprise by-election victories and now UKIP, all speaks to the fracturing of the old party politics, as do flourishing democratic experiments such as the Flatpack Democracy movement in Frome.

This is not just a British phenomenon. The breakdown of party politics can be traced across the continent as new parties spring up – Syrza in Greece, the Five Star Movement in Italy, We Can in Spain, the darker Golden Dawn in Greece and far-right Front National in France. New parties can rise to national importance in months.

But while party politics splinters the idea that we, the people, will simply pass the responsibility of governing us from one or two parties to several parties is fanciful. Politics as representative democracy is now under threat. People will demand and expect an everyday form of democracy – in which our lives as active citizens trump our occasional and weak power as either voters or purchasers. The days of politics being like the Olympics – something that comes round every four years and leaves no trace – are numbered.

We will see deeper forms of deliberative democracy – whereby people are given time and space to consider complex changes. Porto Alegre in Brazil has been setting its city budget like this for years, and Iceland designed a new constitution on this basis. Such deliberative forums will be augmented by more direct democracy as referenda like those of Switzerland and California will be used more often – in part because technology allows it. The debate flourishing in Scotland on independence is a mixture of the two, where the choice to stay or leave the union led to an outpouring of political conversation about what sort of country its people want. When people know their vote counts, politics come to life. And politicians will be cut out of the loop as people demonstrate directly against corporations, to get them to do the right thing on issues like environment and labour standards.

It's tough seeing round all the corners to know where this will take us. We still need political parties of sorts. Someone has to stand the candidates and produce the manifestos. But the future party will be an open tribe that is democratic within and plural without. The job of the political leader won't be to promise things to voters. Instead it will be to help create the spaces and platforms for people to do things themselves – together. Public services will be co-created by users and workers, money will be lent through peer-to-peer networks and energy will be produced through local networks.

The politics of the future will be citizen-centric, not party-centric.

* * *

"Why are you standing down at the next election?" I asked an MP friend.

"Crap job. I thought we could actually change things with political power. I was wrong."

"Crap Job" is a great title for a political autobiography. At least it's honest.

CHAPTER FIVE: THE STATE OF BUSINESS
THE MISSIONARY POSITION

The Missionary Position

Apparently, before the Global Financial Crisis, ███████ ████████, a former FTSE 100 CEO, began executive committee meetings by asking, "who do we fuck today?"

* * *

Sarah is a close friend and also happens to be one of the cleverest and best-read people I know. She is someone Very Important in The City. I absolutely respect her opinion and trust her judgement. Although a liberal thinker, she is convinced that business should never take a moral stance – not because she does not believe in a moral/ethical dimension to business practice (she does) but because businesses are themselves a-moral constructs. People have morals; businesses do not.

The Chairman of one of the UK's largest professional services firms is very clear about the need for a moral compass in business. "The only permanent in business," he told me as I was undertaking stakeholder research for a client project, "is morality." The Chairman agrees with Tom Morris that we cannot compartmentalise our lives – "the most fundamental virtues and principles in private and in public are in fact the same . . . we [cannot] make exceptions to ways of living and treating others. Life is a whole and must be approached as such."

* * *

One of my favourite presentation slides shows a poster of the late economist Milton Friedman, with his beaming image and the headline "Proud Godfather of Global Misery". This may be an over-claim, but it contains more than a kernel of truth.

Friedman's infamous words, written in an article for *The New York Times Magazine* in September 1970, have been subject to some degree of revisionism. At face value, the message is stark: "the social responsibility of business is to maximise profit" – at a stroke subsuming the purpose and responsibility of business under the profit motive. For those of us who lost our economic and political virginity in the late 70s and 80s, this was a singular green light for the worst excesses of Thatcherism. Greed was suddenly good. Money reigned supreme.

While some have tried to excuse Friedman by saying that it is only through profit maximisation that business is able to better deal with the needs of society, others have taken his claims at face value. For them, not much lies beyond shareholder value. The purpose of the modern corporation is to maximise profit and return. Margins matter more than people or planet.

Except that they don't. The problem is that idealism has been crushed by a society that prefers wants to needs and opts for selfishness over generosity. This collective disembowelment of idealism is closely linked to a failure to win the case for social democracy in the past 40 years – creating an intellectual vacuum that has been filled by a posse of market fundamentalists and libertarians. They are quite often mad and wrong in equal measure. How frequently do we hear the phrase "the markets will decide", as though markets have been suddenly impregnated with wisdom?

Markets do not understand values – or indeed limitations, as Professor Michael Sandel so powerfully argues. Real people do. Real people need to be liberated to make decisions, rather than allow abstract instruments of economic imperialism to take hold. As Diogenes the Cynic is quoted as saying, "markets are the places men go to deceive one another."

The real evil of Friedman is not what was said explicitly, but how it has been continually distorted and abused. "The maximisation of profit" ignores the people without whom that profit could never have been possible. It leads to hideous abuses in the supply chain – from the sweatshops of Dhaka to horsemeat in our burgers.

Friedman speaks to the rampant consumerisation of everything – politics, media, business and brands – that would have thrilled Edward Bernays, but which killed trust. Douglas Carswell would have a much-weakened intellectual armoury without the legacy of Milton Friedman. The worry is how much has been polluted by the market-obsessed consumerisation of everything, and how wide-ranging the implications are. Driven by a belief that the mechanism of the market will make it all right, many politicians, for instance, promise (and fail to deliver) irreconcilable sets of changes – lower taxes alongside better public services, or more teachers and more schools in an age of austerity.

Business can and should be an agent, a catalyst for societal change. This is healthy capitalism in practice. Unbridled capitalism ended in 2008, with some of the worst excesses, not least in the financial services sector, still coming to light: businesses being liquidated in order to maximise the profit of the guarantor banks (RBS, take a bow) is just one sad example.

The social responsibility of business has always extended beyond profit. We should not let ourselves be deceived otherwise. It is possible to make a trade-off between profit and purpose, between making money and collective good. It is time for businesses to start thinking in terms of their collaborative edge and for a more honest and explicit contract with citizens that re-examines the balance between wants and needs.

However, the current models of business – and the communications that protect them – do not offer this. As Professor Tim Jackson famously summarised: "people are being persuaded to spend money we don't have, on things we don't need, to create impressions that won't last, on people we don't care about."

* * *

"Greed is good" is a phrase now oft-repeated in reference to an era that has passed, and those who still cling to the Friedman obsession with free markets and the doctrine that the social responsibility of business is to maximise its profits appear about as relevant and convincing in business today as Nigel Lawson on the subject of climate change. However, like Friedman before him and Carswell after him, it was Nigel's own adherence to a near-blind faith in the market mechanism that obfuscated the truth and blocked a more reasoned approach to the world around us. Theirs is – and was – unreason without bounds: a determination that market principles must apply anywhere and everywhere; that there should be no limits to the rampant and rapacious nature of the individual; that companies (and governments) just get in the way.

Citizenship demands responsibilities from individuals. Such responsibilities are rooted in principled and virtuous actions that protect collective well-being, not just personal advancement. Hence I take issue with the Thatchers and the Carswells of the world. There is such a thing as society, and we are all very much part of it. Our first responsibility is to our fellow citizens and to our one planet.

* * *

Sitting in a bar in Malmö, Sweden, in the summer of 2007, having recently become CEO of Edelman in the UK, I was discussing with colleagues what our office of the future would look like. I had already envisioned a democratic workplace – no hierarchies of corner offices or big filing cabinets on which to perch trophy pictures of trophy wives. It was time to destroy the American Dream cliché of office design (which, with the support of my awesome friends, architects and designers Grant Kanik and Gary Wheeler, we later actually did).

"I kid you not," said my colleague Nick over his beer, "when I was a client, one agency actually took us into a room where the ceiling was painted blue. 'This is our Blue Sky Thinking room,' they said, with no sense of irony. To cap it all, we ended up giving them the business."

Such is the power of seduction.

Agency life is peppered with these gruesome tales. I am sure I have often been guilty of some presentational misdemeanours myself (the time we sang a song to Hasbro about the Mister Men springs to mind). But the quest for pointless creativity rumbles on nonetheless. Whole organisations exist to bring out our inner child. That seems to be the only way we are allowed to unlock our creative souls. They charge huge amounts for the privilege. Personally, I find such "awaydays" patronising and humiliating in equal measure. They speak to the constant assumptions of an adult-to-child relationship – telling us what is good for us and what and how we need to learn. They reinforce all the prejudices of vacuous, top-down communication. Beanbags and colouring pens are an unwelcome distraction.

My best awayday ever was hosted, from memory, by an organisation called "What If?" in the Imagination offices in central London. A global mega-brand had paid thousands for the privilege – so we could all step inside the minds of teenage girls for a day. There was not a single teenage girl among us (it might have gone a lot better if there had been).

It would seem that every "Brainstorming Consultancy" has its own proprietary warm-up exercises. At 8am on a chilly day, this one involved forming a circle, jumping into the middle one at a time, saying something that you had done recently, and waiting for others who had done the same to jump into the middle alongside you. I think it was meant to build team spirit.

"Jump into the middle if you are wearing pink," it started. And some people jumped.

"Jump into the middle if you had muesli for breakfast!" Not many did; maybe there were not enough liberal North Londoners present.

This went on, and on.

One Brand Manager was obviously either not paying full attention or had forgotten this was not a drinking game among close friends. Soon it was her turn, and in she jumped.

"Jump into the middle if you have ever had a three-some with your boss!"

Nobody followed.

* * *

Business leaders, especially those focused on energy and financial services, worry about "more regulation" and all rush to agree on the preferable nature of "better regulation" instead. More principled behaviour will transcend the need for such regulation altogether – a new and progressive consensus will understand new boundaries of principle, not just the parameters of scale. Markets may be informative, but civic virtue can speak to a higher moral order. In this context, jostling about to what degree regulation should impact the size of a banker's bonus (a seemingly endless scrap *du jour*) fundamentally misses the point.

Regulation is a mere – and weak – manifestation of a rule-compliant culture, where we have to put (childish) boundaries in place to stop (childish) people offending. Responsibility – not regulation – needs to be the watchword of the responsible society. And that can start from within.

The social responsibility of business today must be to address the new ecology of interests within business on a more equal footing. Business must speak no longer to only the individual or the shareholder, but must embrace the employee as citizen, the customer as citizen, and the corporate entity as a collective citizen of the community and the planet that it serves. No one is trying to undermine the profit motive, per se – but profit without principle has no place in the new business ecology. Companies and brands including Marks & Spencer, Unilever, Patagonia, Zopa, and even The Co-Op are often mainstream, not maverick. What they're demonstrating is that being socially responsible is not just ethically and morally upright, it's good business too.

* * *

One of the working titles for this book was *Biscuits and Bathrooms*. First, because there comes a moment in every CEO's life when they question the cost of biscuits consumed in meetings and organise a biscuit review. Second, because Fred "The Shred" Goodwin famously threatened staff with disciplinary action over the fact that pink biscuits (not RBS's corporate blue) were being served. His email was entitled *Rogue Biscuits*. It was not ironic.

Meanwhile, putting posters on bathroom walls dictating the company's values has become commonplace in modern corporations, as though employees are only ever focused on corporate values when they pee. In the event that staff don't engage with the message, the solution appears to be . . . larger posters. Bathroom poster-posting is an industry whose value must now run into the millions. This is how many corporations genuinely think they demonstrate employee engagement.

Therefore, it is of little surprise that we no longer trust our leaders to make the right judgements or to show the right sort of leadership. They are wrongly obsessed with biscuits and bathrooms, rather than people and society. Business has lost its way.

Nowhere is this more evident than in the domain of employee engagement and internal communications, where the former has, in recent years, become a fashionable misnomer for the latter.

Back in the world of PR and communications, the large network consultancies – who continue to dominate the thinking and under-development of the industry as a whole – have rushed to monetise (an ugly word) this new space (two more ugly words) – chasing the dollars where large organisations have suddenly rushed to spend. Large corporates have themselves recognised the need to invest more in "their people" – now alert to the fact that the cliché that "our people are our most important asset" needed a strategy and a budget, too. Is this really employee engagement – or simply another attempt at using old-style PR to manage the message *to* the people in a rather anachronistic, top-down fashion?

* * *

I would suggest that future business establishes some fundamental principles around which better decisions can be made. Public Leaders need to ask, for example, what is the "right" amount of profit? How do we know whether our organisation is "maximising" its purpose? Is the purpose of our business "missionary" or "mercenary" – or both?

Critically, these principles should be respectful of the capitalist model; they are not a manifesto for its destruction, but rather its reform. Profit *is* compatible with a trusted and ethical organisation. Profit is not a dirty word, but sustainable profit optimisation is better than profit maximisation. It's about being fair and proportionate.

However, profit must be balanced with purpose. Business Purpose and Social Purpose must be fully aligned. The profit of an organisation should never be placed ahead of employee and customer *needs*. All businesses should be explicit about their stated purpose, and about what they are, and are not, prepared to accept and do. This applies to both their business model and their role in society.

Transparency and accountability are also key. This should include the creation of plain English explanations for the mechanisms of making money and a much higher level of openness in the way organisations conduct their business.

Under the future business model, values-led leadership becomes more important than tick-box compliance. Martin Wheatley, CEO of the UK's financial regulatory body, the FCA, has observed that banks, specifically, should move beyond what he called the "ethics of obedience" in order to establish better cultural frameworks – extending right through the supply chain, as well as externally, to customers. This means that leadership and management can no longer make decisions in isolation. Customers and employees need a democratic voice (and not just through carefully managed focus groups). Ideas and plans should be co-created with them, making the organisation's leadership co-produced and citizen-centric: hence the call for the establishment of wise crowds. At the same time, active participation in communities must extend beyond PR-led or philanthropic gestures and must be baked into the organisation's business model.

External validation is essential, through active Public Engagement and accountability to the assembled crowd. Best practice will be determined by what an organisation does, not (as happens elsewhere so frequently) by what it claims or promises, through its PR and advertising. An organisation can then only be deemed "trusted" (or, in the case of the banks, "socially useful") as a result of its actions, not its words. It cannot self-anoint.

Organisations should also *not* view their ethical or trusted status only in the context of their immediate competitors. There is no point simply being the best of a bad bunch. That is to enjoy a calamitous race to the bottom. There is a wider universe of purposeful brands that should be considered as peers.

First and foremost, however, any business needs to be a good, socially useful community. People have values: faceless organisations do not (that's why they create mission statements). Purpose has to be defined, built and curated by real people, from within. In this way, increased trustworthiness and better judgement enjoy stronger roots and are more likely to flourish.

* * *

For those of us who have worked with financial services companies, and especially with banks, the failures of their version of employee engagement are often all the more acute.

Walk into the Bishopsgate headquarters of RBS, and you will be struck by the "Our Values" messaging plastered on the walls, not unlike Monty Python's *Romani Ite Domum*. "Our Values" are Serving Customers; Doing The Right Thing; Working Together; Thinking Long Term. Nobody thought to take a paintbrush to these phrases in the wake of RBS's meltdown and super-impose them instead with *Under Review*.

Maybe the words were painted more recently than we might imagine.

The RBS example highlights the fundamental disconnect between how organisations so often see the world and how the world actually sees them. "None of this," as the Fairbanking Foundation noted, "is rocket science." It does not take a rocket scientist to understand that paying huge bonuses to investment bankers (under the pretext that employee retention is otherwise a problem) while denying staff on the front line a pay rise (or, worse still, threatening them with redundancy) is unjust and morally corrupt. This is why data continually shows the general public's belief that the major obstacle to restoring trust in banking and financial services rests with the bankers themselves – and the culture they protect. (Fairer products and services would help, too).

A thousand words, wherever they are painted, will not mask a single indecent act.

* * *

"There are two Paul Polmans."

These words were spoken openly by ▮▮▮▮ ▮▮▮▮▮,
one of his senior colleagues, just as Polman fever was
reaching its annual dizzying pre-Davos heights. Despite
his great media profile and commitment to change, Paul
Polman can still polarise opinion.

Polman is the CEO of Unilever, the world's second-
largest Fast Moving Consumer Goods (FMCG) company.
Seven out of ten households around the world use
Unilever products. Polman is also the pin-up for a new
generation of chief executives – thoughtful, responsible
and challenging of convention. His stated mission, to
double the company's sales while halving its environmental footprint, boldly goes where few CEOs have gone
before.

Cynics might argue that what has become known as
the Unilever Sustainable Living Plan (USLP) offers little
more than a better type of greenwash: more coherent and
consistent and applied across the company, but still the
brainchild of someone who is, at heart, a mercenary first,
not a missionary. The pursuit of common good, the cynics might argue, has simply been applied as a marketing
differentiator, much as traditional television advertising
(long the obsession for all FMCG companies) was many
decades before.

Polman's philosophy is now well-trodden – and most
recently articulated in the pages of the McKinsey Quarterly (May 2014) and *The Guardian*. "Capitalism has
served us enormously well," he wrote in a commentary
for the former, "yet while it has helped to reduce global
poverty and expand access to health care and education,
it has come at an enormous cost: unsustainable levels
of public and private debt, excessive consumerism and,

frankly, too many people who are left behind. Any system that prevents large numbers of people from participating or excludes them altogether will ultimately be rejected. And that's what you see happening."

In May 2012, Paul Polman received an Outstanding Achievement Award from the Atlantic Council. During his acceptance speech, he noted that "now is the time for business to step-up and lead." This echoed, word-for-word, the key message of the 2012 Edelman Trust Barometer, which Richard Edelman had shared with Polman while at the World Economic Forum in Davos a few months earlier. Likewise, this leadership message had been cascaded through the ranks at Unilever by many of us (Unilever was, at that point, Edelman's largest global client) and by sharing articles we had authored with Polman's backbench of advisers and speechwriters.

Richard Edelman called me from the awards dinner, dead chuffed that Polman, speaking about the crisis of trust in business, had been so spot-on. In truth, the genesis and ownership of the precise phrase matters little. The substance matters more.

"The need for responsible business has never been greater," continued the Unilever CEO, citing the immediate challenges and dangers surrounding food security, climate change, and social and economic development.

"We have to act before it is too late . . . the demand for change from citizens is growing – social media is giving them a voice," he said.

Polman's position then was clear: "capitalism isn't dead – but it needs a fresh expression."

Whether or not there are "two Paul Polmans" ("what a double-talking slimeball," reads one comment from a clear Polman detractor calling themselves *westcoastlogik* on the YouTube channel page), Polman rightly links the erosion of trust, the catastrophes of consumption and the issue of leadership – all the more surprising given that the livelihood of the corporation he leads depends on consumption itself. He stops short of calling for revolution – as he noted in a later McKinsey piece, "capitalism needs to evolve, and that requires different types of leaders from what we have had before." That said, "business simply can't be a bystander in a system that gives it life in the first place."

Corporate leaders, Polman observes, cannot make these changes alone. There also needs to be political will. In addition, pension fund managers are key agents for change – pension funds own up to 75% of the capital on the US stock exchanges. Better systems; long-term, purpose-driven thinking; greater transparency; more partnerships; agile and imaginative incentive and compensation schemes – these are the hallmarks of Polman's new corporation, along with what he calls "a more mature dialogue" with Unilever's investor base.

Campaigner George Monbiot is eviscerating in his condemnation of Unilever. He is certainly prominent among the sceptics. Railing against the delegation of political power to profit-hungry corporations, in an article for *The Guardian* in April 2014, Monbiot admits that he would prefer companies to be more like Unilever than Goldman Sachs, Exxon or Cargill. About Unilever, he says:

"I can think of no entity that has done more to blur the lines between the role of the private sector and the role of the public sector. If you blotted out its name while reading its web pages, you could mistake it for an agency of the United Nations.

"Its people inhabit (to name a few) the British government's Ecosystem Markets Task Force and Scientific Advisory Committee on Nutrition, the International

Fund for Agricultural Development, the G8's New Alliance for Food Security and Nutrition, the World Food Programme, the Global Green Growth Forum, the UN's Scaling Up Nutrition programme, its Sustainable Development Solutions Network, Global Compact and the UN High Level Panel on global development.

"Sometimes Unilever uses this power well. Its efforts to reduce its own use of energy and water and its production of waste, and to project these changes beyond its own walls, look credible and impressive. Sometimes its initiatives look to me like self-serving bullshit."

Like Monbiot, my *Citizen Renaissance* co-author, Jules Peck, has also raised doubts about the "other" Paul and Unilever's most recent iteration of its Sustainable Living Plan. Called Project Sunlight, the plan certainly carries the airs and emblems of a more blatant marketing programme. Writing for *The Huffington Post*, Jules commented:

"There is much in Project Sunlight that is heading in the right direction. But critics are saying that Project Sunlight ultimately suggests we can shop and consume our way to utopia, that it mixes calls to action associated purely with the consumer side of our psyche in with more progressive messages. It is suggested that this risks undermining the overall effect of the Project Sunlight campaign and set [sic] up a cognitive dissonance which at best will freeze us into confusion and inaction, but more likely send us scurrying back into what we know – extrinsically orientated consumerism, atomised, individualistic actions and the hedonic treadmill."

* * *

Nowhere is this missionary/mercenary debate more resonant than in Unilever's commitment to the people and economy of Pakistan. Pakistan is regarded by many as a failed state and shunned by global corporations, Unilever has become not only the single largest inward investor in the country, but also its largest advertiser. It continues to support the economy in numerous ways, some of them highly innovative, including a for-profit microfinancing scheme to support women in rural districts.

As the *Financial Times* reported:

".... it is in the countryside that Unilever has developed its most innovative outreach programme: a form of microfinance, but for profit. It recruits village women and teaches them beauty skills – for example, training them in how to apply conditioner to newly washed hair and how best to apply make-up. It then helps them to convert a room in their homes into an informal beauty parlour, where they can pass on expertise to their neighbours and sell them Unilever products in the process. These sales earn commission for the women, with the most successful earning up to Rp10,000 a year."

This could be seen as feeding the consumption fetish and further promoting "wants" over "needs". Alternatively, it could be seen as enlightened self-interest but also as empowering and democratising. Those who think that society-first thinking must sacrifice profit for "good" are (a) wrong and (b) usually scare-mongering.

We would be thoughtless if we did not respect George Monbiot's warnings of the corporate takeover but, equally, we are missing a huge opportunity if we do not embrace the potential for transformation that global corporations bring. The challenge is to ensure that business leadership can be trusted – meaning that it has to be activist, co-produced, citizen-centric and society-first.

* * *

Paul Polman at Unilever is not a lone crusader.

"Tata is a microcosm of India. It is huge, sprawling, complex, full of heritage, and it needs to change. But it's difficult to change." So is quoted R. Gopalakrishnan, Senior Director, in 2011. *The Economist* took a different tack: "Westerners tend to associate it [Tata] with unre-constructed tradition and messy family politics."

Tata's founder, Jamsetji Nusserwanji Tata, recognised commercial activity as the most effective way to effect social change. In a similar vein to UK pioneers like Cadbury and Rowntree, Robert Owen and Titus Salt, Tata engages in a number of community activities, including creating an Endowment Trust that sponsors international education. The founding principles were extended to the workplace: Tata was one of the first companies to institute the eight-hour day in India and implement other key initiatives such as maternity benefits. The flourishing of Tata also closely mirrors the development of the Indian state and its escape from British colonial legacy, not least via the development and pioneering of national industries. Tata built the first national steel plant in India, for example, and launched the first domestic airline. The list is extensive and impressive.

"Reverence for Jamsetji Tata, the group's founder," continued *The Economist*, "borders on ancestor worship." His ever-present busts are garlanded with fresh flowers daily and there is a yearly march to celebrate his birthday.

Tata values citizens (employees, clients and society at large) above all else. The company's success is determined not just by capital assets, but also by social capital. Society is not a mere stakeholder – it is the purpose of the business' existence. Society has played a role in its advancement, and Tata recognises the need to pay back.

Tata sees itself as a societal steward and trustee.

Gopalakrishnan said in August 2009: "Business is a servant of society... when you have earned a lot of money whose money is it? Did that money come to you entirely because of yourself or is it possible that you are merely an instrument through which you should canalise it back to society?"

This list of social benefits and strategic philanthropy continues: Tata establishes and finances research, educational and cultural institutes in India. It founded the National Centre of Performing Arts and the Tata Institute of Social Sciences (growing educational facilities). It reaches out to the bottom of the social pyramid – the Tata Medical Centre earmarks 50% of beds for the free treatment of the poorer sections of society.

Tata Steel sets a budget for social security to improve access to healthcare and education. Its company town, Jamshedpur, has all city institutions run by Tata Steel and has developed services and infrastructure such as sports arenas. The philosophy extends to the social utility of product and service innovations. Tata's Nano car was developed as affordable (each car costs $2,500) transport for Indian families and a safer alternative to scooters, and the company has designed and donated a software package that can teach adults to read in 40 hours, thereby using its core competencies to aid social development and make this development more accessible.

Tarun Khanna, a Harvard Business School authority on Tata, argues that this particular private sector role makes sense in India, where there is often weak government and under-developed institutions. But Partha Sengupta, Vice President of Corporate Services Tata Steel, sees it in very straightforward terms: "for us, [community support] is a fixed cost of manufacturing."

* * *

Some of the older "general" corporations – the behemoths of the 20th century – are now embracing a more progressive agenda. This is not always because of altruistic ambition. Honest, enlightened self-interest is OK but, as I have argued, profit can be aligned with purpose. It does not have to be a binary choice.

GE's CEO Jeff Immelt is credited with the company's EcoMagination and HealthyMagination programmes. He is clear that it is OK to make money as well as do good. He says, "Green is green" – it is fine to make money out of environmentally better products. Immelt wants to reduce greenhouse gas emissions by 25% and improve the energy intensity of operations by 50%, through *profitable innovation programmes*. EcoMagination revenues continue to grow at twice the rate of total company revenues. In 2012, it accounted for approximately $25 billion in sales.

* * *

Patagonia is a Californian outdoor technical and casual apparel company that has been recognised as a leader of socially responsible business practice. Acclaimed as a corporation that is able to deliver profit while minimising environmental impact, it is celebrated by business schools and journals the world over.

Patagonia's 2013 annual revenue was $575 million – an increase from $543 million in 2012 and $417 million in 2011. Its gross profit margin was 52.6% – proof that it is possible to do the right thing and still make money.

As inspirational founder Yvon Chouinard said in 2005:

"If we wish to lead corporate America by example, we have to be profitable. No company will respect us, no matter how much money we give away or how much publicity we receive for being one of the *100 Best Companies*, if we are not profitable."

Patagonia's corporate aim is pretty simple: to balance sustainable ideals with business growth. Its mission statement reads thus: "to use business to inspire and implement solutions to the environmental crisis."

In Chouinard's 2005 autobiography *Let My People Go Surfing*, he railed against the ugly ethos of traditional corporate behaviour. "I wanted to distance myself as far as possible from those pasty-faced corpses in suits I saw in airline magazine ads. If I had to be a businessman, I was going to do it on my terms."

Chouinard expanded on his vision for the company's primary function in an interview with *The Wall Street Journal* in 2012: "I never even wanted to be in business. But I hang onto Patagonia because it's my resource to do something good. It's a way to demonstrate that corporations can lead examined lives."

The Wall Street Journal observed in response: "His [Chouinard's] approach to leading a company is perhaps best understood as a sort of performance art – less about bottom line than about providing a road map for future entrepreneurs."

Patagonia was one of the first companies to register as a Benefit Corporation (subsequently known as "B-Corps") in January 2013. This functions as a legal entity that holds directors accountable for their treatment of people and the planet, alongside their goals to optimise shareholder return. In its articles of incorporation, Patagonia includes among the fiduciary duties of its executives "consideration of the interests of workers, community and the environment," and the purpose of creating "general public benefit". Or, as others might call it, common good.

The company continues to walk the walk. Its *Footprint Chronicles* makes public significant information about its supply chain, cataloguing Patagonia's environmental impact at each stage. It is presented in a map format, providing details of each component of the chain, including employee gender mix, the language they speak and the location of the activity.

In one of its most celebrated acts, Patagonia took out a full-page advert in *The New York Times* on Black Friday, 2011 (traditionally, the busiest retail day of the year). It was entitled, "Don't Buy This Jacket" and featured one of the company's products. It gave the exact environmental impact of the production process of the R2 jacket, which requires 135 litres of water to make, and the CO_2 used during its journey to the store. The ad concluded: "the environmental cost of everything we make is astonishing."

Harvard Business School Professor Forest Reinhardt recalled: "I have never seen a company tell customers to buy less of its product." Patagonia had established a dialogue on the issue of consumerism. The ad alone generated 30,000 signatures towards a pledge to exercise more consideration before making purchases. It also increased consumer loyalty and brand identification over a longer period and cemented its status as a mission-led business. Uri Nehen, in a later *Harvard Business Review* blog post, characterised this as "Systemic Authenticity". Raj Sisodia, in his 2012 study for Conscious Capitalism, asserted that mission-led businesses outperform the market by a factor of nine to one.

* * *

The social successes of brands like Tata and Patagonia notwithstanding, recent research from advertising agency group Havas is wonderfully telling: "Most people worldwide would not care if more than 73% of brands disappeared tomorrow." This is a shocking indictment of the world of advertising, gloss and spin. The Havas report summary added ruefully, and apparently without irony, "think about the money spent globally on marketing, communications and public relations."

If we want people to start caring about brands again, brands (and the organisations and leaders behind them) will have to show that they care about people and values too.

* * *

CHAPTER SIX: SOCIAL DEMOCRACY
"WE ARE ALL CHILDREN OF THE GREEKS"

"We Are All Children of the Greeks"

Public Relations was, according to popular legand, the brainchild of Sigmund Freud's nephew, Edward Bernays, created as a means of control over the masses, whose democratic judgement he did not trust. From the 1950s onwards, PR exploded into a global industry of business and political propaganda. It celebrated its low point with the ugly moniker of spin and spawned a sibling, Corporate Social Responsibility, which favours compliance over values. Mission statements, constructed by PR teams with the tokenistic acceptance and "approval" of employee focus groups, became the outward expression of this propaganda. Say something often enough (five times, according to the old adage) and people might even believe it.

Senior business leaders and PR executives, apparently blind, still fail to see that we live in the age of US whistleblower Edward Snowden, not Edward Bernays. That is why they stick to their faithful mission statement rhetoric, even while radical honesty and radical transparency prevail.

Companies that legally commit themselves to honour ethical values, while still seeking to optimise profits, can and do exist. These companies, such as the much-vaunted B Corporations in the US, want to positively impact society and the environment, and consider the implications of their actions not only for shareholders, but also for their employees, the communities in which they work, and the wider world in which we all live.

This new model can re-shape business and therefore has the ability to altogether remove the need for Public Relations and its redundant verbal paraphernalia. This new model is activist, co-produced, citizen-centric and society-first. It is *social*, because it is of and among real people, and *democratic*, because it gives voice to all. At its most fundamental level, Public Leadership returns "purpose" to the core of business. And "purpose" has a clear moral and ethical dimension.

"Capital is blind," argues Thomas Piketty in his now controversial book. Excesses in executive pay are a product of "meritocratic extremism." Rising wealth inequality now imperils capitalism, rather than protects it. "The gap between rich and poor threatens to destroy us."

* * *

"Common good" is often regarded as a pejorative term. Some consider it a cloak for a socialist agenda. But this is, I think, because market fundamentalists and libertarians have spent the best part of four decades trying to discredit the wording, and are essentially winning the argument. "Common good," to them, belies state intervention and the ascendancy of equality of condition over equality of opportunity. They are wrong. "Common good" is a hallmark of principle, not one of top-down intervention. It simply means a return to the core Aristotelian principle of fairness and (social) justice. Its roots run far deeper than the birth of the socialist movement or the current mission of the UK Green Party.

Sir Philip Dilley, Chair of the UK Environment Agency and former Chairman of pioneering engineering firm Arup, is under no illusions. "Yes, people are interested in the common good," he argues, "with doing things that are socially useful." Arup is a global firm of 11,500 people

– yet still united by a common purpose that traces its origins to what is referred to as "the key speech" by legendary founder Ove Arup in September 1970.

"From time to time," runs the more recently added introduction, "we have asked ourselves whether what he [Ove] said in 1970 remains valid for us, despite the fact that, inevitably, some specifics about the firm's organisation and individuals' roles therein, to which he refers in passing, have changed over the years. On each occasion we have found that it does, and thereby reaffirmed our commitment to these principles.

"The Key Speech is required reading for each person who joins Arup or who wants to be reminded of what we are all about."

Dilley, a warm and thoughtful man, describes Arup the person as "the original rebel in Bohemian Fitzrovia," who was determined that the firm's early (franchise) partnerships would "fight together for the common good." Early principles became embedded values – "straight and honourable dealings," "*reasonable* prosperity," "social usefulness" – all reminders that what, for many, went awry in the past 30 years has, for others, long been been core philosophy.

Purpose and context, for Arup, remain as one. These are not the vacuous mission statements or promises of an Enron ("integrity, communication, fair compensation and excellence"), Arthur Andersen ("integrity, passion, service, excellence"), Goldman Sachs ("integrity, honesty and our client's interests always come first") or even RBS (hilariously, "how we do business today drives how we are Building Tomorrow").

Readers may not be surprised to learn that Ove Arup started his adult life as a philosopher.

* * *

I think Aristotle was an early social democrat. If he had been alive today, Aristotle would no doubt have been an advocate of Public Leadership as we are beginning to understand it. He would recognise the citizen state within business (as well as within the body politic too). He would have revealed the hidden and dynamic authority of real people within the organisation – seeing them as the active *polis*. It is real people that are authentic and who legitimise power. They are thus transformative, if properly empowered and not institutionally suppressed. Technology is their happy bedfellow, enabling participation and accountability in equal measure. Websites and apps like "Rate My Boss" or "Glass Door", deserve wider application. Embracing the citizen state in business offers a vital first step in the better reform of business itself.

Hence the need to shift away from the redundant model of Public Relations. The future of trust belongs to the citizen in a vibrant eco-system of peers, not to the leader protected and defended by his (usually, *his*) PR team.

* * *

Two books published in relatively quick succession helped catalyse my thinking about the fall of Public Relations and the rise of Public Leadership. Both intensified a personal sense of outrage about the distortions of the unfettered free-marketeering of the consumer society and the communications industry that egged it on.

The first, Tony Judt's *Ill Fares The Land*, was published in 2010; the other, Michael Sandel's *What Money Can't Buy*, followed a couple of years later. Both are, at heart, pleas for the restoration of social democracy and reveal an angry conviction that the world – or we – cannot go on like this.

I had been drawn to the fledgling Social Democratic Party in the early 80s, with its Limehouse Declaration commitment to an "open, classless and more equal society." Looking back a quarter of a century later, *The Guardian* examined the SDP's "enduring relevance," noting that its formation, for some, "remains a vivid and traumatic event that has shaped their lives." I am one of that number. David Owen spoke at the launch of the SDP about "freeing Britain" from Thatcherism. I would contend that we are still not free yet.

* * *

One of the finest-ever treatises on politics, Judt's *Ill Fares The Land* is polemical and passionate in equal measure, and despite Judt's untimely death this is in many ways *the* book for our times: the perfect re-articulation of social democracy and the need for a better way of being; a redefinition of common good; a cry for fairness; and a clear argument for the necessary end of placing selfish, material well-being over a higher moral order for society as a whole. Judt's call for a return to the radicalism of social democracy wonderfully connects the intellectual past with a progressive future in a way that so many of today's political pragmatists all too readily deny.

"Much of what is amiss in our world can best be captured in the language of classical political thought," he writes. "We are intuitively familiar with issues of injustice, unfairness, inequality and immorality – we have just forgotten how to talk about them. Social democracy once articulated such concerns, until it, too, lost its way."

Michael Ignatieff sees the victory of social and cultural progressives in the 1960s as having been won at the cost of an equally resounding defeat in matters of economics. Since 1969, US GDP has tripled in real terms, yet 60 million Americans have household incomes of less than $20,000 a year. "Welfare reform," he writes, "has destroyed the social safety net. Inequality is now at pre-New Deal levels. The minimum wage is 25% lower in real terms. Six million Americans live in households with no income at all."

* * *

Sandel's work is equally compelling – comparing the ethics of "fast lane" queuing at Disneyland with the same behaviour within hospitals and health services. Likewise, the perverse use of market mechanisms to help protect Black Rhinos from extinction, contrasted with the odd markets created by Canadian native seal culls, or the introduction of "Stranger Originated Life Insurance" (pay-outs for the corporates on an employee's death) or, still worse, viaticals – the death bonds championed by ███████ ███████, even after the Global Financial Crisis had hit. Companies would, apparently, buy out the life insurance policies of AIDS patients – later widening this to a pool of life-threatening diseases in order to mitigate risk – and ride the odds on when their charges would die.

"Over the past three decades," Sandel argues, "markets – and market values – have come to govern our lives as never before." That said, Sandel is neither anti-capitalist nor anti-market. "No other mechanism for organising the production and distribution of goods," he writes, "has proved as successful for generating affluence and prosperity."

Sandel focuses our attention on a more profound loss of our collective moral compass. "The most fateful change that unfolded in the last three decades was not an increase in greed. It was the expansion of markets, and of market values, into spheres of life where they don't belong."

Sandel's concerns were captured by Christine Bader, a BP employee until 2008, in *The Evolution of a Corporate Idealist*. She is incensed, whether by the Rana Plaza building collapse or the Deepwater Horizon oil spill, that the corporate world "does not ever learn." Her conclusions are stark: people lie; people don't talk to one another; safety and responsibility cost money – and no one ever gets rewarded for disasters averted; few people bear witness; no one really understands what corporate responsibility really means; and consumers refuse to pay more. "We are therefore in a free for all, where CSR means whatever a company wants it to mean." Consumers must bring real pressure to bear, because "we all have a role to play."

I had long been a fan of Sandel – a truly accessible moral philosopher. In his 2009 Reith Lectures, Sandel observed prospects for the common good and called for "A New Citizenship." Much of what he said then chimed with the central tenet of *Citizen Renaissance* – namely the prevailing confusion between consumer and civic values and the urgent need for a reversal that places "citizen" ahead of "consumer."

Sandel called for a richer and more morally courageous public discourse, later echoed in *What Money Can't Buy*, to question what a good life should really look like. He was challenging some of the rule-based dogma that has exacerbated many of the crises we currently face – economic, political and, of course, environmental. As the philanthropist politician David Sainsbury noted in his 2013 essay for the Royal Society of the Arts journal, "the past thirty years of market fundamentalism has allowed the idea that there is such a thing as public interest to atrophy."

Judt and Sandel would, I think, both argue that leaders must stop treating the *polis* with contempt and stop using PR as a means to hijack and part-own the agenda on their shaped terms. Better leadership and full engagement with citizens to "do what is right," fair and proportionate, is needed instead. And, while none of this is hugely revelatory, leaders in both business and politics seem incapable of making the step change. This is because the system in which they co-conspire, protected by that thin gossamer of PR, inhibits them. They have lost touch with their inner Greeks, demonising the concept of common good along the way.

* * *

"I think we should create a stakeholder crowd and let them help us on the journey towards greater trust," I said to ███████ ███ ████████, a City CEO, in late 2013.

"Why would we do that? We might not like what they say."

"Isn't it better to know what people are thinking, in order for us to put things right again? Don't you always talk about listening to the customer, putting the customer first, etc.?"

"Yes, but not like that."

"Why?"

"We cannot listen to everyone. They might not be, well, right."

No leader can learn if they do not listen. And listening to the wise crowd – the 91% – must surely be smarter than making it up.

* * *

In 2007, on the eve of the Global Financial Crisis, it was clear that we were already on a collision course between profit and purpose – then crystallised through the twin lens of climate change and well-being – and that, as the Head of Emerging Markets at Hermes, Gary Greenberg, later observed, we may have to start thinking about a "post-growth" world.

Jules Peck is more radical in his call for no- or low-growth economic thinking. I am a firm believer in *better* growth. We are both aligned on the need for a different model of capitalism. There is no doubt in our minds that too many organisations, governance structures, markets and indeed leadership teams were built for yesterday and are no longer relevant or fit for purpose today. Radical, revolutionary action is needed to step forward into a new era of Public Leadership. Evolve only slowly and "they will get you."

This does not make me an anti-capitalist. As fund manager Jeremy Grantham said in early 2014, "capitalism does millions of things better than the alternatives. However, it is totally ill-equipped to deal with a small handful of issues. Unfortunately, they are the issues that are absolutely central to our long-term well-being and even survival."

The *Financial Times'* Martin Wolf makes a similar, powerful point. He has written poignantly about how the current model of capitalism "privatises profits and socialises risks," also arguing that "managing… a combination of market dynamism with effective redistribution is one of the defining political challenges of our era. It will take purposive action by states and greater co-operation among them, notably on taxation."

But what has all this to do with trust and, beyond this, with the world of Public Relations?

Even the most basic trust data has, for the past decade at least, spoken to the need to embrace societal interests over pure, corporate interests: in very simple terms, to re-calibrate the relationship between profit and purpose. Even before the surge in social media and peer-to-peer communications, NGOs were scoring higher than business in the trust stakes. Although often un-elected and unaccountable, they were nonetheless filling the conscience deficits created by global multi-national corporations.

Meanwhile, the great TED Talk words of Professor Tim Jackson continue to sound a truth: "we spend money we don't have on things we don't need to make impressions that don't last on people we don't even care about," Jackson says, concluding "that ecological damage should be the result of a series of consumption practices which clearly fail to increase wellbeing has all the characteristics of a social pathology."

* * *

Sir Titus Salt was an early 19th century wool magnate and the founder of Saltaire, a model village in Bradford, Yorkshire. Like Robert Owen's New Lanark Mills several years earlier, Saltaire combined housing, employment, social services and education in what became one of the pivotal developments of enlightened town planning. Workers were provided with homes away from the prevailing slums; wash-houses enjoyed running water; a hospital was available for all, to help develop the concept of public health; education was fostered not only through a village school, but also with a library, reading room, a concert hall and a gym; and the public spaces included a park, allotments and a boathouse. This was new model living, enlightened values setting best practice for the public sector to follow.

Salt's model is not unique. John Spedan Lewis founded the John Lewis Partnership with the conviction that the success of the business was tied to the happiness and well-being of its employees and by its service to the community as a whole – a philosophy that is upheld to this day.

"The real heart of this business," says Patrick Lewis, great-grandson of the founder and a board member today, "is a real sense of purpose, which is about more than just making money or creating financial value.

"It is all about the long-term," he adds. "We co-produce responsibility, relationships and influence."

Under the John Lewis Partnership model, the Chairman gets the same percentage bonus as a shelf-stacker. The company still has – and fights to protect – a final salary pension scheme for all employees, and offers things like study grants.

Patrick Lewis points out that the first complaints about products or services tend not to come from angry customers but instead from concerned employees (who also happen to be shareholders in the business). John Lewis may not be an absolute saint, but there is a lesson here for a more robust and sensible form of corporate accountability.

"The tax environment," notes Lewis, "needs to change. Employee ownership should be encouraged over PLC ownership. Employee ownership needs to be made easier, for accountants to understand."

The success of John Lewis, Arup or of Spain's Mondragon bears testament to the legitimacy and power of owner-operated businesses, even at scale. Governance structures need to be revisited and refreshed, while, as in cases like some banks, the failures of one man – or the financial greed of some within a senior team – should not be mistaken for the failures of an entire business philosophy.

* * *

The terms "shared value" and "shared interests" have become part of the *Harvard Business Review* buzzword bingo, along with "long-termism" and "engagement." The challenge is to give these principles some meaning. Business has a core role in transforming society – and we, as citizens, must work hard to transform business.

The current middle ground is occupied by Professor Michael Porter. His and Mark Kramer's *Harvard Business Review* piece on shared value, published in January 2011, presented a tempered argument for business and an explanation of purpose in a multiple stakeholder world; a more socially liberal alternative to Milton Friedman's "make money first" thinking.

Others have branded this "Conscious Capitalism" – another steady middle ground between purpose and profit. John Mackey is co-CEO and co-founder of Whole Foods Market. He also co-authored *Conscious Capitalism Inc.* with Dr Raj Sisordia:

"A good metaphor for the appropriate role of business in society is citizenship. A conscious business behaves like a responsible citizen in all its communities. This means that it helps tackle some of the problems that communities are struggling with on a local, national and potentially global basis."

Shared value makes a lot of sense in a networked world, where we need to think in terms of connected communities, rather than controlled audiences dominated by authority and elites. But it is in many ways a bland alternative in a society that demands and deserves more radical action. Points of fundamental philosophical importance have been watered down into an easy CEO sound bite.

I believe that citizen shareholders and citizen consumers should now openly advocate their support for "common good" companies and "common good" approaches – and properly hold to account (i.e. agitate and even remove) those business leaders, businesses and brands who have no real appetite for transition and transformation. Real change is not going to come from the top – either in the financial system or the political system.

As citizens and activists this could be the bare bones of a manifesto for a new citizen capitalism:

1. Demand business reform that moves beyond box-ticking compliance. Citizen capitalism insists on a more fundamental re-examination of *principles*, *values* and – ultimately – *leadership*.
2. Only support businesses that balance profit with purpose to deliver common good, asking for more than the narrow and selfish focus on money alone.
3. As shareholders and stakeholders, play a more active and empowered participatory role, through accountable crowds and via supervisory boards, employee and supply-chain councils and a non-executive presence.
4. Build ownership models on a broader membership basis, safeguarding longer-term value. Establish more mutuals, partnerships and co-operatives.
5. Demand institutional change. Both UK and global government and constitutional organisations need urgent reform. This applies to those that govern business as well as citizens. Many of the legacy

foundations that emerged after WWII are simply no longer fit for purpose.

6. Work hard to improve and share financial literacy across the board.

7. And, finally, collectively measure success in terms of material well-being and ultimately happiness – and not just in growth or through financial metrics.

"Citizen-consumer values are changing fast amid the flourishing of the wikiworld of the 'frictionless' and relationship economy," wrote Jules Peck on www.jerichochambers.com:

"We are seeing the rise and rise of a digital-democracy powered, peer-to-peer, crowd and matrix of citizen makers and doers. From Airbnb to Blablacar, The Mesh, Openinnovationmeetups and The-people-who-share, these innovations and movements are sending shockwaves through the mainstream. As Kevin Keely, former executive editor of Wired has said 'How close to a non-capitalistic, open source peer production society can this movement take us?' Closer than we thought."

Citizen activism is on the march.

* * *

Porto Alegre was one of the host cities for the 2014 FIFA World Cup. It is the capital city of the southern Brazilian state, Rio Grande do Sul. More importantly, Porto Alegre is internationally renowned for its citizens' high standard of living, its commitment to sustainability and as the pioneer for bringing citizen participation into its budget and decision-making processes.

The principles are clear: the executive branch is better represented by the municipality, while the primacy of dialogue with citizenry is absolute. This is, in many ways, the classical *agora* made real.

Participatory budgeting, for which Porto Alegre achieved subsequent global fame, started in 1989 and was formulated in tandem with Brazil's progression towards democracy in the 1980s. It was a popular reaction to the centralised and non-democratic institutions that had previously prevailed.

Porto Alegre's local districts meet in plenary assemblies to discuss and vote on the priorities they want to focus on for budget allocations (20% housing, 30% education, etc.). This is split into two sections – local priorities and concerns affecting the entire city. They also elect delegates for the Municipal Council of the Budget. At the budgetary council, delegates then meet again to decide on a final budget, which is then approved by the city council. It all works from the bottom up.

The process gives voice to delegates representing local communities and their interests. It is not aligned with embedded or institutional powers, and thus avoids bias (or even corruption claims) that often accompanies the vested interests of small, powerful cliques.

Decision-making is facilitated largely through discussions. Voting is recognised as something of a last resort. This is collaborative politics brought to life, and it is no surprise that Porto Alegre has been a frequent host of the World Social Forum (an anti-establishment counterpoint to the World Economic Forum).

Former Mayor Tarso Genro, speaking in 1999, sees it thus: Porto Alegre is a "non-state public sphere... a new interface between state and society that combines the 'direct action' of the citizens – organised around a growing network of multiple local organisations – with the already existing public institutions."

Neighbourhood associations are the main vehicle for popular participation – churches and schools are used as venues for the discussions because they are locally based and familiar to residents. Giovanni Allegretti, senior researcher at the Centre for Social Studies at Coimbra University in Portugal, emphasises the benefit of face-to-face discussions in the decision-making process. Healthy dialogue is established through the consultations.

"[Participatory budgeting] entrusts citizens with budget decisions. Building trust between government authorities and citizens matters very much, and so does dialogue among them."

The Porto Alegre example offers an interesting counter-argument to the campaigning digital democracy espoused by the likes of 38 Degrees and the effectiveness, but potentially detached nature of, online political engagement.

"People are more generous and their sense of solidarity is stronger than you would think. But authorities [still] have to stimulate the exchange," comments Allegretti. "If people stay in privacy, they tend to be more egoistic... the idea is to create more social links between the administration and the people... you have to focus on personal contact."

Science author Steve Johnson recognises Porto Alegre as a success story for "peer progressivism". Change, he argues, occurs most effectively via collaborative networks that operate beyond the traditional controls of state or marketplace.

* * *

In a network of employee-owned businesses, many believe that "distributed leadership" is vital. "Leadership needs to be developed; it needs to be spread widely and it needs to be reproducible." So said Jose Luis Lafuente, Mondragon's Corporate Management Model Specialist, in an interview in May 2012.

Mondragon is the world's largest co-operative federation, with companies operating in four sectors: finance, industry, retail and knowledge. In the post-credit-crunch era, its successful structure of broad-based employee ownership has presented Mondragon as an identifiable alternative to the capitalist corporate model that otherwise prioritises shareholders. Some who have been "moved and inspired by MCC's record, will use it to build their particular non-capitalist cooperative enterprises as innovations provoked by today's global economic crisis," ran a Democracy at Work report in January 2013.

Mondragon's global revenues totalled €14.08 billion in 2012. It employs approximately 83,000 people across 256 different companies, operating under 140 co-operative enterprises. Its principal aim is to remain competitive while promoting co-operative principles. It approaches business and its function from a humanist perspective – largely to improve the individual's moral character. The role of profit in the organisation is subverted to an agency that serves the well-being of the workforce. Its mission statements reinforce its beliefs in fostering solidarity and democratic methods for organisation and management, encouraging worker participation in management, the egalitarian spread of wages and profits, and the development of human and technological skills through training and innovation.

Mondragon employees can become worker-members of the co-operative by committing to the Mondragon Constitution and committing €13,500, which is refunded at retirement. This provides them with an ownership stake in the company. They receive a share of its annual profits and possess decision-making control in the form of an ability to vote on management and policy direction.

It is therefore a workers' co-operative at scale. It is not accountable to outside investors and resists stock-market-driven short-termism. It replaces a goal of profit maximisation at all costs with collective goals supporting the betterment of the company and all those who participate.

Worker-members can influence decision-making by participating through democratic channels set up throughout the company. They can vote on direct management and internal affairs within their own co-operative, while also engaging collectively to decide on the running of the organisation as a whole.

Co-operatives' general assemblies convene annually and worker-members operate democratically to elect upper management. They choose and employ a Managing Director and members of the Governing and Social Council are elected, which are responsible for performing management functions such as overseeing salary levels and recruitment.

The Co-operative Congresses, which comprise 650 worker-members, define the organisation's common principles and policies in the form of four-year strategic plans and annual business plans, thus formulating a self-directed enterprise. Within each individual company, worker-managers have two meetings a month to discuss key business, financial and social topics and the wider position of Mondragon as a whole.

Every member-worker, from manager to worker, has an equal vote in decision-making. This addresses the issue of separating voting rights from ownership rights. Leaders are more accountable to their co-workers. Operating under these democratic principles prioritises consultation and communication with the workers. Information transparency is absolute: any co-op member can ask for the company's financial records at any time.

Mondragon's management structure has been described as an "inverted conglomerate," which places operational decisions and ultimate authority at the bottom of the traditional power pyramid with individual companies and their employee members. This allows for the benefit of their intimate knowledge of operations and local issues, rather than a detached decision-making authority.

Mondragon has been the subject of a great deal of academic study. It "re-unites in one person the functions of worker, manager and owner. Capitalism consigns these functions to three separate persons...re-uniting these functions in each member abolishes the conflict among the three groups," observed Betsy Bowman and Bob Stone in their paper "Cooperativisation on the Mondragon Model".

Analysts deploy Mondragon as a case study to support the wider argument that co-operatives are more enduring and are less susceptible to perverse incentives and other problems of organisational governance than more traditionally managed organisations.

"What helps us stand out is *the combination* of employee ownership and participation," said Lafuente in May 2012. "The two roles of owner and worker are somewhat in tension, but they are also complementary, two sides of the same coin. When co-owners act as workers, accepting the expertise and 'local authority' of others, they know that they have ownership rights that they can and should exercise to ensure accountability and fairness, and this knowledge helps keep things in balance."

Mondragon Chairman Jose Maria Aldecoa sees the benefit in very stark terms:

"In a regular company, the worker thinks: 'you, the boss, pay me, and, if later the company closes I get compensation, and that is not my problem. Here the company is ours, and if there is no company there is no work."

* * *

CHAPTER SEVEN: PROGRESSIVE CORPORATISM
ASK BIGGER QUESTIONS

Ask Bigger Questions

The new model of Public Leadership cannot thrive independently of a new model for corporate behaviour.

In spring 2013, I had started thinking about Progressive Communication (which eventually led to Public Leadership) as the antidote to the regressive thinking of Public Relations. But, as I dug deeper into the idea, I realised that communication could never be anything more than part of a wider corporate re-set.

There is a paradox: corporates are the future (the business states of the 21st century) – but the future is not corporate, as we have come to understand it. It is asymmetrical and activist, and its economies are no longer traditional and rigid, but creative and flexible. The management principles for this paradoxical corporate future must reflect this complex, chaotic creativity.

This requires the effective re-engineering of the DNA of corporations, simultaneously looking beyond shareholder value and rejecting the false orthodoxy of "pure" markets and "maximised" profit. Social is the new normal – not just social media or social business but social impact, social enterprise and social value. (Jesse Norman's *Anatomy* analysis of the Big Society provides some excellent examples here – including, at a national level, how Norway invested its sudden-found oil wealth to safeguard future societal well-being, rather than rushing to consumerise and spend everything at once. It built a trust for the future.)

The lack of research and understanding into the social

impact of business is an acute concern. I sit on the Advisory Board of ETHOS: The Centre for Responsible Enterprise at Cass Business School. In its summary manifesto, the organisation recognises that: "the social impacts of business have not received much attention in management research. Addressing the challenges of sustainability requires a multi-level approach focusing on the broader political economy and the institutions that govern the global economy."

* * *

I would like to suggest a four-part framework and stepped process for the new, progressive organisation that could operate within the context of a social democracy – offering a way for business to exist in this new world. For me, this is what Progressive Corporatism might look like:

- Progressive Goals: Ask Bigger Questions
- Progressive Values: Citizens Before Capital
- Progressive Practices: The Corporation as Social Movement
- Progressive Communication: Actions, Not Words

Critically, communications comes at the end of this process, never at the beginning. Long gone will be the days when a newly appointed CEO or senior politician calls first for their PR advisor. Historically, part of the problem has been that we all think that everything starts with communications because everything *is* communications. It shouldn't and it isn't.

It is no longer enough to ask only, "how can we maximise shareholder value?" without also considering Public Value. The *Financial Times* Business Editor, John Gapper, has noted what we all already see: "the very sense of stockholder primacy is now being challenged."

It is no longer enough to ask only, "what can we sell you today?" without considering employee and customer needs ahead of corporate wants.

It is no longer enough to ask only, "am I doing what is compliant?" without also asking "am I doing what is right?"

Progressive corporations need to ask bigger questions of themselves. They cannot engineer change in increments. They need to throw the nature of those questions open to the wisdom of the crowd. They need to find the courage to both ask and answer them – demonstrating both character and shared beliefs (the Classical Greeks termed this courage "ethos").

Just as Unilever can rightly ask itself, "how can I double sales while halving environmental footprint?" so a bank would be better off asking, "what does it take to be socially useful?" before it asks whether it can be trusted by its customers. Only better, sustained actions can make a bank more socially useful.

Communications will also be better contextualised by asking/answering the bigger questions first. There is no point, for example, trying to "defend" an Amazon, Google or Starbucks on issues of tax, without first understanding what "fair tax" looks like – or even if the company is actually interested in what is right or fair. The better question thus becomes "what is the purpose of tax?" and, having answered that, the rest of the arguments can flow.

Without answering the bigger questions, the actions of the organisation are most likely flimsy, and the urge to spin almost irresistible. This also determines the need to enjoy real expertise to answer those very real questions and challenges.

The (in)ability to ask bigger questions lies at the heart of the greatest corporate issues today. Energy companies might ask themselves not, "how do we defend fracking?" for example, but instead, "what is the future of transport?" or "what does low energy living look like 20 years from now?" Food producers might ask themselves not, "how many more mums can we sell to?" but instead, "how can we make (GM) foods absolutely safe to feed the world?" Property investors will ask less about maximising land values through land banks and more about the global challenges of mass urbanisation and urban migration and making cities human again, with better homes for all. Insurance companies will not ask, "what products can we cross-sell to existing customers?" but, "do we have the right ethical framework for new product development?"

Asking and answering bigger questions with the participation of the crowd will build trust in a progressive corporate future.

As a footnote to this, progressive corporations will admit that they sometimes do not have all the answers: that sometimes they will fail. As we have learned from the tech sector, it is OK to fail (occasionally). Such is the messiness of the real world. A preoccupation with "only success" (the manicured CEO) has fuelled the recent obsession with PR – hence the idea that companies should "manage the message" and can always spin their way out of trouble. In the progressive future, this simply isn't possible – or necessary.

* * *

Progressive Corporatism demands a different form of

leadership and a different organisational structure. In recognition of the new social democracy, it moves from hierarchies and controls towards much more fluid networks of collaboration. It builds ecosystems, not silos. Power and influence is shared, not enforced.

The progressive corporation should think of itself as a social movement. The social movement corporation supports coalitions with employees and stakeholders and empowers employees to build coalitions with fellow workers. Imaginative co-creation within a wider ecosystem of influence helps determine company policy on everything from NPD (new product development) and business planning to working hours and community outreach. By co-funding the ideas and enterprises of the extended community, business leaders can build new models of what we might call entrepreneurial communitarianism. Every leader should think seriously about mutualising the organisation through collaboration and extending share ownership and shareholder participation to allow the social movement to thrive.

Truth and transparency are the accepted and expected norms. The conversation – with employees, customers and civil society – about the importance and priorities of profit is made explicit. As I have argued, it is incorrect to assume that profit is evil and that, somehow, making money has to be fully subsumed in the quest for societal purpose. Trust data confirms that citizen-consumers understand the need for profit. It is the excesses that are deemed intolerable and the fact that curtailing those excesses are within an organisation's control.

This is why the public backlash against banks and financial services firms in particular has been so strong in that these issues are seen to be something leaders can fix but choose not to, perpetuating a view of "greedy leaders" putting their pay packets and their profits consistently above customers needs. Moreover, as many proponents of best practice in this space have commented, profit should be seen as an agent of change (and of societal and citizen/customer well-being).

The social movement corporation encourages open dissent and looks to citizen-employees to ask the challenging questions in a workplace that is open and transparent. Everyone is nonetheless fully accountable to the shared organisation goals and organisational values – and genuine commercial sensitivities are still protected.

The social movement organisation recognises that digital technologies are an extension to the democracy of the organisation, not a threat to it. By active participation in the new social space, business leaders can facilitate reform, not destructive revolution – and they can flatten and remove the hierarchies that have historically created and protected bad practice.

Accountability, responsibility and constant performance review runs to the heart of this culture change. Transparency is not a fetish but a mandatory behaviour. Nor is it an instrument of compliance but rather one of continual accountability for actions taken.

Innovation necessarily plays a central role in the practical application of a more socially useful framework. Community engagement and involvement needs to move to the next level, way beyond the tired conventions of Corporate Social Responsibility. No organisation should detach its workforce from the communities they serve. Instead, it should view them as active participants and agents of change. Their networks can and should support advocacy. They need to demonstrate social leadership and social impact as well as social purpose. This is the best sustainability programme any organisation can offer and by having it as part of its business strategy, it simultaneously removes the need for separate resource and cost-heavy structures and reporting. This is the organisation as social movement brought to life.

* * *

Progressive Communication sees the ultimate shift from adult-to-child conversations (telling, demanding, scolding) to adult-to-adult ones instead (participating as equals).

Pierre Goad, Global Head of Communications at HSBC, sees it thus: "Implanting messages doesn't work with five-year olds let alone with 255,000 grown-ups. We don't waste time crafting the perfect message and the most efficient channel to plant communications in people's heads."

The workplace is the front line. "Work," Goad observes, "is a profoundly social experience. [Yet] large organisations still do everything in their power to deny that."

As David Weinberger, co-author of *The Cluetrain Manifesto,* points out (I paraphrase) – we need to move from the falsehood of simplicity to the realities of social chaos.

Manifestos replace mission statements in the Progressive Communication world, reflecting the shift from controlled "truths" to more participatory and relevant campaigning platforms. It is OK to be an activist at both an individual and a corporate level and to *believe in something,* to drive for change. Under the new model, never would anyone accept – still less believe – the bullshit platitudes plastered across the gleaming reception of RBS Group's London HQ.

Progressive Communication (and the Public Leadership model) sees a continual conversation among multiple stakeholders (the chaotic ecosystem at play) and information shared, not controlled. Opposing and sometimes contradictory views are inherent – offering a final repudiation of the manicured nonsense of press releases filled with meaningless corporate-speak. Communicators should be confident about openly sharing contrary points of view, whether about products, services or people. They can be found with the click of a mouse anyway.

Just as there is nowhere to hide, so should nothing be hidden.

* * *

When I started on my PR career in the early 1980s, I had assumed that here was an industry that had been going forever. But in fact, the formal industry then was only about 30 years old. In the three decades since, there has been much blather but little evidence of change. PR as it has become now is pretty much PR as it has always been. The reason? It is the ugly child of bad politics, bad market economics and the misguided corporatism that enshrined them.

Meanwhile, the next workplace generation already sees that, when it comes to communication, there is a better way. It is time to put a discredited function, PR, out of its misery and to build a new model afresh, for the world as it is now, not the world as it once was. Arguing for the re-branding or evolution of Public Relations will not do. The great, opaque and unaccountable propaganda game of the 20th century is over.

* * *

Wise Crowd Contributor:

The Death of Anti-Social

Celine Schillinger
For a long time, companies have not been good at being social.

They were focusing on manufacturing quality products, delivering good services, optimising resources, and meeting shareholders' expectations. Pushing promotional messages was enough to grow their customer base, and collecting market insights was done through market surveys, focus groups and consultants' analysis. Connecting with experts, policy makers and authority figures was enough. Or, they believed they *were* social. They'd opened a corporate Facebook page. They'd contracted an internal social platform. External Comms departments produced reputation reports based on social media mentions. Internal Comms departments delivered information materials and entertainment activities to keep employees together as a team, bonded by the corporate Vision and Mission.

Alarming blindness.

Some have started to realise how much the world has changed, and what it takes to adapt: a complete transformation. The shrinking lifespan of large companies and the sky-rocketing disengagement of employees across the world are no minor signals. The advent of the connected and empowered customer, the ever-faster pace of disruption of economies and business models and the massive shift toward knowledge work have signed the death warrant of the anti-social corporation.

Finally, it is the end of corporate omniscience, arrogance and social inability.

To engage their audiences and grow their business, companies have to become social. This imperative covers both "social inside the enterprise" and "external social media marketing and customer relations". More than just digital tools, it requires a deep transformation in leadership culture, relational habits and communication processes.

Replacing one-sided communication with two-way conversations is often what comes first when considering a switch to social. Some companies, however, determined to jump in, have set up a corporate Twitter account, administered by a Comms fellow, supervised by Legal and Compliance departments, fed with tweets validated in advance through editorial meetings, to serve the corporate image. Meanwhile, employees are reminded that social media is a major source of risks and deterred from interacting online. In this case, social media is no more than a fig leaf, and it shows. Two-way conversations just can't happen. The same applies to social inside the enterprise, when staff are still viewed as a passive audience, subject to layered cascading of information via the chain of command. The old thought patterns – of rhetoric, mistrust and control – are not breeding grounds for social.

A truly social company is able to connect and engage externally, thanks to a connected and engaged workforce. It bonds internal and external stakeholders by creating the conditions for a sincere and authentic conversation to happen. It involves its audiences (clients, regulators, suppliers, staff) in creating shared value through tangible actions that serve a common purpose and support the company's business.

Those who get it and lead the way into the social era face, as a very first obstacle, the inability of organisations to properly address cross-functional change initiatives. They need agile and flexible structures to quickly adapt to the unexpected. They require a culture that fosters holistic thinking, emotional connections, empathy with diversity, and comfort with complexity and ambiguity. Instead, they have to play with industrial age management models built on extreme task segmentation and control, aimed at reproducibility and predictability, handled by experts and often crippled by bureaucracy.

However, even the most traditional industry can move towards social literacy. Turning the alleged "customer centricity" into an actual focus on human relationships enables people to connect and engage with the organisation's ecosystem. Only then can companies thrive in the new business normal, i.e. the social economy.

It starts with a pretty straightforward move: listen. Social listening is about making sure the stakeholders' voices are heard, wherever they speak – including on social media. Social network analysis, advanced sentiment monitoring and big data visualisation provide amazing insight that complement traditional market surveys and open new strategic spaces for engagement.

Obstacles to listening must be removed by developing relevant skills and tools, and by overcoming corporations' traditional bias toward intermediaries. To accurately hear and interact well with stakeholders at large, organisations need to go beyond the intermediaries (expert groups, consumer associations, unions, institutions) that are usually their focal point for engagement. Social requires direct connections. The good news is: technology now enables them. It is not a matter of possibility; it is a matter of will.

Meaningful interactions are what work best for sustainable

engagement in the social era. To this end, companies must drop the idea that interactions revolve around their products or services: they don't. They revolve around the higher purpose served by those products. Can competitors serve an identical purpose? Certainly. But clever companies boldly embody their "Why" through tangible activities over time, leveraging their stakeholders' input, leaving no share of voice to the competition.

It takes an enabled workforce to become a social business, because engaging at scale requires resources. It is high time organisations realise they seriously underutilise their own internal engagement assets. The media-trained-to-death, waffle-expert spokesperson may have been appropriate for one-sided, controlled communication; s/he is now irrelevant and detrimental to social engagement. Internal gatekeepers must be shown the big picture and educated, to let social initiatives happen. Employee social activism is not a threat any more, it is the future. Enabled employees can become the best social connectors as well as precious resources for monitoring and insights – creating a virtuous circle of internal engagement.

This requires two conditions. Diversity is the first one: a wide range of perspectives, genders, ages, social and educational backgrounds at all corporate levels (including with the leadership team) mirrors the stakeholders' heterogeneity. Diversity is crucial for establishing connections, developing empathy, and increasing collective connectedness capabilities.

The second condition is trust. Authentic, lasting connections require trust – which comes back to the purpose of this book. When corporate executives understand and accept the challenge, the way forward will be pretty simple.

CHAPTER EIGHT: ACTIVISTS AND ACTIVISM COMMUNICATIONS AND THE SEVEN STRATEGIES OF WE

Communications and the Seven Strategies of We

Journalists relish taking large corporates to task: their communications teams, still more their PR consultants, are cheap and easy prey. I have occasionally been that victim.

In a June 2014 article in *The New York Times*, Journalist Timothy Egan took aim at Walmart, accusing the retail giant of being "a net drain on taxpayers, forcing employees into public assistance with its poverty-wage structure" and claiming that its "humiliating wages force thousands of employees to look to food stamps, Medicaid and other forms of welfare."

Walmart decided to meet journalist activism with corporate activism, head-on. David Tovar, its VP for Corporate Comms, used the power and reach of the retailer's own blog to post a red-line commentary against the original article.

"Thanks for sharing your first draft," he wrote. "Below are a few thoughts to ensure something inaccurate doesn't get published. Hope this helps.... WMT."

Some accusations were repudiated as "false" and better facts offered instead. The word "fake" was also used. In response to the charge about being a net drain on taxpayers, Tovar scribbled, "we are the largest taxpayer in America. Can we see your math?"

* * *

On a Saturday morning, sometime around 2005 or 2006, I found myself in a small room in a soulless business centre above Argos in the Holloway Road, London, not far from Arsenal's Emirates stadium. I was there, along with my Edelman colleague and then European CEO, David Brain, to present the communications plan that would bring down the British monarchy.

The plan was originally David's idea – though I was an enthusiastic and willing participant. I have long loathed the institution of monarchy, the constitutional enshrining of the hereditary principle, and the hideous layers of deceitful spin that for centuries have been used to suppress fair and equal citizen representation and participation in society. The argument that the British monarchy is kindly benign does not wash; in fact, its very lack of clarity perversely reinforces the non-accountability of the executive authority.

The divine right to rule had, I thought, been outthought by the Enlightenment. But here is a Greco-German family, blessed by the Archbishop of Canterbury, invoking a non-existent god's given right to allegedly lead one of the world's greatest democracies. It just makes no sense.

The presentation started well. David and I outlined what was then a 25-year plan (whoever said PR was all tactics and no strategy?) that would gradually erode the power and legitimacy of the Royal Family. We readily acknowledged that affection for Elizabeth was too ingrained and that to target an elderly woman – forcing her into homelessness and unemployment – would win us few friends. So we focused instead on the transition to her son, Charles (less popular and a bit odd), and used that as the inflection point to call for a referendum to question who heads the state. Meanwhile, year on year, we would campaign, *inter alia*, to have the word "subject" removed from UK passports; to change the national anthem from "God Save The Queen" to "Jerusalem" or "Land of Hope and Glory"; and to establish the opening of all the family's palaces to all the citizens of the country. It would be death by a thousand cuts.

At the end of the presentation, there was a round of applause – and then questions.

"Do you not think we should bring down the dictator sooner?" asked a man with a real (non-hipster) beard and metaphorical sandals.

David and I exchanged glances. We thought we were radicals, but neither of us has considered the Queen a dictator.

The plan met with universal approval – but then bureaucracy and process intervened.

"I am sorry, gentlemen, but you will need to leave the room while we consider your proposals. We need to take a formal vote," piped up a man who had hitherto been dribbling into his beard.

And so David and I retired to the stools in the corridor (and thereafter, from memory, to the Herbert Chapman pub). The motion was tabled and the proposals were approved. But the campaign never materialised. The Queen is still in power.

* * *

In *Ill Fares The Land*, Tony Judt asks: why do we experience such difficulty even imagining a different sort of society? Our increasingly slavish addiction to profit and loss, consumption and consumerism is, after all, "not an instinctive human condition" but "an acquired taste". Such are the parallels with monarchy.

We have lost our ability to ask the right questions. We fail to challenge ourselves beyond the conventional projection of probable futures and to remind one another that we need not remain passive recipients of bestowed authority. When Elizabeth Windsor tops the Power List of 100 Most Influential Women, we do not see either the irony or the shame in this celebration of the hereditary principle – nor the painful juxtaposition with rightful calls for greater female representation in the boardroom. The only Queen that belongs at number one belts out a Bohemian Rhapsody.

The more pertinent question is: why do we still accept anachronistic power structures and fail to catalyse real change? And what is the role of Public Relations in all this?

The British monarchy is symbolic of the weighty anchors of old elites and traditions. As Hilary Mantel has eloquently argued, this is not a relevant institution for a grown-up nation, let alone a progressive one. But its continued presence – benign or otherwise – tells another story: as subjects who fawn at plastic princesses, we have paid a heavy price. We have evaporated our own curiosity and imagination, and feasted instead on a diet of trash TV and celebrity news.

Rather than driving citizens and state into harmonious proximity, technology has oddly enabled this new distance to fester. We have ended up celebrating crass simplicity through remote relationships and satiating our curiosity by peering into the lives of others through social media, complete with hundreds of make-believe "friends". We increasingly shun complexity (and thus the real world), because simplicity is faster-to-hand and more immediately gratifying, but, in truth, deeply unsatisfying. We have consequently lost sight of real values and lost our appetite to confront the real societal challenges. Our moral compass is awry. We inhabit a self-created awkward land of princess-pink (or Princess Kate) make believe.

This world could simply not exist without the current construct of Public Relations, advertising and marketing. Here we see that the "lipstick on the pig" is more than metaphorical. We have distanced and alienated our audience for so long that not only have they accepted it, they have become apathetic about everything we say. It's time to get involved again, and technology (sometimes part of the problem) also offers the solution – through online communities who don't need a government or a business to tell them what to think, and who can connect and enforce change themselves.

* * *

In the workplace, employee activism is on the rise. According to the Edelman Trust Barometer, regular employees find level pegging with NGOs in the credibility of spokespeople – and surge ahead of more traditional voices, such as those of the CEO. People trust people like themselves and can easily find them within their own networks.

These networks are not confined to shared interests around sport, poetry, knitting or porn. They exist, too, on issues such as executive pay, diversity, working conditions, supply chain ethics, product development and environmental protection. Employees have opinions. They see what we see. Employees are already building coalitions with other employees – they no longer need physical water-coolers to facilitate the conversation – and these coalitions are based on shared values, not imposed rules.

Expectations are changing with the times. Increasing job insecurity, widening pension gaps and falling real wages decrease loyalty in companies and make challenges to the managerial status quo more likely. Trade unions also need to take note of the employee network phenomenon. They may be facing their own redundancy in a connected, activist and asymmetrical age.

All this also sits within the context that businesses are no longer expected just to deliver great products and services and to make money in return. They are increasingly expected to play a more influential societal role. The employee demand is a critical component of this and will inevitably only increase in intensity as more Millennials – better connected and, again, more activist-minded – enter the workplace. This is why businesses consequently need to think, work and organise themselves from the inside out and to demonstrate Public Value.

Within business, the opportunity exists for leaders who embrace the principles of Public Leadership to fully appreciate the employee as advisor, the employee as advocate, the employee as agent for change. These activist employees – possibly co-funded by the employers themselves – will help drive better internal communications, find richer ideas, embed true innovation, protect the social and environmental bottom line, build new coalitions and partnerships, and ultimately deliver a more genuinely accountable system of governance.

The current truth, however, is that many organisations host a fundamental conflict between the prevailing hierarchies – which have historically been built as vertical silos, each led by a power-base executive – and the horizontal, more fluid and slightly amorphous spread of employee networks.

Public Leadership organisations will be those who fully

embrace the activist employee and harness this energy, rather than fight it. In this scenario, the employee ceases to be a passive recipient of corporate dictates or (often) gratuitous and centralised initiatives, and instead sits at the heart of a de-centralised and empowered network of likeminded souls who, collectively, can be a reforming force for good – inside and outside of an organisation – working to a shared manifesto, curated by and accountable to a wise crowd.

Internally, this network sharpens the accountability of business leadership and therefore makes the business itself more stable and robust. Externally, it is also is a network that can spread the (good) word to the outside world of citizen consumers, through family, friends and their communities beyond. Marketing is made all the better and more authentic – and therefore more credible – by being built from the inside out.

Demographic shifts will only increase activism and accelerate change as old authorities' grip on power inevitably is weakened. Progressive business leaders – Public Leaders – will therefore be those who get ahead of the change curve and begin to lead by tomorrow's rules, not today's.

* * *

In late April 2012, I joined the Reverend Giles Fraser (the outspoken former Canon of St Paul's Cathedral) and Occupy Activist Naomi Colvin at St Bride's Church, Fleet Street, in a discussion on the future of capitalism.

Colvin had previously written of the need to build "a new, participatory politics" and on the imperative of seeing consumers as citizens. The consumerisation of everything – as New Citizenship Project's Jon Alexander later wrote – remains a vital flaw in capitalism's societal role.

But tents on the streets (or on the steps of the great cathedrals) and articles in *The Guardian* are not the only answer. David Graeber of The Democracy Project saw it thus: "only when a movement appeared that resolutely refused to take the traditional path, that rejected the existing political order entirely as inherently corrupt, that called for a complete re-invention of American democracy, that occupations immediately began to blossom across the country."

A version of Occupy movements can start in the workplace and the shopping mall, not just on the streets. The leader who thinks and behaves like a social activist will rightly channel the activism of others, employees and customers alike, with no deference to hierarchy or institutional niceties. They will become the incumbent disruptors.

Positive activism from employees can spread wisdom across otherwise stultifying organisational silos, finding others of like minds and shared interests. Positive activisim from employees can take top-down, philanthropic initiatives and turn them into grassroots movements that can scale social success. Positive activism from employees can demand both greater accountability from, and transparency within, the body corporate – web-based campaigning within organisations can replace the old-fashioned threat of the withdrawal of labour.

Positive activism from employees can find a political voice within a reformed participatory politics and an economic voice within better forms of business organisation. Positive activism from employees can inform the process of renewal, rather than forever waiting for it to emerge, courtesy of those on top. Positive activism from employees can curb the wilder excesses of either corporate pay or environmental bad practice.

In other words, we no longer have to wait on others – but should instead recognise that the power lies within. Positive activism from employees can add human values – real values – to the disembodied made-up values of corporate constructs.

Too often, as with Occupy, commentators speak and write of "employees," "consumers" and "protestors" in the separated abstract – failing to recognise that they are in fact people, just like you and me: people in jobs; people with votes; people buying things in supermarkets.

David Graeber, also one of the key architects of Occupy, writes: "the system is not going to save us, so we are going to have to save ourselves." This chimes with the John Kotter view, expressed in the pages of the *Harvard Business Review*: "people use the word leadership to refer to those at the very top of hierarchies.... this is also a mistake and very misleading."

* * *

The failure of the Occupy movement to build on the collective energy of global anger, however, would seem to undermine the argument that it is within networks that big changes happen. From spontaneous protests on the steps of St Paul's and in Wall Street, in Madrid and São Paulo, this was a movement where dramatic change was surely the logical outcome. And yet, despite the initial energy, the momentum fizzled and the movement died.

In his brilliant analysis of the new global revolutions, journalist Paul Mason tells the story of a social activist whom he first encounters on Twitter. Inspired by Mason's book (*Why It's Kicking Off Everywhere*) and the revolutionary zeal of the activist, I started following ██████,through social media. The fact that they are now, I think, the Press Officer for a major corporate probably says it all.

Mason makes the point that the great revolutionary year of 1848 was also preceded by a communications revolution: "the telegraph, the railway and the steam boat formed part of an emerging transport and communications network clustered around the cities that became centres of the social revolution."

As Mason writes: "the revolutionary wave of 1848 ended in defeat: all the monarchies under threat survived, except the French, which upgraded to Empire status. But it nevertheless ushered in modernity."

Noam Chomsky has made similar points about not getting overexcited about the power of the internet to fully dismantle traditional elites. Yes, it has become an essential tool for activists, but do not write off the corporate manipulators or propagandists just yet, he warns.

"Capitalism," Mason says in a later keynote, "needs to mutate to survive."

As reported later by Phil Teer, Mason "argues that the fight is now between network and hierarchy, this pervades everything and we do not know yet where it ends. He believes it will come down to the Networked Individual: someone with weak ties, lack of hierarchy, massive ego in the sense of massive personal space around them and a 'don't touch me, don't harass me, don't get in my way' message. They are not very collective but are very powerful. They are like the Spanish people in the Occupy movement who organised collectives after the crash. They want something different, they have different ideals and they are not going to take what an unchanged capitalism is offering them."

Professor Manuel Castells asks us not to give up on optimism. In his brilliant analysis of Occupy (fittingly titled *Networks of Outrage and Hope*), leadership within networks, he argues, does not have to be anarchic. For him, horizontalism therefore works and big changes can happen.

The PR of the past, complete with its protection of elites and its unspoken passion for authority and control, is not fully equipped for the networks of the present and the future.

* * *

The history of the internet is, as we know, peppered with examples of where bright lights are (often humorously) shone on corporate misdemeanours. An angry United Airlines passenger, furious at his treatment as a customer, famously sang "United Breaks Guitars" which, last time I looked, had received over 14.2 million views on YouTube. United has no doubt treated their guitar-carrying passengers with greater care and delicacy ever since.

Corporations often try and reverse this energy flow – to build what have become known as social movements from the top down, with no sense of shame. This is the twitching body of PR trying to exert a last vestige of control.

Just as organisations have no real values (they are hollow constructs; real people have values instead), they do not have the legitimate authority to engineer viral campaigns or social movements. (M)ad men have moved quickly to try to monetise this potentially fertile space, promising their large corporate clients that they can "do an M&S" or "do a GE" and create a branded social movement for good. They make similar nonsensical claims about "going viral". Advertising does not make things go viral – people do. Instead, ad men can only create a revised form of advertising. We the people create the social movement and spread it according to our whims and needs.

* * *

38 Degrees, like Change.org, is an interesting organisation that shows the true power of "bottom up" activism. Launched in 2009, 38 Degrees has, at last count, over 2.5 million members.

The organisation represents, in many ways, the possible future for politics – more single-issue, more focused, and, in so many ways, more passionate. Here is a network of the like-minded on some issues (but not on all) that is prepared to challenge the conventions of authority. Saving a local hospital from closure is, to some, more resonant and more motivating than endless posturing about, say, issues around Europe, immigration or welfare.

Bound together and accelerated by technology, 38 Degrees and others find the *polis* at its most active – brought to life almost through the immediacy and interdependency of the web. If politicians had better beware then so, too, should business leaders. Versions of 38 Degrees (in case you are wondering, the tipping point at which a leaning human falls over) will most likely start popping up within major corporations, just as campaigns are conducted within Great Britain PLC. The radical and smart leader is the one who encourages employees to form such groups, thus creating an inherent and entirely legitimate system of accountability through radical transparency. This is channelled activism, not old-style PR, with the leader as social activist, not remote controller.

Rage against the corporate machine is nothing new. Even before the arrival of the internet, the equivalent of "I'm Hatin' It" (a play on McDonald's famous "I'm Lovin'

It" slogan, utilised in a campaign by PETA) and "Shell Hell" (another anti-Shell activist group) would have existed, but most likely in less accessible domains. Technology has made the art of protest and discontent possible, immediate and global – and this is not a trend that will now diminish or reverse. Public Leaders will seek to learn from the malcontents, to welcome them into their crowds, to be open about their failings, and to use criticism, where justified, to drive reformation and progress. This distinguishes them from older-style Servant Leaders. Within corporations as within countries, the active *polis* has finally found its reforming power. Public Relations will fall because it simply cannot contain the groundswell any longer.

38 Degrees was one of the early consequences of the 2010 Conservative Liberal coalition in the UK, particularly in contributing to an assortment of legislative reversals. Its victories have ranged from the local (a government U-turn over the future of Lewisham Hospital being maybe the most notorious) to the national (petitioning to save bees, preserve forests, or for better child protection) and even international (lobbying on Palestine or on EU-US trade deals). It has, however, faced criticism over its style of campaigning and has become a focus for the debate regarding the nature and, to an extent, validity of political engagement via digital platforms. In 2011, 38 Degrees was named the Oxford Institute's Best Internet NGO but, despite its popularity with the commentariat and its growth, it remains a relatively small-scale venture: in the financial year ending September 2012, the organisation received £1.4m in donations and charity grants and spent £1.1m on campaigns and running costs.

People power is at the centre of 38 Degrees' organisation and operation, with campaigns decided and implemented through the engagement and mobilisation of its members. It is a multi-issue platform: its initiatives are loosely united by the fact they are presented as apolitical, although broadly contributing towards liberal and progressive outcomes. Its advocates argue that it is strengthening the process and operation of democracy by providing a greater voice to citizens and increasing the platform and channels that they can engage across. There are voices that are desperate to be heard.

The Conservative MP Robert Halfon sees 38 Degrees in more binary terms, as left-wingers proving more successful than the right in the digital space. "The left have leapfrogged over us. Instead of Web 2.0, they have gone straight to 4.0, creating interactive campaigning websites, American-style, that have changed the nature of how pressure groups operate." In response to the "mass database of centrist floating voters, albeit with a sizeable majority from the centre left," Halfon established Right Angle to mobilise conservative online engagement. Online campaigning had thus been opened to the forces of competition.

* * *

In autumn 2013, the leader of the UK Labour Party, Ed Miliband, launched a very public broadside on the *Daily Mail*, a right-wing newspaper, which had run a particularly unpleasant, personal and unrepentant attack on his late father, a Marxist historian. While the tone of the paper's venom was not surprising, the robust way in which Miliband fought back was. Very few politicians ever dare to take on the might of the media. This was partly symptomatic of a strategic "core voter" play by Miliband, but more a recognition that it is now possible to go over the head of former media elites and call bullshit on their prejudice and nastiness by speaking directly to the people. The media had been dis-intermediated.

The fall of media can also be linked with the fragility of trust. To be more precise, the fall of traditional media, which coincides with the rise of more social forms of media, is happening as we become increasingly trusting of "someone like me" over conventional authority figures and institutions. Hence CEOs are effectively half as trusted as fellow employees, and we trust our government much less than we do our friends and family.

Social media, as organisations such as Mumsnet and the amazing charity Mothers2Mothers show, can be a force for good, can offer a voice to the many, can connect the otherwise disconnected – and yet, in the case of Mumsnet, still display incredibly trivial dimensions. Maybe this last point satisfies the old adage that we end up with the media we deserve, but it is all too easy for leaders to dismiss the Twittersphere with the arrogant waft of a hand (as the old guard, including those like Lord Tim Bell, is often wont to do). But social media is so much more than a media channel. It speaks to the connected society – and thus to the commonality not just of cause but of effect, too.

That said, technology can divide as well as unite. It is easy to see it as an empowering tool, but this is not always so. In "Power-Curve Society," a 2012 paper by David Bollier for The Aspen Institute, the author notes:

"The challenges of the power-curve economy are formidable indeed. In the more optimistic scenario, the coming surges of productivity, innovation and economic growth will be disruptive, but tolerable and hopeful because they will also usher in enormous efficiencies and bounties that could eradicate poverty and improve standards of living. Under this scenario, the transition we are in must be understood as something on the scale of the Industrial Revolution itself.

"In a more troubling scenario, the power-curve economy poses a series of disruptions that have no easy or recognised solutions. We appear headed for a greater polarisation into haves and have-nots and more acute economic hardship and unemployment. Greater social and political unrest seem inevitable if no interventions are taken."

However, for the next generation of Public Leaders technology is a friend, not a foe. They must recognise that the time of managing the message, still less the media, is finally over. As Edward Snowden testifies, truth will out and the windows of deceit and apology are closing fast. This is a call for radical honesty and radical transparency across society – in business and in politics – fuelled by rightly activist citizens of the new *polis*. Radicalism starts not with the massaged truth or the half-truth but the full truth in all its glory. This is a significant departure from where we find ourselves today. Custodians of new trust will be those who accept the underlying principle of all this – that a time of citizen-centric power demands citizen-centric leadership.

* * *

I spent the 12 months after leaving Edelman sharpening what has become known as the "Seven Strategies of We" – a series of strategies for how businesses can better communicate in an activist, co-produced, citizen-centric and society-first world. This thinking has already been pressure-tested across a range of global enterprises and industries – from energy to property and professional services, from the UK and Europe to the Middle East and Asia.

In today's world, however, we can only offer suggested frameworks, not absolute commands. These seven strategies are therefore not a series of hard-and-fast, "must be obeyed at all costs" rules. Each organisation must fine-tune its own actions around this framework. People are activist and power is asymmetrical – our organisations need to reflect this.

1. Strategy One: Accept Chaos as Reality

The world is interdependent. Events are interdependent. Communities are interdependent. This is not complicated. It is (systems) complexity at work. More systems build more complexity. More complexity means chaos as reality.

The Fukushima accident in Japan led, incredibly, to the cancellation of Germany's nuclear programme. We also see interdependency in the relationship between lower fuel costs and increasing energy efficiency in the US having a direct impact on the oil revenues and therefore the social investment funds of Middle Eastern states and ultimately their mid-term political stability.

Accepting complexity means accepting chaos. This means shifting communications from command-and-control (telling people what to think; broadcasting messages) to participation and engagement within networks. The conversations are happening anyway. Corporations and brands should join them and have their say.

Many companies have real expertise to share beyond their immediate universe. They should offer expert opinion and proactive advice more publicly, to build authentic engagement and trust. In order to participate and engage more effectively for the betterment of society, they need to liberate their thinking by asking and answering the bigger questions. Novo Nordisk, for example, has followed this path and become the recognised global expert on diabetes.

Expertise also offers a point of competitive advantage. Companies need to explain, rather than seek to control or apologise. Experts continue to score well in all trust data – they are twice or three times more trusted than CEOs, for instance.

In accepting complexity, companies also need to accept fragility. This, too, has implications for the state of trust. Trust is fragile as well as complex. As we have seen, trust is harder than ever before to win but easier than ever before to lose.

* * *

When I was leading the Public Engagement work at Edelman, I suggested that the starting point had to be "embrace chaos".

"We cannot say that."

"Why not?"

"It will scare clients. They want us to give them a simple, single answer."

"But the real world isn't like that. We need to be honest."

"We cannot use it."

So "embrace chaos" became "navigate the complexity" because it was an easier sales message.

2. Strategy Two: Radicalise Honesty and Transparency
There is no space for spin.

Today's progressive Public Leaders are those who start with the truth – and make it openly available for all. This includes the uncomfortable truth, even when mistakes have been made. Admission of error builds trust. Public Leaders explain with evidence.

Transparency needs to be the partner of honesty and

can work on many levels. Corporate transparency is not so much an issue of legal compliance but one of accountability, within the Public Value framework. Research tells us that transparent organisations are more trusted. Transparency also means being accountable for your actions to the many, not just the few. It means being prepared to open up businesses to everything bar the commercially confidential. I appreciate that this scares people – but what is there to fear from being open in a world that sees through you anyway?

* * *

Open data is an important component of transparency. Specifically, it brings huge benefits to communication and society.

New York City is an example of how shared public data can foster creativity and innovation. The NYC Open Data Plan includes 440 city-agency public data sets and ensures the constant release of public data. It includes information about things such as natural gas consumption per Zip Code and energy efficiency projects.

Rahul Merchant, Chief Information and Innovation Officer of New York City's Department of Information Technology and Telecommunications, talks of a revolution that makes the city run smarter. By breaking down the walls between the public and agencies, non-public information is now accessible and is inspiring innovation amongst tech entrepreneurs and SMEs through sustainable living apps and solutions. Innovation, technology and transparency are working together.

In Boston, the government's Citizens Connect smart device app empowers Boston residents to be the city's "eyes and ears", allowing them to alert the city to issues such as potholes and graffiti by uploading images, locations and other details. Again, advancing technology becomes one of the most powerful tools within the Progressive Communication and Public Leadership armoury.

* * *

Puma was probably the first global company to place an economic value on its environmental impact. It subsequently set a gold standard for transparent reporting.

The Environmental Profit and Loss Account places a financial cost on Puma's use of "natural capacity". Puma is able to evaluate water intensity used, matched against regions where the availability of water is scarce. The report places an impact cost – real monetary value – on elements such as water, air, biodiversity and land.

Puma applies this across the company's entire supply chain. It can identify where important work needs to be done and where radical changes must be made.

Rather than opt for conventional environmental reporting, Puma chose the progressive option. It is grounded not just in transparency but in radical honesty. It reframes the conversations between an organisation, its citizen-consumers and the regulatory environment. While the financialisation of all metrics may not be the perfect answer, it does demonstrate an accountable commitment to its employees, customers and society beyond.

3. Strategy Three: Build Coalitions ?

Public Leaders should not try and fight the battles alone. In a networked world, coalitions mitigate risk and build both resilience and trust.

This means collaboration with governments, NGOs and think tanks, co-operation with experts and academics, new forms of partnerships with media owners, and shared actions with employee and customer networks.

Manifestos should be co-produced after an extensive period of listening.

In building coalitions, leaders need to identify shared value, as articulated by Michael Porter, on their journey towards Public Value. Porter quoted Nestle, Johnson & Johnson and IBM, as well as GE, as examples. These should be considered as starting point companies – the more powerful universe is one of common good.

* * *

Basel-based Syngenta, with whom I worked briefly when at Edelman, is another good example of a company that is building coalitions with stakeholders and is also emphasising its more transparent approach and expert credentials.

The Syngenta Good Growth Plan is open about its targets. Like Unilever and GE, it wants to increase productivity without using more land, water and inputs. It is creating a coalition between the company (and its scientists), farmers and smallholders, government and NGOs. The project has its roots in the 2007/8 price spike in agricultural commodities.

Syngenta's CEO, Michael Mack, is expecting criticism as part of the process. "We welcome it," he told the *Financial Times*. "The whole point of the initiative is to have a dialogue." Mack argues that industry and technology must be fully represented in the sustainability debate. "There were a lot of ideas out there," he has said, "but they weren't progressive."

The global debate around pesticides and GM crops had been seriously impacted by the poor communications, over a decade earlier, by Monsanto. The original Monsanto campaign was ignorant and arrogant. It reminds us

of the damage regressive, rather than progressive, communications, can do to an industry sector.

* * *

Now is the time for a genuine Coalition of the Informed –
bringing together the world's leading companies to each
make a difference, in their own sectors, to the well-being
and protection of people and planet. Examples might
include TetraPak on packaging, Shell on energy, Sygenta
on food production, Unilever on consumer goods, etc.
This is common good, shared and Public Value made real.

The World Economic Forum is an obvious point for corporations to convene and align. But the WEF is not a progressive movement: it is more about words than actions.

Coalition building sees new partnerships emerging
between corporations, cities and states. You can detect
an emergent theme here. Companies like Siemens and
IBM are already doing this well, with their Smarter Cities
projects. Others, like Dutch-based paint and chemicals
giant Akzo-Nobel (a client), are just starting out. And
cities like Bogota, Poznan, Oslo, and Mexico City are
leading the way in creating new, imaginative and inspiring coalitions between public and private sectors and
states and citizens.

4. Strategy Four: Take to the Social Dance Floor

Many organisations fear technology, and especially
social media. In the changed world, it is essential to
embrace technology as a friend.

All leaders, corporations and governments should be
active on Twitter, LinkedIn and Facebook – as participants, with an authentic voice. This is not just about
social media but also about social *business* in a networked
world. Technology, as I have argued, connects across
coalitions and flattens hierarchies.

Together, organisations can take to the social dance floor – a wonderful phrase brought to life by Celine Schillinger, whose 2014 TEDx talk demonstrated how Sanofi Pasteur has begun think about "social impact, not just social networks" in fighting Dengue fever.

Smart technologies – through platforms and devices – are essential for the delivery of Progressive Communication and Public Value, not least because of their integral relationship with driving behavioural change. Smart apps – such as AC Mobile Control from LG or British Gas' "Hive" or even Sky's "Go" – allow us to control home devices remotely.

Companies can introduce technologies, but it may be that governments still need to reset expectations for social norms. India's Perform, Achieve and Trade Scheme attempts to do just this by issuing penalties for companies that do not reach their energy reduction targets. The Indian government has also introduced a mandatory CSR tax on big businesses which Deborah Doane, former Director of the World Development Movement, sees as little more than "enforced philanthropy".

5. Strategy Five: Be the Media

Every company can be a media company now.

In the old world, PR intermediated between a company and the media. Advancing technology and collapsed hierarchies have killed the need for intermediation. Companies can "go direct" – through their websites, through social media platforms, with podcasts and film – even through their own TV and radio channels. They just need compelling content.

* * *

Red Bull is frequently quoted as the best example of how

companies can "be the media". This principle can be applied to any product or service space. Building a company's own media channels provides another opportunity to emphasise expert credentials, to show depth of knowledge, to crowdsource ideas, and to lead the conversation.

Companies who think like media companies need to think from the outside-in, as well as the inside-out: to consider how they are "consumed" by people, not how they currently organise themselves in the workplace. The traditional model of "earned, paid and partner" media – with the first represented by PR, the second by advertising, and the third by the blurry "advertorial" – is long since bust. Edelman lovingly constructed something they wrongly called a cloverleaf, which aligned "paid", "owned", "social" and "hybrid". The "owned" represented the company's own media channels (correct), but I think "hybrid" was only there for geometrical and sales purposes. I never really understood it.

In a world dominated by Google, outside-in thinking means that companies should consider their share of search or share of social. Citizen-consumers don't really care about how the information found its way onto the Google landing page, or through which internal corporate department. They just want decent and honest content.

6. Strategy Six: Love the Citizen Crowd

This is a recurrent theme. Everyone now has a voice. "Opinion" is no longer the preserve of business or media elites.

Loving the crowd means involving a wider stakeholder universe in awareness building, decision-making and accountability. It means listening as well as speaking. It means ceding control to those who really do now shape opinion. A new relationship exists between a company and its citizen stakeholders. That is where the manifesto is co-produced.

Most importantly of all, therefore, loving the crowd provides the measurement and accountability mechanism for Public Value.

* * *

Ultimately, the citizen crowd helps hold large organisations to account for their promises and commitments. It builds more sustainable communications strategies and helps inform better decisions.

Loving the citizen crowd runs to the heart of co-produced, progressive leadership. As an example, on the theme of energy consumption, Management consultancy McKinsey has called for a consensus research group to address energy efficiency – involving all stakeholders in the co-design of proposals for "new hardware, skills, norms and rules that can collectively encourage sustainable household consumption practice." This is not far from what we see with India's HCL Technologies (co-produced business strategies) or with Agora drinks – crowd-designed products and brands.

Movements are happening all over the world that are making participatory planning real – from Porto Alegre in Brazil to the Community Energy Coalition in the UK. These are social movements that explore new ownership models and fiscal incentives to innovate through technology and sustainable consumption. They are also often backed by government.

7. Strategy Seven: Communicate Through Action, Not Words

It is what an organisation does, not what it says, that counts, set within a publically-acceptable, ethical framework, understood through Public Value.

Corporations often need to change their behaviours before they change their communications. They should certainly not try to defend the indefensible or to spin their way out of trouble.

Unilever is a good example of a global organisation that is changing the way it communicates through the substance of its actions. Despite allegations of bribery in China and Poland in 2013/14, GSK is another example, with, as Jim Woods has noted, its open-sourcing of patents and its commitment to lower-priced drugs in the developing world.

Unilever and GSK demonstrate corporate Public Leadership and Progressive Communication together in action.

* * *

These seven strategies are axiomatic. They are the only way to intelligently navigate the communications world today – especially for those organisations that sit, critically, at the heart of the water, energy and food sectors, which are inextricably linked. Organisations that adopt the strategies will be more authentic, more credible and more trusted. They will enjoy competitive edge – or, as we have learned to call it, a "collaborative" or "co-operative" edge.

There is no place to hide. The Prime Minister's former Director of Communications, Alastair Campbell, filmed for a KPMG Tax Conference where I was a speaker, sees it thus:

"If you cannot defend it, it is not defensible.
If it is not defensible, don't do it.
If it is defensible, change the terms of engagement.
Don't think a problem will go away, because it won't."

* * *

In a spring 2014 article for *Forbes*, the management expert Steve Denning wrote of the shift from the "Traditional Economy" to the "Creative Economy" – to a world where companies are "better, faster, cheaper, lighter, more convenient and more personalised." We see this in greatest evidence among the tech entrepreneurs and on the campuses of Silicon Valley.

Steve Denning is in no doubt about the unfolding drama:

"Suddenly power in the marketplace has shifted from seller to buyer. Suddenly the customer is in charge. The customer is now collectively the boss. This is an epic social and economic development."

To "customer", add "employee" too. In an article based on his original Scrum Alliance piece, Denning writes:

"Just as dinosaurs became birds, not by becoming better at crawling or walking, but by sprouting feathers and learning to fly, so organizations have to become different kinds of animals, with different mind-sets, attitudes, values and capabilities. It means different ways of thinking, speaking and acting in the workplace. It means change at the level of the firm's DNA.

"The phase change is as fundamental as the Copernican revolution in astronomy — a shift from the view that the sun revolves around the earth to a view that the earth revolves around the sun."

* * *

Meanwhile, as we have seen with 38 Degrees, organisations such as Change.org are introducing new methods of campaigning and accountability. Change is famous for its petitions. Its motto is "*Victories Every Day*". The group was described by *The Guardian* as "the fastest growing website for social change in the world." This is Progressive Communication from the bottom up, not the top down. One of the reasons that GE and Walmart, Unilever and GSK are changing their behaviours is because they know that active citizens will otherwise hold them to account through organisations like Change.

Greenpeace's "Unfriend Facebook" campaign (2011) gained over 700,000 supporters and forced Facebook itself to move away from coal – and to power its data centres through renewables. Here, we see the worlds of global corporations, social media and citizen power collide – on this occasion, through the prism of energy.

* * *

As we move towards the Seven Strategies of We and activist communications, so there is also an important shift to be made from Corporate Social Responsibility to Corporate Social Enterprise.

We can consider this through the story of Francesca Findlater – a somewhat unlikely social activist.

Fran's appearance in *The Independent*'s 2014 Happy List ("people who make life better for others") as a "rehabilitator" hardly does her justice:

"Four years ago, Francesca, a London businesswoman, started Bounceback, which helps rehabilitate prisoners. The project's success – 90 per cent of participants avoid trouble when out of prison – inspired Francesca to open a training centre for former prisoners, in Brixton."

Glamorous, brilliantly quick and a professional

designer, Fran is a close friend and one of the crowd-funders of this book. More importantly, Bounceback is fast becoming one of the most influential social enterprises in Britain today. It helps train prisoners for painting and decorating jobs after their release, and maintains a duty of care once they are out.

A June 2014 report on Bloomberg covered the Bounceback story in the context of what has become known as London's "construction crunch". A couple of weeks before it was published, in a speech to the London Real Estate Forum, Mayor Boris Johnson claimed that there were 19,000 job vacancies in the capital's construction industry. While the city needed to build over 40,000 homes a year to satisfy an acute supply crisis, he said, there simply were not enough skilled workers to help build them.

Bloomberg reported on the everyday reality: "People are going around construction sites in London, offering more money to tempt workers off one site to go onto another," said Mark Farmer, head of residential advisory at consulting firm EC Harris LLP. "There are not enough people to go around to build what's currently coming forward."

And, as I know from my own work with clients and with the Centre for London, where I am an Associate, what's currently coming forward is nowhere near enough.

The Bloomberg article continued: "Construction demand is so high that rates charged by subcontractors increased at the fastest pace since Market Economics and the Chartered Institute of Purchasing & Supply began to track the data more than 17 years ago."

Bounceback – even with its constrained resources and relatively limited geographical reach – holds at least one solution to help resolve the current crunch. The prisoner community can be both rehabilitated *and* trained to address an urgent societal need, beyond the prison walls.

Bloomberg told the story of Lorenzo Dorsett, "a former Arsenal Football Club youth team soccer player, who [had] spent more than three years in prison for drug possession. Today he works as a painter and decorator in London, where a building boom is creating jobs that benefit more than just the economy."

After Lorenzo went through a training programme for current and former inmates, he said, "I've worked consistently since I finished . . . [before jail] the only career path was football and when that stopped, I didn't know what else to do."

I know how hard Fran has worked – often with no real resources beyond ingenuity and chutzpah – to get the big "corporates" to support her projects. Nine times out of every ten, she would have to go through the bureaucratic compliance processes of FTSE 100 companies, hoping and cajoling for what was, in effect, a philanthropic hand-out. It is all the wrong way around.

Everyone with a commercial interest in resolving London's housing crisis – from developers to construction firms, think tanks to the hand-wringing commentariat – should support organisations such as Bounceback. They should hire them in their homes and, when wearing corporate suits, sponsor start-up social enterprises of their own. Responsible corporations should help channel and support the community-focused causes of their own employees, rather than offer simplistic, if convenient, headline-grabbing millions to the giant NGOs. We can all be activists now. We do not always need a panda badge on our stationery.

The construction industry is a brilliant example of how companies can – through enlightened self-interest if nothing else – move from a world of Corporate Social Responsibility to one of Corporate Social Enterprise. Building sites can become training sites. Large employers can establish their own welfare-to-work schemes. Traditional industries can adopt a *creative* industries approach – using social enterprises, apprenticeships and local communities as effective social accelerators. This can all be achieved in conjunction with the public sector – from local and regional authorities to some of the arms-length funding organisations of which central government is so proud, such as NESTA. Private foundations (Young, Rowntree, Fairburn, Peabody) can play their part, too. At last, we can begin to express ourselves in terms of human capital, not just financial capital.

None of this is beyond either reason or practice. It simply takes ambition, vision, courage and leadership to make Public Value real.

* * *

There is a community of "activist nuns" on the East Coast of the US, who have been buying shares in "do bad" corporations in order to gain representation at their Annual General Meetings to fight for the rights of the poor – and to vote down excessive pay and, more recently, challenge the likes of Chevron on fracking.

These nuns are the Sisters of St Francis of Philadelphia. *The New York Times*, in an article from 12th November 2011:

"Long before Occupy Wall Street, the Sisters of St Francis were quietly staging an occupation of their own. In recent years, this Roman Catholic order of 540 or so nuns has become one of the most surprising groups of corporate activists around.

"The nuns have gone toe-to-toe with ▮▮▮▮▮▮, the

grocery store chain, over farm worker rights; with ▇▇▇▇▇▇, over childhood obesity; and with ▇▇▇▇ ▇▇▇▇, over lending practices. They have tried, with mixed success, to exert some moral suasion over Fortune 500 executives, a group not always known for its piety.

"'We want social returns, as well as financial ones,' Sister Nora said, strolling through the garden behind Our Lady of Angels, the convent here where she has worked for more than half a century. She paused in front of a statue of Our Lady of Lourdes. 'When you look at the major financial institutions, you have to realise there is greed involved.'...

"'We're not here to put corporations down,' Sister Nora said, between bites of broccoli salad. 'We're here to improve their sense of responsibility.'"

Last time I looked (April 2014), the sisters had turned their attention to oil giant ▇▇▇▇▇▇. They successfully forced a shareholder vote to demand the company publish its risk analysis on fracking. The sisters are social activists. Among the many religious communities, they are not alone.

None of this is rocket science. We can all find our own ethical anchors.

* * *

Wise Crowd Contributor:

Is Diplomacy Dead, Too?

Tom Fletcher

Robert Phillips makes a powerful critique of traditional PR as having drawn too much from its origins in a now buried age of institutional authority. He argues that PR insufficiently reflects the new realities of a world in which the balance of power between citizens, business and government is shifting from hierarchies to networks; that PR prioritises bureaucracy and generalism over transformation and expertise; and that PR has prioritised pumping out a message over changing society. As a result, he argues, it has lost trust.

Sound familiar? Substitute "traditional diplomacy" for "PR" and we can see a similar challenge.

Diplomacy has detached itself from public debate through meaningless platitudes; much of its form (summits, communiques) was designed in 1815 for an age of monarchies and great states; and it has been slow to adjust to the next wave of disruption. Let's be honest, we are also, post Snowden, Assange et al, less trusted than we were.

The iGeneration has more opportunity than any before to understand, shape and engage with their world. In the ten years since 9/11 that world has been transformed more by American geeks in dorms than by Al Qaeda operatives in caves.

It was citizens who took the technology and turned it into something extraordinary. We should hesitate to talk of "killer apps", not least in a region where there are plenty of those already. But if Middle Eastern societies can find a way to meet the aspirations of their people for security, justice and opportunity, they are on the way to a very different social paradigm by 2020. In years to come, people may say that the most powerful weapon in the Middle East was not sarin gas or Iran's bomb, but the smartphone. We have seen the power of the best of old ideas allied with the best of new technology: regimes can ban the iPhone, but iFreedom will get through in the end.

Equipped with the right kit, and the right courage, diplomats should be among pioneers of this terrain. We're already writers, advocates and analysts. We must now become digital interventionists. We must learn the language of this new landscape in the way we learn Chinese or Arabic.

Set piece events are being replaced by more fluid, open interaction with the people whose interests we are there to represent. I ask colleagues who are not convinced about the power of these tools to imagine a reception with all their key contacts. You would not delegate it, stand quietly in a corner, or shout platitudes about warm bilateral relations. You would be in the mix, exchanging information. With or without the Ferrero Rocher.

Like the best traditional diplomacy, iDiplomacy comes down to authenticity, engagement and purpose. It is raw and human. The internet brings non-state actors into the conversation. That's part of the point. Once they're in, they can't be ignored.

I am not saying that we need to throw the traditional diplomatic skills – networking, discretion, negotiation, tact, expertise – out with the bathwater. We still need secrets, and direct conversations, however many of us become what *The Economist* calls "Tweeting Talleyrands".

There is real peril for us if we begin to see ourselves as driven by our PR. The sound bite follows the substance, not the other way round.

But our business does need to shift from digital engagement to digital influence. We need to drop the diplomatic baggage. We need to make the case afresh for why we matter to the citizens we represent. We need to re-establish trust.

I wouldn't say diplomacy is dead. That would be pretty depressing for a diplomat. But we need to take a hard look at ourselves. Are we too selling generalism over expertise; too rooted in selling stuff to consumers rather than societal transformation? Have we responded to the challenges of big data, digital citizenship and social media? Up to a point yes, in that we are now on social media. But I'm not sure many foreign ministries have a big data plan, nor a honed view on whether the inevitable empowerment that digital allows is a good thing. I suspect many would agree that it was important in more repressive societies, especially those we disagree with – think Russia or Iran. But we would not necessarily see how it is going to change our relationship with those we represent. We are only peeping over the precipice towards activism and participation – we are not yet as social, progressive or democratic as we need to become.

Technology and society are being transformed, with or without diplomats. This presents threats as well as opportunities. But so did the printing press, the telephone, air travel. Now that anyone can be a diplomat, we have to show that you can't live without diplomats.

Diplomacy has often been about finding ways towards progress and development that don't involve killing each other. We need to reconnect with that – yes – idealism. And we do need to embrace a more activist, insurgent, citizen style of diplomacy if we're to survive.

I always ask people who will influence the 21st century to a greater degree – Google or Britain? Most say Google. Diplomacy in the 21st century matters too much to be left to diplomats.

* * *

CHAPTER NINE: ACCOUNTABILITY THROUGH PUBLIC VALUE
THE ONLY WAY IS ETHICS

The Only Way is Ethics

I managed to upset Lord Tim Bell, "Maggie's favourite PR man," on a TV show, without even making any reference to some of his more controversial views.

The route to the *Bottom Line* studio in BBC Broadcasting House had been an odd affair, not least because I had spotted an ex-girlfriend of 25 years earlier in the Green Room. Inevitably, she turned out to be the show's producer.

We were on air to discuss ethics within communications. His Lordship has famously long been an advocate of the "cab rank" rule, as practised by barristers. You simply have to take whoever comes along as clients (or who insists on paying), regardless of any moral or ethical discretion. I have long thought this is nonsense. The cab rank is important for the law (so everyone has access to justice and a fair defence) but it is not applicable to communications. We are all able to make our own choices.

Evan Davis is a gentle host and the show meandered somewhat. I can't remember much of it, apart from a couple of feisty exchanges.

Tim Bell, colleagues say, is a lovely man – exceptionally generous, kind and protective of his charges. But for someone whose politics were forged in the darkest days of Thatcher's Britain, I always struggled to understand him.

With fellow panellist Julia Hobsbawm, the conversation focused on how we are all able to make ethical choices. We do not simply have to work for anyone and everyone.

Lord Bell took issue with something Julia had, I think, just said about working with clients with questionable ethics, such as unpopular regimes or dictatorships.

"Well, I don't think Julia would have acted for Augusto Pinochet," I started.

Tim Bell turned quite red. He was steaming.

"Nor did I, so don't just repeat claptrap."

A short squabble followed and Evan Davis intervened:

"Let's just clarify.... what was the relationship with Pinochet?"

"I worked for an institute called the Pinochet Foundation. I have never met General Pinochet in my life," said the good Lord. "Incidentally, I wouldn't mind meeting him and I can't now."

* * *

In September 2014, I attended a roundtable on Sustainable Value Creation. Contributors from leading consultancy firms, NGOs and think tanks were tasked with developing a uniform dashboard for chief executives, so that business leaders could measure (and then compare) sustainable value and "trust".

As is so often the case, the convenor started by asking the *wrong* questions.

First, "sustainable value" must extend beyond financial metrics alone. Second, "trust" or "trustworthiness" is an outcome – personal and behavioural – and not measurable in the absolute. Third, the group made another classic business school mistake: dashboards no longer apply.

Responsible businesses need to move beyond the last-century uniformity of competitive benchmarking. Collaborative, not competitive, edge is the future way.

Accountability is more important than absolute measurement. Public Leaders should read Margaret Heffernan before they return to early Michael Porter. (Margaret Heffernan believes those who see competition as everything are wrong, that hierarchies stultify and place ego over collective performance. She argues that short-termism places return on shareholder investment over sustainable growth and that efficiency is deemed more important than safety and well-being).

Conventional measurement, just like traditional communications, was born in an age of hierarchy and command-and-control. It holds little relevance in an age of networks and extreme sharing, however much we crave reductive simplicity everywhere in our usually complex business lives. The real world is messy, chaotic and contradictory and it is time we all came to terms with it.

Those present at the roundtable were looking for the right answers in the wrong places.

The "responsibility of business" must extend to employees, customers and society itself, not just to a shareholder few. It is within this context that we need to reappraise the concept of Public Value and the methods by which we judge success. We have to place purpose up there alongside profit.

Real people, including regulators and politicians, of course instinctively know what "ethical" or "good" looks like. "Good" is mostly common sense – an avoidance of the abuse of power, authority or profit, for example; something that contributes to the flourishing of the many, not the few. "Good" extends beyond mere compliance. The good company is led by values. Even badly behaved corporations know this to be true.

This thinking now needs to be made relevant for every

organisation. Business leaders must shift from making – and then testing, through patsy focus groups – platitude statements ("we are committed to being good"; "trust is central to everything we do"; "we put our people first", etc.) to the practical application of being "responsible", "socially useful" and "societally relevant". They must be assessed on what they do, not what they say – and convene stakeholder crowds to judge their actions.

In this way, they can become accountable to Public Value.

This measurement of Public Leadership by Public Value fuses an evolved concept of Aristotle's and Aquinas' common good and, yes, Porter and Kramer's shared value (Buddhists call this *sanga*). The temptation of course is to build yet another rigid compliance framework. This is to be resisted at all costs. Every corporation must have its unique version – based on its own co-created manifesto – precisely because Public Value is better co-produced with wise crowds of employees, customers and stakeholders, through open consultation and engagement.

The co-produced manifesto becomes the anchor for the corporation's accountability to the many, not the few – what the Occupy movement might call the 99% or The Crowd might recognise as the 91%.

A bank that thinks in terms of Public Value outcomes and actually listens to its employees and customers first, for example, would quickly address the classic Lord Adair banking challenge of being "socially useless".

Gap analyses and sentiment shifts, set within this accountability framework, become more important than relatively meaningless, absolute statistics, as expressed on uniform dashboards. Old hard-and-fast measurements represent the false controls of the old world, often used by corporate bureaucracies to boast competitive advantage in a race to the bottom or to defend budgets and justify existence. Rarely do they place employees, customers, citizens or society first.

* * *

The concept of Public Value, historically used in relation to the public sector, was brought to prominence in 1995 by Harvard Professor Mark H. Moore, who saw it as a translation of shareholder value.

From a 2002 report by the UK Cabinet Office's Strategy Unit on "Creating Public Value": "*trust...refers to the relationship between citizens and public authority. It is often the most neglected element but a lack of trust, even where services are well delivered, reduces public value and can hinder a public service's capacity to create it elsewhere.*"

The BBC used Public Value as its platform for licence renewal in 2004 and, two years later, Accenture launched the "Institute for Public Service Value". Two years after that The Work Foundation came up with a paper entitled "Public Value: The Next Steps in Public Service Reform".

The notion occasionally comes up in the private sector, too. Vogel Wakefield, which describes itself as "the counter-consultancy," recognises Public Value at the heart of much of its corporate advice. The German medical devices company Fresenius Medical Care is also often quoted in this context, while Wikipedia cites Bayern Munich football club as a champion of public and societal value – "counter-balancing its status as a global entertainment brand with an organisation that holds deep roots in its local community."

The property sector, where I advise extensively, is rich with such examples. Commitments to affordable housing, more green spaces, higher environmental standards, enhanced transport infrastructures, and more are often regarded simply as the demands of new property development. Yet these are also tangible demonstrations of Public Value, often financed through the benefits of private sector capital and profits. If, as Lord Andrew Adonis has argued, London is to realise its Vision 2030 with the construction of six new "city villages", it cannot do this through the public sector (or the public purse) alone. But nor does it have to descend into the murky depths of post-Thatcher PFIs.

Growing shareholder value can help grow Public Value in harmony. This does not necessarily mean, to borrow from Peter Mandelson, being "intensely relaxed" about the super-rich, but it does demand a real dose of reality as to how, for instance, major infrastructure projects – healthcare included – can be responsibly funded and deliver social impact.

There is a distinctive "type" of Public Value demonstrated by, say, a bank, which needs to take demonstrable actions to prove social utility, for example by setting fairer lending practices and/or capping excessive pay and bonuses.

Unilever would argue that it demonstrates Public Value by halving its environmental footprint over time; Puma by opening up its environmental impact reporting and setting quantifiable metrics; Tom's Shoes by giving a "free" pair to someone in the developing world for every pair that it sells. For some, environmental campaigner George Monbiot included, none of this is enough. For others, it might be a starting point for a new way of being accountable to a Public Value framework.

The "universe of good" liberates companies from only ever judging themselves against their competitors – a practice which only leads to a race to the bottom, as with the financial institution which aimed (not very high) to be the most trusted bank in the sector. Unilever needs to assess its Public Value alongside Puma; the BBC alongside Shell; the World Economic Forum alongside Syngenta. A Coalition of the Informed would then be able to self-identify by its existence within a universe of good, and it would be clearer to everyone who is striving for positive change and who is just opting to conduct business as usual.

Whatever different business leaders may choose to call it, demonstrating Public Leadership (activist, co-produced, citizen-centric, society-first) and embracing Public Value (being "socially useful" and/or a "business with purpose") should become the central organising principle of the future corporation, thus proving that it *is* possible to be held accountable for being ethical, trusted and good. It is a responsible measurement framework that speaks to the common good.

This may all be rather complicated and time-consuming. It may fly in the face of traditional and much-loved CEO dashboard measurements. But at least it is real and rooted in purpose.

* * *

The Danish pharmaceutical company Novo Nordisk specialises in diabetes treatment. It has enjoyed 40 consecutive quarters of double-digit sales growth, while also being recognised – according to the Corporate Knights 2012 survey – as one of the most sustainable multinationals in the world. The company's ultimate goal is to wipe out diabetes, which would, ironically, render the company redundant.

Novo is the largest company in the Nordic area by market capitalisation. It operates across 75 different companies, with production facilities in seven, and has 35,000 employees. Its 2012 revenues totalled DKK 78,026 million (10.5 billion Euros – up 18%) and its profit growth was up 25%. By the end of 2012, Novo's share price had quadrupled from its 2009 post-crisis low.

Novo Nordisk's stated aim is to expand the scope and accessibility of global medical treatment along a trajectory that pays proper consideration to social and environmental responsibility. The "Novo Nordisk way" is centred on the notion that all actions must be conducted responsibly and towards a positive social goal. This functions as the values-based DNA of the company, to serve as an underlying guide to every facet of the company and specifically provides a framework for strategic decision-making. Its commitment to triple bottom-line accounting (financial, social, environmental) was incorporated into the company's by-laws in 2004. This framework also serves as an engine for business development, by facilitating co-creation with stakeholders. It has become a source of both employee pride and external recognition.

"The main foundation," according to CEO Lars Sorensen, "is protecting our license to operate, our license to innovate, our license to be a business. And that begs and obliges everybody working in the company not only to see that we become a business...but that we do so in a way that is socially and environmentally responsible."

Novo's insulin market strategy in China reflects this. It has trained over 50,000 physicians and invested extensively in local healthcare systems (affecting an estimated 140,000 patients) to drive greater levels of diabetes diagnosis, treatment and care. Its investments have developed a profitable $1 billion market in China for insulin, with a 20% growth predicted for 2013. This is enlightened self-interest, with clear social benefit.

The company takes its environmental responsibilities seriously. Between 2004 and 2009, it achieved a 35,000 tonne reduction in CO_2 emissions, meeting its target five years ahead of schedule. It has recently initiated 580 energy saving projects and invested a further $21 million towards global energy efficiency campaigns. Within this, every company production site has to appoint energy stewards and conducts energy screenings every three years.

Novo Nordisk is one of the co-hosts of the World Business Summit on Climate Change (COP 15). It collaborates with Denmark's biggest utility company, DONG Energy, and has signed a 20-year contract to buy electricity exclusively from wind farms. The company provided capital to develop the farms and led a coalition to encourage other major manufacturers to join.

Novo Nordisk's share structure as a foundation is consistent with others within the Danish business sector. At least 120 other companies are similarly organised. Theirs is a culture of recirculating profits not through philanthropy but via direct social engagement and research into a better way.

* * *

"Power and responsibility," comments Dr Bruce Lloyd, Professor of Strategic Management at London South Bank University, "are simply different sides of the same coin. They are the yin and yang of our behaviours. They are how we balance our relations with ourselves with the interests of other, which is the core of what we mean by our values. Power makes things happen but it is through an appropriate balance between power and responsibility that helps ensure as many 'good' things as possible.

"In almost all ethical debates," he continues, "the ultimate objective is to try to achieve the appropriate balance of rights and responsibilities. If individuals behaved more responsibly and ethically towards one another, it would be much more likely that the net result would be a higher standard of ethical decision-making overall."

"The bankers have got away with it," wrote columnist Philip Stevens in January 2014. "They have seen off politicians, regulators and angry citizens alike to stroll triumphant from the ruins of the great crash... We were fools. Bankers are still collecting multimillion-dollar bonuses even as they shrug off multibillion-dollar fines."

The answer to the banking crisis is, at its core, cultural. The Barometer data consistently shows that that the lack of trust in financial services stems from the institutions' failure to address their own *cultural* behaviours: what they do, every day, in putting their own interests ahead of those of their employees and their customers.

████████ ████████, a former bank CEO, described himself as "institutionally blind on an industrial scale." It was a moment of great self-realisation – he had, by his own admission, been cocooned in his City bubble for the entirety of his 30-year career. He simply did not see what the rest of the world sees now: bonus payments defying gravity, let alone common sense, were just one manifestation.

Justin Welby, the Archbishop of Canterbury, condemned the "rotten culture" in banking, at about the same time that Lord Adair Turner called many banks "socially useless". If banks can become socially useful again, then we will have travelled a long way towards the reformation of business itself. In other words, if the "socially useless" bankers can find their renaissance as Public Leaders, there is genuine hope for us all. This will be a journey of substance and, as ███████ ███████ ██ ███████████ discovered not one of spin.

* * *

███████ ███████, like nearly every senior banker I have met in the past five years, told me how he admires Handelsbanken.

The Swedish bank, proud of its communitarian approach, avoided the bloodbath of the Global Financial Crisis through a combination of community focus and common sense. It proved, in very simple terms, that there is a better way.

Handelsbanken happily eschews practices such as the bonus culture in favour of what some still see as old-fashioned values. In the post-credit-crunch environment, where hostility to banking greed is more acute, its principles have captured the zeitgeist, while strong financial performances have attracted the attention of courters, not least the UK government.

Handelsbanken, unlike Zopa, is hardly a niche player. It is one of Sweden's largest banks and boasts over 700 branches in 24 countries. It was named in Bloomberg's 2013 list of the top ten strongest banks worldwide.

The company's aim is to maintain a sustainable banking model that emphasises customer service with the ultimate goal of generating profit by maintaining a higher return on equity than its peers. Its trajectory originated in the work of Jan Wallander, who restructured the bank in the wake of the financial meltdown of the 1970s. In particular, Wallander rejected what he considered inappropriate US management methods of the banks, and instead undertook counter-measures such as decentralised decision-making and the transfer of authority to local branches.

This was all underpinned by a wholly conservative approach to funding – exactly the opposite of the casino banking fiasco that would later lead to the downfall of previous luminaries, including Lehman Brothers, RBS and the Co-Op. Handelsbanken's specific growth model is openly risk-averse, avoiding high-leverage, high-yield options. Before the Global Financial Crisis, for example, Handelsbanken was offered Triple A assets of mortgage-backed securities by US investment bankers. But the bankers could not provide underlying documentation on the mortgages, so Handelsbanken's Chief Executive, Par Boman, visited some of the houses on the West Coast that were part of the securities before declining the offer. They were clearly sub-prime, in every sense of the word.

This return to an old-fashioned banking function emphasises the value of face-to-face encounters for banks in nurturing customer relations. Each Handelsbanken loan and service is bespoke to each particular applicant. This sits in stark contrast to many banks today who, while admiring Handelsbanken from afar, do little to emulate its practices. In June 2013, Barclays CEO Anthony Jenkins argued that setting up stores was a waste of assets because consumers mostly act online and stood by his decision to offer huge bonus payments to under-performing senior staff.

Handelsbanken relies primarily on consumer reputation and word-of-mouth for new business growth. It has no marketing department and deploys no national advertising. To my knowledge, there is no distinct emphasis on Public Relations. Trust and better communications are built from within.

Handelsbanken TV is a video channel that was set up

as a free service on the website providing financial information. It provides daily and varying economic reports
and has become one of Sweden's leading online video
news services, with 100,000 daily visitors. Initial success
led to the evolution of an independent service, EFN –
proof that any company can be its own media outlet.
Inter-mediation is no longer necessary.

Above all, Handelsbanken has learned the lessons of
history. The bank's management is highly aware of the
fluctuations in financial systems and holds a long-term
perspective on the business cycle. For this reason, it was
one of few banks that survived both the 1992 and 2008
crises without any government financial aid. The bank
holds key documentation of the board meetings from
the past 140 years to give an appreciation of historical
trends. That said, stability and profitability are not mutu-
ally exclusive. In Britain, the bank has delivered an 11.4%
return on capital – the highest return on allocated capital
of the international home markets, bar Norway. It has
the best returns but highest capital ratios of any lenders,
which attracts the (positive) attention of overseas regulators and investors.

* * *

It is now nearly two decades since I first attempted to
ban Advertising Value Equivalent from the PR lexicon.
For those unfamiliar with the term or the practice, this
is the so-called measurement tool with which PR traditionally measures itself. In very simple terms, you figure
out what the article would have cost in advertising terms
and then apply a multiplier. Yes, that's right – because
PR, with its implicit third-party endorsement, is deemed
to carry exponential value. The traditional multiplier was

three. In the travel sector – where word-of-mouth recommendation is so vital – it occasionally rose to seven.

In order to assess the value of PR, all that was needed
was a ruler (to measure the column inches), a handbook
(to see what the ad guys were paying) and a calculator.
I guess that first-time readers of this practice will think
this strange.

90% of current PR consultancy CEOs will tell you that
AVE is a wicked discipline. As a latest guess, at least 50%
of those are still using it to justify "success" to clients
– all the more bizarre given PR's long-held chippiness
about not living in the shadow of advertising. Whole con-
ferences, dating back nearly a decade now, have come
and gone on this subject – once enshrined as "The
Barcelona Principles" – but, in reality, not much has
changed.

The measurement itself is ridiculous and anachronistic. But there are wider principles at stake (setting aside
the one about not indulging in false self-justification).
Here are just two:

First, AVE speaks to a world of broadcast and not one of
engagement. It assumes that all audiences are equal and
that mass awareness is the name of the game. We know
this to be a wholly pointless argument. We now live – and
communicate – through our communities. We are networked and we overlap with one another through shared
interests and passion points. We are not any longer passive recipients of information – little points at the end,
at the mercy of large corporate or media spokes. We are
one huge Venn diagram.

Second, AVE speaks to the measurement of outputs,
not outcomes. This is the hideous verbiage of endless
press releases, corporate narratives and mission statements that are, quite frankly, mostly ignored. "They" –

the corporates – may want to land their narrative, but we are no longer listening. In the many Achilles' heels that bedevil today's PR industry, the obsession with outputs over outcomes is probably the most fundamental. Someone needs to turn off the loudhailer.

Data changes all this. With better data, gathered in real time, we can begin to track sentiment in media – just as supermarkets can move stock between aisles and at different heights in immediate response to customer demands and preferences. We can now not only focus on *what* is engaging, we can also determine *when* best to engage. We are guided not by the corporation's blind supply, but by the citizen-consumer's real time demand. This makes the media relationship more authentic, more legitimate and more direct – simply through the re-consideration of the measurement tools.

In an article in the *Financial Times* on Tuesday, 8th April 2014, the journalist Emma Jacobs noted that some business leaders were turning away from PR because they failed to see where it demonstrated value. AVE is not a good enough measurement, but the problem runs deeper still. "I do not know what [PR] does for us," quoted one executive, "except add corporate-speak."

* * *

I never expected to find myself in agreement with *Daily Mail* columnist Simon Heffer, still less wondering whether he actually sat to the "left" of me on issues of banking and ethics. But, early on in the establishment of Jericho Chambers, Simon delivered a lecture on the future of capitalism, in which the banks and the bankers featured heavily.

"Members of the public have to be given full information about risk. Then, if they wish to deposit money or buy shares in a bank that has a casino element to it, so be it... Honest capitalism," Heffer continued, "requires that workers can trust their bosses and that customers can trust the firms with which they do business."

"The casualties of the great financial crash were pensioners, shareholders, rank-and-file employees and taxpayers ... directly affected by the stupidity, recklessness, self-service of those for whom greed trumped not just sense, but decency."

Banks and bankers have become the near-pantomime baddies of the corporate world. (I say "near" because, in the West at least, they pretty much brought the prevailing model of capitalism to its mercy-seeking knees). The banks would not have embarked upon LIBOR-rate fixing or PPI mis-selling if they had exposed themselves to the scrutiny of real people and a wise crowd. Social democracy in action is a safeguard against mad market fundamentalism and the pursuit of profits at all costs.

To signal the all-important cultural shift, bank CEOs need to find a new honesty and slay some dragons by capping crazy bonus payments and establishing fairer wage ratios between the highest paid and those in the banking front line. They need to banish cross-selling and thus ensure they put customer needs ahead of bank "wants". They should remove, not excuse, any staff who fail to reach or do not maintain competency standards and, first and foremost, they must stop talking about trust and ethics – and instead demonstrate leadership through deeds, first and foremost.

* * *

The launch of Snapple is one of my favourite pieces of work of all time. I probably learned and innovated more on that campaign in the mid-1990s than on any single piece of work since. We were "doing social marketing" before social marketing went mainstream; we were developing user-generated content long before that, too, became a cliché.

Snapple was the brainchild of Arnie, Hymie and Lenny – three 70-something New Yorkers who had previously owned a fruit juice store and a window-washing business, among others. When asked by my business partner, Jackie, how they knew Snapple was going to work, Arnie said: "We didn't. Our carrot crushing business, for example, that failed."

The three pioneers went on to make many millions from the sale of Snapple to Quaker and, without even knowing it, provided a brilliant marketing strategy ("Made From The Best Stuff On Earth") for the likes of Innocent Drinks to later follow, including offering free tours of their HQ.

When I was an eager young Social Democrat in the early 1980s, we ran a photo-call for Dr David Owen. For some reason, we had hired a double-decker London bus. The good doctor was at the wheel. I asked him to wear the driver's cap. He scowled at me (probably with the same scowl that later withered the political reputation of the Liberal David Steel).

"I have one piece of professional advice for you," he said. "Never wear a silly hat." And to this day, I never have.

One session with two of the Snapple founders turned into an equally illuminating lesson about the value of independent thinking.

"Conventional business school thinking says that you have to think in terms of pie charts – taking a percentage slice from your competition; adding another percentage slice from your pricing policy and distribution; attributing another slice to TV advertising or similar. Everything is framed in terms of the competition – what you are up to and what you need to take from them.

"That's how people want us to handle Coke and Pepsi," they said.

"The thing is. We never went to business school. We didn't know about these pies. We just went ahead and baked a pie of our own."

It is good to challenge Harvard orthodoxy. Things can be done differently.

* * *

George Pitcher is legendary in many ways. And not always for the right reasons.

I once had to feign deep religious conviction to stop a drunken oaf punching George in the Garrick (a place, not a metaphorical part of anatomy). George is a priest of the Anglican Communion, as well as being the co-founder of Jericho Chambers and a noted iconoclast. It is, as they say, a very broad church.

In one of his many previous lives, George was advising McDonald's. It was sometime between the McLibel case and the moment they saw the green salad light and went all healthy on the world. They were getting some (justifiable) stick. He tells the story thus:

Many senior McDonald's executives were present, alongside a phalanx of the usual advisers.

"How can we deal with all this negative commentary about our animal husbandry?" they asked.

Much breath was sucked between teeth.

"I know (someone) on the *Telegraph*. He could do us a favourable piece," was the first response.

"We need to get to members of SelCo (glossary: Parliamentary Select Committee) for sure," tried another. "Get our message across. Make sure they understand our narrative."

George, unusually for him, was silent. The roundtable kept on spinning.

The names of supposedly "friendly" journalists were chucked in with carefree abandon. Everyone was showing off their knowledge of media figures and politicians. The clients seemed oblivious.

Finally, they turned to George.

"What do you think we should do, George?"

"Treat your animals better," George tells me he said.

* * *

Wise Crowd Contributor:

Death of the Passive Leader

Is There a Way Through the Climate Impasse?

Paul Westbury

We have been worrying about the negative impacts of climate change in a serious way since the Kyoto Protocol of 1997 – an agreement of sorts amongst leading developed industrialised nations that aimed to limit global greenhouse gas emissions. It was an attempt to wrestle climate change under some sort of control and it was a start, although it later proved to be a rather weak one as the full support of major economies fell away. Since this time atmospheric CO_2 levels have rather alarmingly passed the upper limit recommended by scientists at the time of Kyoto, and governments still don't seem to have much to show for all of the talk that we have since seen.

In 2013 the UN Global Compact completed their largest-ever study of the attitudes of the CEOs of the world's 1000 largest businesses, across 107 different countries. 75% of the leaders of the planet's biggest businesses confirmed that they struggled to convince customers to pay more for truly sustainable products. So 75% of our biggest bosses were in effect admitting that they didn't yet have a business model that worked for sustainability, and with 83% agreeing that government policymaking and regulation will be critical to future progress they also appeared to be looking for others to solve the problem.

It's a classic impasse. Businesses can't sell sustainable products to customers who aren't prepared to pay the higher prices that they want to charge for them, so they ask for government to legislate in order to force the shift. Democratic governments are understandably reluctant to act in this way as the voter mandate is tremendously hard to achieve and is, in the eyes of the modern career politician, rather risky to attempt. So when faced with the simple honest truth surrounding the essential need to act in the best interests of a warming world, politicians can too often opt out and instead do what is required to secure another term in office. This retains power but without the necessary mandate they are left to work within the short-term time horizons that this strategy inevitably brings. The big fixes become near impossible to deploy. So there are three parts to this impasse: businesses who won't raise prices to deliver the right products, governments who dare not take the true cost to the voters, and voters, denied strong political leadership, act in their short rather than long-term interest. We are locked in a tri-partite paralysis.

The recently published Fifth UN IPCC Climate Change Report says that the effects of climate change will be severe, pervasive and irreversible. We must quickly break this paralysis if we are to address significant global challenges. But who will lead the way?

If career politicians are too infrequently prepared to take some risks for the sake of progress then the only answer lies with business, but it is only through the emergence of a new style of leadership that we are starting to see a way for businesses to now step in and show the way forward. Capitalism is set up to maximise profit within the regulatory frameworks that contain it, but some businesses, their leaders, and their employees, are making a conscious decision to plan for longer-term success that is measured across social and environmental as well as fiscal factors – even if it is at the possible expense of short-term financial gain. A new type of business leader is taking a different approach, is acknowledging their responsibilities, and is offering a new way forward for the longer term by promoting the right products and solutions, even if customers aren't immediately prepared to fully pay for them.

This is a tricky balancing act, but these smarter leaders seem fully aware of the upside of following this approach. The circular economy is being embraced more openly in strategic planning and time horizons are being stretched further out into the future. The majority of businesses aren't charities, so financial stability and surety is still important, but there is a middle ground emerging that is rightly attracting a lot of attention and support amongst those weary of what appeared to be the endless pursuit of short-term gain at all costs. In some enlightened cases, this new sustainable approach is actually allowing businesses to improve their near term performance and demonstrate that smarter, broader and more responsible strategy does indeed attract attention and can be used to drive positive results pretty quickly, contrary perhaps to popular opinion.

What of the climate crisis? The carbon dioxide potential in the world's proven fossil fuel stocks is widely regarded to be around 3,000 gigatons. It is generally acknowledged that to control global warming we will need to find a way to leave a large proportion of the remaining fossil fuels in the ground. Super-clean new technologies can facilitate smarter energy generation from fossil fuels during a relatively quick transition to a low, to no, carbon economy. However, we will still need to leave about two thirds of all of this remaining global oil and gas in the ground. So with that in mind, why did the oil and gas industry invest something like £400 billion over the last year to find more oil and gas? Investors are increasingly asking whether these carbon assets become stranded assets in a carbon-constrained future world.

The Guardian recently reported a high profile case where investors in ExxonMobil asked exactly this, and that the Exxon-Mobil board seemed to work pretty hard to try and avoid answering their questions. Eventually, on the day that just happened to coincide with the 25th anniversary of the *Exxon Valdez* oil spill, the board agreed to disclose their carbon asset risk assessment. Their answer was, in a way, a confirmation that they were not concerned. They felt that the future scenario where governments restrict hydrocarbon production to meet accepted carbon reduction targets was highly unlikely, and that society would not be able to supplant traditional carbon based forms of energy with renewables soon enough. In other words, they felt it unlikely that the world would meet future carbon reduction targets; that the low carbon futures that climate scientists were demanding were unlikely to be achieved; and that there will continue to be a constant demand for carbon well into the future. On this basis, the risk of their carbon assets becoming stranded was considered to be low.

In contrast, Shell, Unilever and 68 other companies with a collective annual revenue of $90 billion have come together to call for a cap on post-industrial carbon emissions at a trillion metric tons – the cap required to hold global temperature increases within the accepted upper limit of 2 degrees. It's a far better example of businesses acting as governments should; coming together across international borders, having a plan that unfolds in the medium term (we are estimated to reach a trillion tonnes of carbon by 2040) and showing that with enough critical mass they can create market change. The businesses involved still need to ensure their own successful futures, and this will not have been easy to set up and deliver, but with a new style of business leader driving the way forward and with global alliances being struck to maximise collective firepower, it is a great example of how businesses can start to effect positive change.

Engineers have been at the heart of the climate debate for many years and have been encouraging government and business to take the longer-term strategic view. Experts at assessing options from the perspective of triple bottom line, and in finding solutions that are optimised and smart, engineers have been ideally placed to shape future models for a controlled climate and advise on how businesses and governments can get there. It now feels like change is coming, a change driven by a new style of business leadership that recognises the need for smarter action for the long term.

We have seen throughout history, with products such as the mobile phone or the motorcar, how the private sector can get behind a new idea and drive transformation beyond what most thought possible. This drive for change needs to come from within industry. For a sufficient critical mass to be behind it, others soon need to get concerned about being left behind and join the movement. But couple this with the power of the inquisitive investor, who is no longer buying into the usual short-term responses from the markets, and we have a powerful collective force for change.

In time, as more people and voters are exposed to the long-term truth that has been lost in noise for too long, they will at last be able to make their own minds up without the influence of near-term spin. Activist businesses and educated voters are leading governments towards a smart long-term plan created and made possible by engineers; our future depends on it.

CHAPTER TEN: ENLIGHTENED PUBLIC LEADERSHIP
AN END TO PALE, MALE AND STALE, "MANDY" CEOS

An End to Pale, Male and Stale, "Mandy" CEOs

"So, what do you think is the hallmark of an enlightened CEO?"

"Er...."

"It's really not a difficult question."

"I'll ask my PR team to come back you within a few hours."

* * *

There are some CEOs who feel comfortable answering this question directly and without hesitation. Unfortunately, they remain in a lonely minority. It speaks volumes about the state of business today that so many business leaders feel the need to hide behind their PR teams to provide answers that should otherwise be instinctive and immediate.

Some answer in their stride. Kingfisher CEO Ian Cheshire is one of them. Asked in the context of input for a Crowd sustainability session, Cheshire wrote:

"An enlightened CEO is one who really cares about what their business' true overall impact is today and also how they can ensure the business will still be here and sustainable in fifty years' time."

Ronan Dunne, CEO of telecoms giant O2, addressing the same brief, also saw sustainability as key:

"The modern and enlightened CEO must place sustainability at the heart of business planning – a strong business performance cannot be achieved without a strong sustainability performance. A vital role for the CEO is to show leadership and commitment to the sustainability agenda, inspiring others and constantly seeking new ways for the company's skills, assets and brand to deliver wider benefits and opportunities to the communities they serve."

Clear. But a cynic may argue, also carefully crafted (and he was answering to a session on sustainability).

There is certainly a fashion among Chairmen and CEOs for this way of thinking. The question is whether it is defensive "fashion" that comes from fear of regulation or a heartfelt, enlightened belief. Business leaders are understandably anxious to be seen to do the right thing, which is somewhat different from an intrinsic commitment to do what is right.

For the same session, John Maltby, CEO of the challenger bank Williams & Glyn (at the time of writing, being spun-out of RBS at the request of the EU under challenger bank legislation), characterised the enlightened CEO:

"One who has a clear sense of business and social purpose and understands their role is to listen to and deliver for customers, colleagues, society and shareholders – not the other way round."

Data substantiates this mindset. The 2014 UN Global Compact Report stated that "93% of CEOs surveyed believe that environmental, social and governance issues will be 'important' or 'very important' to the future success of their business."

Mandy Rice-Davies was the socialite and "showgirl" who, along with Christine Keeler, became a central figure in the 1960s Profumo scandal. When Lord Astor denied, in court, having an affair with her, she famously replied: "well he would, wouldn't he?"

I sometimes wonder whether other CEOs are merely

inviting the Mandy Rice-Davies riposte. They would say that, wouldn't they?

* * *

In 2011, *Business Insider* reported that 25 global corporations enjoyed turnovers in the previous year that exceeded the GDPs of entire nations – in their own words, "often with a few billion dollars to spare." Matching turnover with Gross Domestic Product (GDP), the US behemoth retailer Walmart is roughly the same size as the Republic of South Africa. Amazon is bigger than Kenya and Oracle larger than Lebanon. Visa is bigger than Zimbabwe, and McDonald's larger than Latvia. Moreover, these private sector business states are often relatively unencumbered by the problems that real politics brings. They are better organised, more efficiently structured, enjoy access to deeper expertise and boast greater financial resources to boot. And they certainly have more marketing clout. This is why organisations such as the World Economic Forum should play such an important role in shaping world and societal events beyond politics – and why they are such a wasted opportunity.

The HSBC Global Climate Change benchmark, a tracker for the performance of sustainable companies, revealed that sustainable investments delivered 19.8% growth in 2013 – out-performing the global equities market for the first time, as well as indicating that investment in the sector is beginning to grow. The burgeoning Social Impact Investment market (now championed by the likes of JP Morgan and Goldman Sachs) equally symbolises this trend. We Create's Nick Jankel-Elliot likewise quotes a 2012 IBM study: "entrepreneurs who are committed to a mission beyond profits are [those] most likely to succeed."

2013 Accenture analysis ("Why Green is the New Gold") argued that transformational leaders "display significantly superior performance to their peers, out-performing 65% of their respective industries in total return to shareholders and 59% in profitability and revenue growth."

Transformational leaders are those who, according to the report's authors, are the CEOs of companies "regarded as high performers on both sustainability and business metrics."

The enlightened, transformational leader, however, should do what is right because it is the right thing to do, not because it simply maximises profit or return.

Tim Cook, the otherwise usually reserved CEO of Apple, expressed rare anger at a 2014 shareholder meeting when challenged by a member of the National Center for Public Policy Research, a Washington DC lobby group "dedicated to providing free-market solutions to today's public policy problems."

As Joel Makower later reported on GreenBiz.com, Justin Danhof from the NCPPR "demanded that Cook pledge that Apple wouldn't do anything related to the environment that didn't follow a clear profit motive." In short, they wanted to make sure that anything Cook, and Apple, did was going to make them some money, regardless of any possible social or environmental motive.

"When we work on making our devices accessible by the blind," Cook said, "I don't consider the bloody ROI."

* * *

In *The Key*, London Business School Professor Lynda Gratton works in similar vein of thought:

"To create a good future, it is crucial that those who lead corporations become increasingly transparent about their actions and intentions and see themselves as part of the wider world they inhabit."

As a blurb for her book puts it, "The world's business leaders must make a decision: either connect your company's interests with those of the world at large – or watch these separate interests crash into each other. You have the resources to save the world."

"I think the new role for the CEO is to be the 'chief engagement officer'," Richard Edelman wrote in the *McKinsey Quarterly* in April 2014. "A CEO is going to have to go and meet the community and... actually make relationships personally and listen. And not just go and formulate policy, but listen first and participate in the community – only then be an advocate."

In this context, CEOs might consider a shared oath to personalise the mission – but *not* if this is simply the equivalent of posters-declaring-values on washroom walls, or the parallel madness of RBS "values" being emblazoned across its reception area. This is the old, rock-star way. Progressive Public Leaders will co-produce manifestos from within the organisation. A wise crowd will help inform and shape them into a more meaningful commitment that demonstrates substance, not sound bites. That crowd therefore becomes central to the wider drive for cultural relevance.

Genuine empowerment (a trust builder) needs to be a guiding principle for any culture change programme. With empowerment comes ownership – a personal commitment to delivering the manifesto, and therefore an implicit weakening of control "from the top" and more trust inherent at all levels of the organisation.

If we can manage 360 degree reviews, why can we not

deliver 360 degree compensation initiatives, as management expert Gary Hamel has argued? "Compensation has to be a correlation of value created, rather than how well you fought that political battle."

There can be no trade-offs: a company cannot do what is right in one area of the business and something less purposeful, less trusting elsewhere. Nothing works in isolation. Similarly, what is internal is external, and vice versa. What an organisation says inside is what defines it outside. Maybe this is what Richard Edelman meant. Until everyone really understands this and the transparency required to deliver it, no culture will differentiate itself sufficiently to be recognised as successful, sustainable and trusted.

* * *

And then there is the "L'Oreal CEO": the one who justifies his excesses because, to borrow from the cosmetic company's famous advertising strapline, *he thinks he is worth it.*

The following is a warning tale:

Once upon a time, a senior PR practitioner found himself counselling a scandal-ridden CEO who thought it "appropriate" to take a double-digit percentage pay rise, despite the collapse in the company's share price. Corporate morale was at an all-time low. Media coverage was hideous. The business had not only declined in absolute terms but had also significantly under-performed against its competitive set. Under no circumstances did this person deserve a pay rise, while their employees could expect little more than, at best, an inflation-linked increase and, at worst, redundancy through the ugly-phrased "right-sizing" (a classic word progeny of PR "message management").

The PR adviser was in the back of a car when he received the call, asking him to talk some sense into the CEO. "He might just listen to you' was said, more in hope than expectation. He quickly fired off an email, offering an opening statement for the CEO to his company's AGM. It started, as I understand it, with the words, "I'm sorry."

"I'm not the person who matters most in this organisation. There are tens of thousands of employees who are much more important than me. They are the ones who deserve recognition and reward. They – not me – are the ones most vital to our business' future."

There was some optimism that the speech – and, more importantly, its theme of contrition and humility – would stand and that, despite the remuneration committee's recommendation that a significant pay rise be awarded (an odd call anyway), the CEO would see sense and decline the offer. Only 90 minutes later, however, the CEO had changed his mind. His stance had instead hardened to the point of obstinacy.

The PR advisor called the Comms Director and suggested that, if the Labour Party Manifesto in 1983 had famously been "the longest suicide note in history," this AGM speech might become one of the shortest. "But he genuinely thinks he deserves it," he was told. "He thinks it simply reflects his market worth." The truth is, as many would agree, it simply didn't.

The adviser was about to mention this directly to the CEO (like me, he has long believed that 100% of fuck-all is still fuck-all) but instead suggested, more gracefully, to the comms chief that taking the pay rise and failing to open with an intelligent *mea culpa* would hasten the CEO's downfall. It would leave the media and institutional shareholders baying for blood. The company chairman would be forced to make a choice – and, at the very least, offer a sword on which to fall. The CEO would hear nothing of it. Wilful blindness had combined with absolute arrogance and total hubris. It was a toxic mess. And thus the "L'Oreal CEO" eventually departed.

Real Public Leadership and Public Value inverts this model, while old Public Relations protects it. Old PR paints lipstick on pigs.

* * *

And here is my very personal view on Richard Branson.... why I believe Richard Branson is a phoney.

Richard Branson is not an enlightened CEO. He is not a Public Leader.

I do not understand why so many people are persuaded by the mythology of Branson. As journalist Jonathan Ford commented: "Few entrepreneurs have grasped as clearly as Sir Richard Branson the importance of public relations in modern business."

The Branson story is well and often told. A privileged background; a rebellious under-achiever at an elitist school; a passion for music; a youthful sense of entrepreneurial ambition; his first record store; the music label; a love of aviation (and then ballooning); fearlessly taking on the big boys; endless publicity stunts; a conversion to environmentalism; Blair & Mandela; Davos and the B-Team; Necker Island; etc etc.

Oh, and the ding-dong between BA and Virgin over BA's alleged "dirty tricks"; the hugely complex business structures (there are apparently eleven corporate entities, in various jurisdictions, between Virgin Atlantic and its ultimate owner); the record on environmental commitments within his own companies; and more. In his critical book on Branson, *Behind the Mask*, Tom Bower observes that Branson is in essence a traditional "monarch" with a passion for self-reinvention. "Much of the cash flow," he comments, "has come from businesses that, far from being 'challengers', are incumbents in highly-regulated industries, such as the state-subsidy-guzzling railways."

In rebuttal, Branson himself was quoted by the *Financial Times* as saying Bower's work is "a foul, foul, piece of work from the first words to the last."

But, let's be honest, nobody seems to mind whether Bower or Branson is right. In an age of lazy 24/7 media, Branson's is the easy sound bite, the free rent-a-quote, the immediate money shot. We do not stop to think "why?" when we see him first in line to congratulate the new Prime Minister outside the Royal Festival Hall in 1997, or, 16 years later, sitting alongside Oprah Winfrey at the stadium funeral for Nelson Mandela. He is our business Obama, a commercial Stephen Fry, an apparent national treasure.

The Branson mythology is of the quintessential leader – charismatic, witty, fearless and entrepreneurial. But it is precisely that – mythology. A careful PR construct. Conventional wisdom sees Branson as a trusted leader, yet Branson defies what a trusted leader should be about – from his position on the sustainable health of the planet (even some of my greenest and most altruistic friends seem taken in by him) to less-than-clear financial transparency that is characteristic of many of his corporations. Abundant media skills (or manipulation) should not be mistaken for enlightened thinking, transformational ability or commitment.

Richard Branson is a very deliberate, imaginary construct, not unlike Bob Dylan (a legitimate hero). But Dylan's prose is infinitely wiser. It is no coincidence that Branson is widely regarded (sadly, applauded) as a master of spin. He is not merely an anachronistic, charismatic leader, but a creature of PR.

In my personal view, Richard Branson behaves like a buccaneering hippy because the reality is that he isn't one. It is all a PR smokescreen.

* * *

Klaus Schwab is founder and Chief Executive of the World Economic Forum. "His people" declined the opportunity for him to be interviewed for this book.

I wanted to say this to him: it is time to have an honest conversation about the legitimacy of power and leadership. That could start at Davos, atop the real and metaphorical mountain.

As Professor Andrew Henderson of the University of Texas has written: "people who get to the top tend to be both skilled and pretty fortunate, which gives them a certain level of self-confidence and makes them less open to new ways of thinking." We can express this in many ways. Some believe that eight years is the maximum tenure for a business leader; others simply say that the world has had enough of a "male, pale and stale" elite.

Why are we surprised that the Eurozone spent the best part of five years in crisis (before the story slowly, and somewhat bizarrely, faded away)? That global inflammation issues as diverse as poverty or religious fundamentalism remain unresolved? That American kids are still being shot in the streets, despite the horrors of Newtown or similar? That austerity lingers where (better) growth can prevail? Is it because we are mistaking power for leadership; power for authentic authority; power for a real hunger for change? Is it because the power status quo offers a comfort blanket, shabbily knitted by the devil we know, and that "power", if not corrupted, has certainly become inert? Is it because our leaders have failed us? It is because we are looking for trust in institutions that now lack relevance and for trust in people who have debased both the "t" word and, quite often, the trust principle itself?

Power, as currently constituted in business and in government, too often locks the wrong people in the wrong roles and blocks the emergence of a new leadership. Reimagined power, leadership and authority perhaps lie with the young and (often) disenfranchised; not, by design of fate, with the older elites.

Speaking at an event at HM Treasury in June 2014, I was asked for my best advice on how to facilitate the shift to networks and away from hierarchy. "Skip a generation of leadership," I offered. "Don't let every generation of 50-something white males always hire successors from among a bunch of 40-something white males." There was widespread nodding in the audience. My career ambition is to make this thinking real.

It is time to question existing gatekeepers and institutional authority at a fundamental level. This is the challenge for tomorrow's Public Leaders. The social contract, once implicit, now needs open reconsideration and a more explicit affirmation of the relationship between rulers and the ruled, citizens and state. Plato and Aristotle, Rousseau and Hobbes, even Rawls: none of these had to really contend with the implications of a properly empowered citizenship – with either the transparent accountability of the web or the contention of business empires of scales that outstrip the GDPs of entire nations. The new conversation needs to be open, honest and immediate.

This is more than a rage against vested interests. Progress can no longer be entrusted to those (business leaders) who simply sway with happenstance in a world that is properly shifting. To ignore these shifts is to have learned nothing from the trauma and crises of the past half-decade. These have been seismic and irreversible changes. Reimagined power, authority and legitimate leadership needs to reside elsewhere if a real change is going to come, especially as more millennials enter the workplaces and polling booths – increasingly debt-ridden, sometimes unemployed and uncertain about future security.

* * *

In a couple of articles in 2011 and 2013, John Kotter of Harvard Business School captured what many had probably known instinctively for years. First, that management should not be mistaken for leadership. And, second, that hierarchies remain important for management but it is within networks that real leaders operate and the big changes happen.

These two statements should be read together to make most sense. The Kotter argument does not deny or decry the need for management. It exists to bring order, discipline and focus to any organisation or campaign. But it simply is not the same as leadership. Leadership brings vision, hope, progress … and change.

Management, meanwhile, brings process, not progress.

Leadership, Kotter argues, is "about vision, about people buying in, about empowerment and, most of all, about producing useful change." Leadership is not about attributes; it's about behaviour.

"20th century, capital 'H' Hierarchy (a sort of hardware)," he writes, "and the managerial processes that run on it (a sort of software) do not handle transformation well."

Trust, likewise, may well be an attribute, but it also serves a higher function, with greater authority, as a behaviour. Does this mean that we are more likely to trust our leaders rather than our managers – or will we simply trust only those whose behaviours in fact demand and deserve our trust? The latter argument insists upon a new level of accountability, where said leaders are rightly judged by their actions and not (wrongly) by their words. Which makes sense. Seen through this prism, so many who talked themselves into the trust trap might have thought about the walking of it first. Just ask any one of the reverse poster boys of recent corporate trust woes.

Managers create and protect hierarchies as logical instruments of expression, command and control. Those hierarchies exist within institutions that are themselves often hollow creations: reality-show constructs that we are then expected to trust simply because we are told to do so by those "in control". This makes increasingly less sense in a borderless world that sees networks supplant hierarchies, and where hierarchies tend to view change as anathema. Conversely, in Kotter's words, networks see the urgency for transformation around "tomorrow's possibilities". PR, meanwhile, constantly and obstinately protects "today's rules".

Luke Johnson, in an article in the *Financial Times*, reinforces this point: "Technology, globalisation and changing behaviour mean many previous assumptions and hierarchies are falling apart. The end of authority across so many aspects of life is palpable: the barriers to entry for upstarts are collapsing. Loyalty too is evaporating ... Better informed, empowered citizens are deserting old media because they want to participate, rather than be lectured."

Or, as Clay Shirky puts it: "sharing changes everything." We want leaders, not managers. We want to be involved in the discussion and decision-making process, not dictated to.

We live in a time of technocracy – where management has been elevated far beyond its deserved status. Technocracy has in turn bred a culture of compliance that, in a vicious circle, has created more managers and fewer leaders. Managers like to keep their heads beneath the proverbial parapets, which is probably why so many so-called leaders went missing in the immediate aftermath of the 2008 financial crisis. It turns out that they were never leaders after all. Their PR advisors were advising silence and, worse, those leaders took that advice.

In business, Corporate Social Responsibility is the equivalent of a managerial coup of what should be a leadership discipline: usurping true, values-led actions with a compliance culture that is *de facto* the enemy of powerful, progressive thought. The CSR space has increasingly been occupied by a combination of reformed PR practitioners and sustainability "experts", but it might as well be populated by lawyers (obey the rules, please) and accountants (assess the cost-benefit analysis).

* * *

I hate Starbucks.

And I told them so. It was all deeply ironic.

✻ ✻ ✻

Jorge Mario Bergoglio is now better known to the world as Pope Francis I. "Elected" to the Holy See in 2013, only time will tell whether Francis is truly a transformative leader – or possibly the most brilliant brand marketer and communicator of his age. He may well be both.

The Pope is a Jesuit, his name taken in honour of St

Francis of Assisi, whose own prayer was mutilated by Margaret Thatcher and her PR team on the steps on 10 Downing Street in 1979.

Wonderfully, he travelled by bus to check out of the hotel in which he had been staying during the Cardinals' Enclave that elected him. That must have been one hell of a surprised Roman receptionist, when the new Pope, Christ's embodiment on earth, offered his credit card as payment.

Francis also took the first papal selfie. He is very much a man of the moment.

The Catholic Church, beset by global scandals about issues ranging from banking to child abuse, made a brilliant brand choice in electing Jorge Mario Bergoglio. His Jesuit humility was the perfect antidote and antithesis to everything that had come before. His apologetic tone, open manner, sense of forgiveness (who can forget the early money shot of him washing the feet of a black Muslim woman?) and even wry humour suddenly repositioned what, to the outside world, looked increasingly like a moribund and out-of-touch institution. He instinctively knew what every great incoming CEO knows: that he had to immediately slay some dragons. Hence the second-hand ring, the basic apartments and the refusal of new robes. The banking equivalent would have been no bonuses, capped salaries and expanded peer-to-peer lending and community investment. When it came to transformative status, Francis got there first.

Doctrinally, little has changed. I do not want to enter into a debate of faith, but Pope Francis has not yet overturned Papal doctrine on, among other things, the role of women in the church, homosexuality, abortion and contraception. His views are not new here (and his tone is always tempered) – he believed the same when tending the flock in Buenos Aires. I have no doubt that Pope Francis is a man of great integrity and personal moral courage. But are his actions symbolic or transformative? They are certainly a recognition of the need for a different style of leadership in a changed world; old structures are collapsing and new techniques are needed. But, as *The Spectator* magazine in July 2013 quoted one conservative Catholic who views such moves as contrived: "Frankie is less Assisi and more Howerd... All those naynays and titter-ye-nots are scripted, not spontaneous."

Could this be little more than great PR in humble disguise?

* * *

What is beyond doubt is that Pope Francis intends to build a clear, ethical framework for the Church in his image. Whether for Church or (business or political) state, this has to be the start-point of true, Public Leadership – ruling both in and out what is deemed as "acceptable" and "doing the right thing". The latter is not, I would hasten to add, the preserve of the liberal left – who, on so many occasions, have proved wholly intolerant of what many would see simply as a plurality of views.

The April 2014 defenestration of the Mozilla CEO, Brendan Eich, is possibly the most recent example (he had earlier helped fund an anti-gay marriage pressure group). There is no moral absolutism in business – each one of us must be able to freely choose who we support and who we shun. With this in mind, we all need to use the networks and the technology available to us to make those choices visible and audible – whether it is bringing change to organisations (as activist employees or shareholders) or whether it is refusing to buy goods or services from certain companies or brands.

Amanda Mackenzie, CMO of insurer Aviva, speaks to moral and ethical relativism in business:

"When you are struggling with a 'where do we draw the line?' kind of conversation, it sometimes has to be less about staying within the letter of the law or the rules and more about what feels right or wrong.

"As leaders, there are certain decisions that are absolute and others that are relative. The absolute ones are comparatively easy. It is the relative ones that are more difficult to gauge and those are the important conversations to have."

* * *

Roxanne Wilson is Jericho Chambers' first Communications Pupil. She is a graduate of the Taylor Bennett Foundation, run by the brilliant Sarah Stimpson and the brainchild of the legendary Heather McGregor, otherwise known to millions of *FT* readers (and attendees at the Edinburgh Fringe) as Mrs. Moneypenny, and one of Lynda Gratton's modern masters. The TBF was created to address the urgent need for greater diversity in the Public Relations and communications sector and to bring more people from BME backgrounds into the profession. It does important work. Roxanne, 24 and with a degree in Fashion Promotion, is a wonderful exemplar and ambassador.

As part of its ten-week cycles, those on the TBF courses enjoy internships at many of the leading PR consultancies in the UK.

"What do you make of your first week at Jericho?" I asked Roxanne.

"Well …. Interesting."

"Go on."

"Almost everything you are writing and saying is pretty much exactly the *opposite* of what me and my mates were taught at all the big agencies during our time there."

* * *

I met Dagmara Wojciechowicz, a 28 year-old CSR graduate from Liverpool John Moores University, on Twitter, via the crowd-funding of this book. Dagmara had read my blog post on "Why CSR Makes Me Angry". I had originally called it "Why I Hate CSR". In one of her tweets, she noted: "I think my tutors will be happy when I leave Uni... I ask too many #uncomfortablequestions".

Dagmara and I exchanged a few notes, swapped ideas and then spent an hour on the phone together. It was clear that she remained wholly unconvinced by the conventional thinking around CSR and how, in essence, it has been deployed as both an instrument of compliance and an essential part of the PR industry's make-up bag. Or, as one of her friends said to her, "*sprinkling glitter on a pile of poo to make it look prettier.*" More politely, Dagamara referred to CSR as "corporate wallpaper". Changes don't happen on paper, she added.

Dagamara has decided that, on finishing her degree, she will not seek employment with the traditional consultancies. Activism, she believes, is the future and, like Celine Schillinger before her, she is determined to be an agent of change.

While finishing the book, I stumbled across this tweet from Dagmara. I had not realised that she was also the mother of a young child:

"My child is now familiar with: YouTube, Instagram, Facebook and Twitter – that's at 17 months old! I ate dirt when I was his age!"

Ours is a future of Instagram and Twitter, Dagmara and Roxanne. They see through the corporate poo. They do not need to manufacture glitter because they are determined instead to be honest and activist. Their generation is now in control, insofar as control is anyhow possible. The smarter ones among the older generation will lead and be the change. We will be the incumbent disruptors while they, the Roxannes and Dagmaras, will help engineer the shift to Public Leadership and Public Value. Believe and trust them we must.

Back in the academic world, Kotter argues that, without strong leadership, "we end up with over-managed and under-led organisations, which are increasingly vulnerable in a fast-moving world."

That, I am happy to report, is the truth.

Wise Crowd Contributor:

Leadership is Dead

Professor Cliff Oswick

Is leadership dead? Maybe not yet, but it is in terminal decline. In a rapidly changing and highly connected world traditional forms of leadership are becoming increasingly redundant and irrelevant.

As a viable and effective means of organising and coordinating collective activities, leadership has been over-hyped, over-used and over-stretched. It is a slippery concept. It is everywhere, encapsulates everything and applies to everyone. It is the solution to all social, political and organisational ills. It is the modern day equivalent of snake oil.

Vague Vernacular and Dodgy Determinism

Beyond the conventional notions of leadership as the process of managing a group of followers, more abstract descriptions of the phenomenon have recently entered the lexicon. We now have: "thought leadership" – leading ideas rather than people; "spiritual leadership" – leading beliefs and values; and "self-leadership" – leading oneself. This begs the question: what aspects of life are not leadership? If I express a view in a tweet am I engaged in a process of thought leadership? Is organising my commute to work an example of self-leadership? Leadership has become an empty signifier. It is a sort of "death by diffusion".

In addition to semantic questions around what constitutes (or does not constitute) leadership, there are significant pragmatic issues concerning the track record of leadership. There are three fundamental and interrelated problems with the prevailing logic around the performativity of leadership. First, the attributes and characteristics of effective leadership remain highly contested and illusive. Hence, the meaningful measurement and replication of "good leadership" is at best extremely difficult, and at worst futile.

Second, there is a problem associated with the over attribution of agency (e.g. great things happen because of great leaders). The *Harvard Business Review* is replete with heroic stories of how charismatic CEOs have turned around flagging businesses or initiated processes of unprecedented growth or innovation. Through a comparable process of attribution there is also a propensity to directly link the failure of an organisation with the poor performance of a key leader. Although the performance of a leader is often a factor in organisational success and failure, it is not the only factor and it may not be the major factor. Some organisations might succeed despite the CEO, rather than because of the CEO. Equally, a string of poor performances by a football team might have more to do with the effort of key players rather than the leadership of the manager – but it is the manager who is likely to be sacked. The point here is that the connection between leadership effectiveness and organisational success is often tenuous.

Third, leadership is becoming increasingly difficult to position as a rational, ordered and predictable endeavour. It is better captured by chaos and complexity theory. A seemingly insignificant utterance from a leader may be equivalent to a single flap of a butterfly's wings in Brazil, insofar as it causes the organisational equivalent of a Texan tornado. The inference that can be drawn here is that it is unclear, possibly unknowable, which micro-flap of a leader's wings is likely to have highly significant, or even catastrophic, macro-organisational consequences. Hence, trying to make deterministic claims about leadership is like weather forecasting, only far less predictable.

From Perennial Problems to Millennial Machinations

In addition to the tranche of content-based concerns about the utility and effectiveness of leadership, there is also a massive context-based elephant in the room: the alluring and enchanting draw of leadership for the Silent Generation and the Baby Boomers is not shared by the Millennials or Generation Z. As Andrew Davidson observes:

"For traditional employers, Millennials pose new problems. Command-and-control is out. Having grown up with constant feedback from parents and teachers, they want dialogue, not orders, and a world of work that offers more opportunity and less hierarchy, and always new ways of doing things."

Millennials want to be engaged, not lead. This presents an explicit challenge to organisational leaders. This challenge will become more acute as the number of baby boomers decreases and the relative proportion of millennials grows. This inexorable shift in power and prevailing social attitudes will drive a concomitant shift in the nature of work itself as we see the established pillars of authority, hierarchy and leadership giving way to democracy, networked activity and self organisation. The highly individualised tenets of leadership, where the leader knows best and exhibits vision and charisma, will be displaced by a collective and distributed mantra for organising (ie. a "wisdom of crowds" logic).

The emergence of more spontaneous, fluid and connected forms of decision-making has been facilitated by technological advances and social media. As a result, hierarchical, leader-based forms of decision-making are beginning to be replaced by networked forms of "organisational crowdsourcing" and "employee flashmobs". In the future we might expect to see organisations which more closely resemble social movements than they do traditional organisations.

The abject failure of leadership to meaningfully deliver on its promises, combined with a seismic shift in social attitudes and digital technology, has created a perfect storm situation from which there is no stepping back. The death knell for leadership is ringing.

* * *

CHAPTER ELEVEN: RETURN TO HONESTY
IT'S OK TO BE AN ASSHOLE

It's OK to Be an Asshole

Michael O'Leary, Chief Executive of low fares airline Ryanair, has enjoyed an epiphany. Having built a brand with about twice the market capital of British Airways almost entirely on the disrespect of its customers, he has decided that now is the time to be nice.

Publicly, O'Leary attributed this to becoming weary of taking abuse from the general public when he visited McDonald's with his kids. Privately, he might admit that he needed to do something to counter a resurgent Easy-Jet, his main competitor, who were championing low fares and decent customer service, together.

I prefer the old O'Leary approach. He may have treated his passengers with apparent contempt, but he was at least honest and explicit about what they got in return: low fares and on-time flights. His manner was refreshingly direct, honest and free from annoying corporate PR-speak. He was saying what British Airways and Virgin, among others, probably felt. He often seemed like an asshole, and was open about it.

* * *

"You need to abolish free banking, if you want to be trusted. And get rid of ridiculous bonus schemes for senior execs."

"You know we can't do that. Free banking is too central to our business model and lower bonuses would lead to a flight of talent."

"But you keep on quoting John Lewis as your most admired organisation. They don't allow crazy bonuses."

"That's not the point."

"And companies like Handlesbanken and Metro Bank have changed the model, so that's not impossible either."

"It is for us."

"Then stop going on about how you want to be trusted, ethical and good if you are not prepared to challenge some of the fundamentals."

"What do you mean?"

"Maybe you just have to accept that you are in fact an asshole brand. Stop promising one thing and doing another."

Assholes don't need to be hypocrites.

* * *

We are still unable to resolve the conflict between the firm market fundamentalists and the passionate believers in common good. I think they are in fact irreconcilable positions – the profit maximisers versus the profit optimisers, if you like. There is little point continuing the argument – the views are too entrenched and the arguments become tediously circular.

I am firmly in the common good camp; an angry adversary of the Milton Friedman school; a believer in the need for corporations to drive transformation and not simply to make money; to balance profit with purpose. I am equally comfortable with those who want only to make loadsamoney and maximise profit at all costs. I just wish they would be more honest about doing it.

* * *

I am a Jewish atheist.

I have long lost my faith and indeed struggle to understand how others find theirs. But religion still offers an important framework for ethical, honest behaviour and quiet contemplation. The late Dr. Albert Friedlander, a wise Rabbi and inveterate name-dropper, taught me that it is just as easy for a good Muslim to enter heaven as it is for a good Christian or a good Jew. "Good" is open to interpretation, but the essence of "good" rests with doing the right thing and embracing concepts of common good and shared society.

A world that continually deifies the false gods of corporations and brands (and, worse still, celebrities) needs its own mechanisms for atonement and apology. In his Jericho Chambers lecture in September 2013, fellow atheist but political opposite, Simon Heffer, argued that we have forgotten how to apologise – that we have become institutionally resistant to admitting error. In an increasingly godless society, he continued, we need to put in place temporal safeguards to protect systemic abuses of trust and truth.

Heffer makes an important point. There should be no acceptance of deceit in business – financial services or otherwise – just as we cannot condone lying as an acceptable, human behaviour. There is no room for massaged truths or half-truths. Only truth-truths will suffice.

Several years ago, I was approached by the Marketing Director of one of the major UK train operators. It turned out that its poor standing was well-deserved – the Marketing Director boasted proudly about how they shortened train lengths at peak times and lengthened them off-peak. This way they met the averages demanded of them by the regulator but paid less in fees. So what if the customers were packed like sardines? They had to get to work, so would put up and shut up – because they had to.

I responded with a pitch I knew would never win. I suggested (with feigned sincerity) that he and his CEO create a National Apology Day – a collective *mea culpa* for all those "do evil" asshole companies and brands that consistently betray the trust of their customers and employees. The train company would lead the way, spearheading the campaign (and first mover advantage would be theirs). Even then, there were a fair few financial institutions on the list, alongside some energy providers and the monarchy. Nothing has really changed.

Japanese in style, the train company's CEO and Marketing Director would meet disgruntled (and no doubt irritable and sweaty) customers on a ▉▉▉▉▉ station platform and offer humble apologies. They would symbolically bow low – atoning for their abuse of trust through financial compensation and commitment to a better way: an improvement timetable to which they would hold themselves accountable, their own jobs on the line.

Obviously, this "crazy" idea was ridiculed and rejected. As a brand marketer, I was meant to conspire with their fraudulent idiocy – to spin and protect, rather than expose and decry – just as my occasional detractors in the current Public Relations industry would like me to co-conspire with them in denying a changed world, because it hurts their dinosaur business model.

"Do evil" corporations should atone for their sins, the first stage of which should be self-awareness and confession. Their public will respect them more for it. Atonement teaches us to know ourselves better and to find our own honesties. It teaches us to learn from our mistakes and not to repeat them. Some religions require (self-) flagellation, others mere contrition.

I would like to put National Apology Day back on the agenda. It might lance the festering boil of animosity towards the bankers in particular, but could sweep others into its healing path. Once they say sorry, we can all move on.

Companies know when they have done wrong. Companies know when they have substituted the convenience of tick-box compliance for the imperative of values-led behaviours. And they know when they really should apologise – not that they do. No one needs to "have god" to understand this. But everyone needs to have a core humanity and a very real sense of purpose and values – of what is right and what is wrong – in business, as in life.

* * *

"Democracy needs whistleblowers," says Bonnie Raines, one of two burglars of the FBI's offices in Media, Pennsylvania in 1971, who sought to expose the organisation's dirty tricks. "Dissent and accountability are the lifeblood of democracy."

Edward Snowden, one time consultant to the US National Intelligence Agency and subsequent whistleblower, likes to tell the truth. He probably competed with Pope Francis and Nelson Mandela for 2013's Person of the Year.

Snowden is an unlikely hero (or, depending on your view, villain) and the purpose is not to re-tell his story here. However, his truth does represent the future world for businesses and brands – a world of raw transparency, for those elected or otherwise.

"When everything becomes digital," noted a McKinsey report, "private public and civil institutions become... more vulnerable to attack by sophisticated cybercriminals, political 'hacktivists,' nation-states, and even their own employees. As a result, all our institutions will have to make increasingly thoughtful trade-offs between the value inherent in a hyperconnected world and the risk of operational disruption, intellectual property loss, public embarrassment and fraud that cyberattacks create."

Being connected in a digital world will mean an institution will have to be transparent: technology not only allows this, it demands it.

* * *

The former Labour Party Communications Director, Alistair Campbell, has noted that, in today's corporate environment, "one man can start an avalanche," and, if Wikileaks' Julian Assange threw the first snowball in 2010, it was Snowden who launched the *force majeure*.

The Wikileaks saga was still in its formative stages when I was asked to speak at a prestigious event in Berlin. The previous speaker was Mario Monti, addressing the future of the Italian economy.

I was honoured, if somewhat bewildered, to have been invited to address the European Roundtable of Industrialists. I am known for my radical thinking on the future of communications and the state of trust. These were the CEOs of the 50 largest manufacturing companies in Europe. Not all of them are necessarily known for their progressive edge. But it seemed a good opportunity to share the progressive agenda and to talk trust in its new context.

I had been put through my paces by the CEOs' "sherpas" in a dry run in Paris a few weeks before. I was absolutely worked over by them – a good thing, on reflection, as they sought to protect both their charges and their own reputation for putting me forward as a guest speaker. They had given me hell.

We were now in Berlin. It was October 2012 and the huge ballroom filled with meaningless foliage was an incongruous setting for the meeting. Triffid pot plants spilled everywhere. Forty-four of the CEOs were present. There was only one woman. Bar her, everyone seemed to be wearing grey – myself included.

I walked through the state of trust, using my Edelman Trust Barometer slides as a statistical comfort blanket. The bottom line, I explained, was that trust was shifting from institutions to citizens, whether in business or in government. The status of old elites was being eroded.

I told the truth. "They" (or "you") are no longer in control.

My scheduled slot was about an hour. In the end, the argument raged for another 30 minutes. It was fascinating.

When I closed, one of those worrying silences hung in the air. Either what I said was total bollocks or so dull that nobody felt like asking anything.

How wrong I was.

Apres moi, le deluge.

"What you don't understand," came the opening volley, "is that people like ME pay people like YOU to keep us in control."

His finger was wagging furiously.

Before I could answer, another CEO jumped in, this time passionately in my defence.

The room then split 50-50 during what could only be described, in diplomatic terms, as a "full, frank and robust exchange." The technology company CEOs led the way – brilliantly articulating the power shift from state to citizen, employer to employee, corporation to citizen-consumer, empowered and emboldened by technology.

"They" are no longer in control – however much they pay "people like me" – and need to get used to it.

* * *

Every organisation of scale potentially conceals a proto-Edward Snowden. The technology certainly exists for any employee, in either the public or private sectors, to blow secrecy apart. Hence the inevitable fall of PR, where it seeks to massage or disguise, deceive or spin.

The smart organisation is the one that channels transparency to advantage and creates a new culture of openness that then properly discriminates between the commercially confidential and the involvement of all its citizens. Just as organisations can share values, so they can share information and opinion. Control passes to a new culture of "we". By being fully transparent, "we" become properly accountable – not to once-powerful elites but to an empowered *polis*. Relationships shift from adult-to-child (we will tell you what is good for you and when) to adult-to-adult (a mature conversation of equals). Trust is thus engendered with employees and customers – properly built on mutuality and respect.

Fear often holds back an organisation from opening itself up. But fear is a derivative of the managerial culture – the commands and controls necessary to ensure compliance with process. True leaders are not fearful but courageous. Public Leaders are those prepared to stand naked, while Public Relations offers only thinning, cold comfort blankets instead.

Within a decade, if not sooner, corporate nudity will become commonplace – the legacy of Snowden and Assange.

Individual empowerment will only increase transparency, just as advancing technology and costless communication will only accelerate the process, driving power away from old hierarchies and towards new networks of influence.

However, we should beware the fetishisation of transparency. Simply publishing a lot of information is not going to build or restore public trust; this is just another attempt, as with CSR, to *appear* transparent and socially responsible. This cannot be used as a smokescreen for better governance and ethics. One of the unintended consequences of Freedom of Information requirements is that not all reports are thorough, accurate or honest any longer.

It is within all this that we find the real accelerants for the fall of Public Relations and the rise of Public Leadership: atomisation, activism and the asymmetry of power and influence. This makes us paradoxically more atomised and yet more connected; more potentially activist as individuals but stronger still when joined with those with whom we find common cause; and more unpredictable as our networks weave and spread their webs through sometimes unexpected commonalities. The context spells the end for PR as it was built by the likes of Dan Edelman and Harold Burson in the 50s and 60s. And it is both a recipe for ongoing instability (hence the enduring fragility of trust) and a powerful aide to accountability. As Evgeny Morozov has said: "the Snowden saga heralds a radical shift in capitalism ... personal data [is] emerging as an alternative payment regime ... with democracy the main victim."

* * *

In the future world of progressive business, communications will become a threat to trusted status and therefore itself a corporate risk. Any slippage into the bad old ways of spin or message management are likely to be ridiculed or punished.

The culture of Public Leadership is one of intelligent accountability. Public Value is not a one-off statement or event. Every member within an organisation will have it front-of-mind every day, and bring it to life through everyday actions – from the top to the bottom and vice versa. Constructive dissent is to be encouraged. No one should ever be allowed, let alone rewarded, to walk on by.

In his September 2013 lecture, Simon Heffer noted: "To blow the whistle is an act of leadership. It should be identified as such, celebrated as such, and rewarded as such."

This is an important and necessary culture shock.

* * *

Breakthrough campaigns of the future will be grounded in both business purpose and societal purpose, just as the modern corporation needs to be rooted in beliefs and behaviours and not in clever branding mechanisms. An increasingly transparent and activist world exposes flimsy brands, and increasingly holds companies to account. In some ways, over-played branding is very 20th century – essentially another propaganda tool of Bernays and Packard.

Progressive Communications appreciates individualism and enterprise, with technology enabling networks of shared interests to coalesce around common causes. In organisational terms, leadership companies will be those with hyper-connected local communities, spread across business areas and geographies – which in turn shape strategic thinking about everything from employee engagement to brand marketing, co-created strategy and creative development to brand and corporate trust.

As one communications chief of a Fortune 150 company who gets Public Leadership excitedly shared with me as I finished writing, "we are now a belief-and behaviours-led organisation." The business world needs more people like this.

Activist communicators are *de facto* change agents. They have a manifesto to bind their company and a series of commitments and proof-points to make their activism real. They stand for something; they are not just part of Vincent de Rivaz's wallpaper of the banal. Activists believe that they can transform the company from within and that, in turn, the company can help transform the communities that it serves – employees and customers alike. Their activism speaks to local and community values and makes emotional connections. It rails against homogeneity and values-less corporate-speak. It is inclusive, not exclusive.

This is in tune with the business zeitgeist, supporting the shift from the traditional to the creative economy that Steve Denning describes. It speaks to agility and individual empowerment, localism, partnership and coalitions, and respect for employees as potential corporate and brand activists and advocates themselves. It places real people at the centre of everything, co-producing leadership for a better world, and communications at the end of the four-stage process that we identified in The Paradox of Progressive Corporatism: Goals, Values and Practices and, finally, Communications.

This is communications for the new corporate citizenship of the 21st century. It eschews the broken models of Corporate Social Responsibility and PR. It demonstrates leadership through actions, not words, matching beliefs with behaviours. It confirms that new capitalism and better business needs new and better communications.

This approach is authentic, radical and breakthrough. It connects the internal and the external communities. It is emotional but still speaks to experience. It is distinctive and brings focus. It enjoys a clarity and simplicity of purpose. It is, above all, agency in the truest sense of the word.

* * *

A number of corporations are getting it right. Where "social usefulness" has been successfully embedded within organisations, it is usually because a practical framework was established that promoted and protected an ethical and trusted *culture*.

Even the much-maligned RBS Group was applauded by the 2013 Fairbanking Foundation report, which gave it its first ever five-star banking product award to the RBS/NatWest Instant Saver Goal Planner.

We have already seen Sweden's Handelsbanken being congratulated for its "Church Spire" model, allowing autonomous and empowered decision-making at a bank branch level (96% of decisions are taken locally) – and matched with a company policy against "mad" bonuses.

Similarly, Whole Foods champion autonomous decision-making with small teams in each store who run their own profit and loss accounts and enjoy authority. The flip side is that they are held accountable for challenging targets and are rewarded accordingly. As a creative economy model, this increases agility and reduces bureaucracy.

Examples should not be limited to the private sector. "Gamesmakers" were one of the heroic successes of the London 2012 Olympics. That principle, a shared identity among an army of volunteers, has since been translated into the King's College Hospital Foundation Trust, where over a thousand uniformed volunteers work alongside those with qualified medical expertise to offer care for patients. This is the Big Society made real in a good way.

There is no reason why global MNCs should not borrow from it to build a better community partnership model with shared values and shared purpose.

The New York Police Department reversed its fortunes and reputation in the 1990s with behaviour-change based on respect. Even those arrested were done so with a polite "Sir" or "Ma'am". Putting mutual respect at the heart of the customer and employee experience is fundamental to building a better and more purposeful culture for any company or brand.

* * *

Lawyers maintain that transparency increases risk; Ops Directors argue that something obviously remedial is simply not planned; CFOs that it isn't budgeted. Some, but not all, Comms Directors suggest transparency is just too open and too honest – as though these are matters of degree. Then there are those who would like heads to remain firmly beneath the parapets and who often find comfort in external consultancies, with their over-complicated message management (small firms are particularly vulnerable to this).?Whatever the scale of the business, not engaging is not an option. Participation and honesty is everything.?Progressive business leaders know consumers now see what we all see; that the truth will come out anyway; and that any sense of deception will be met with justifiable anger. Instead of building trust, half- or massaged truths will erode trust. Only honesty, however uncomfortable, will suffice.

Progress demands honesty and engagement, transparency and accountability. To "manage the message," as has historically been PR's job, is now to manage reputational decline. This is the incontrovertible message business leaders must share with their communications directors, their teams and to those who advise them.

* * *

Wise Crowd Contributor:

Is Internal Communications Dead?

Lucy Adams

Over five years as HR Director for the BBC I sent a number of all-staff emails. Unfortunately I never got to launch the new Drama season on BBC1 or the lineup for *Strictly Come Dancing*. My emails, in an era of cutbacks, were rarely pleasant to write or read. They typically announced the removal of some perk, some new rule to follow or, worse still, another below-inflation pay deal, or even redundancies. I always hesitated before pressing send, knowing that the message's arrival in 20,000 inboxes would spark a deluge of angry responses.

I found each new email more problematic to write and dreaded the inevitable backlash. One day, I got a call from a guy in News who explained to me that "my emails were crap" and I should "get someone else to write them for me". I was slightly taken aback, because this was precisely what I had already done. My emails were usually written with several other people – people in HR, people in Legal, people in the press team and, of course, people in Internal Communications. But as I re-read the most recent communications, I realised with dismay that he was right. My emails *were* crap. They seemed pompous and sterile, lacking any humanity or humility. This was not the fault of my co-authors. I was the one who had signed the communication off. Moreover, they rarely achieved what I had hoped to achieve – an explanation of a decision that would be understood and accepted, if not necessarily liked. Instead of increasing understanding, they served to exacerbate a belief in management incompetence, or, worse, a conspiracy.

The all-staff email is possibly the most loathed of all internal communications, but the reactions I experienced over five years at the BBC is perhaps indicative of a wider point. Internal communications as a narrowly defined function and approach is dead, and a fundamental re-think of communications – and more importantly, relationships – with our employees is needed.

Let's start, as the strategists say, with the context for the death of traditionally defined internal communications. First and foremost, we have to finally accept that the old "deal" is dead. The financial crisis and recession killed off the last remnants of the old employment relationship, the post-WWII contract where I work for and am loyal to you and you provide me with a job for life and a generous pension when I leave. We made one in seven people redundant in the UK during the recession, we cut or froze pay, and the once ubiquitous final salary pension schemes are now as rare as hen's teeth. Moreover our business leaders proved themselves unworthy of our trust. We came to know the guilty by name – their photos blazoned over every newspaper – ███ ████ ███ ████, "███ █████ ███ █████. A post-recession missive from the executive suite is no longer read through a lens of unquestioning deference.

A new generation of millennials, who are not burdened with the boomers' need to be promoted and achieve in corporate life, will comprise 70% of the workforce by 2025. Their distaste at the actions of the Captains of Industry is infectious. No more grumbling to a few mates down the pub. The rise of citizen power and increasingly, employee power through sites such as "Glassdoor" (think TripAdvisor for places to work) and other social media outlets makes them louder and more impactful on the reputations of their bosses.

The concept of "internal" communications belongs to the days when a company email would remain within the walls of the company itself. A contentious BBC all-staff email appears on every news outlet within minutes. Whilst the BBC, with its thousands of journalists on the payroll, is an extreme example of the blurring boundaries between internal and external communications, it is indicative of the trend.

Yet we persist with the tired old methods that belong to a pre-recession century. We are so concerned about getting our written communications correct that we "lawyer-out" any personality or emotion. We compile our data-intensive PowerPoint slides and ignore the power of honest storytelling. We survey our people just once a year to find out how they are feeling and then produce meaningless action plans that they don't believe anyway. We use the most primitive of market segmentation techniques to communicate, grouping employees into homogenous lumps based on geography or department. We have only begun to think about how social media, or smartphones, or digital technology could enable discussion. Instead we use technology to create barriers, emailing and broadcasting our one-way messages. Our nervous forays into social media are rarely authentic and a Tweet from your uncomfortable CEO is a bit like watching your dad dance at a wedding.

Only one in five employees believe a business leader will tell them the truth when confronted with a difficult issue. The future knowledge-based economy will rely heavily on employees making a conscious choice to give their creativity and their knowledge to their employer. The volatility and uncertainty of the future economy requires even greater levels of trust in our leaders to steer us through. If these statements are true then the ability to build meaningful, adult relationships at work has never been more important or more difficult. Internal communications as a traditional approach to a narrowly defined function is dead. Relationship building, though, is very much alive.

* * *

CHAPTER TWELVE: CHANGE THE LEGACY
IT'S WHAT YOU DO, NOT WHAT YOU SAY

It's What You Do, Not What You Say

Khaled is a progressive thinker.

After 9/11, Khaled received 86,000 hate letters from around the world – the majority from the USA. He was then editor of *Arab News* and is a Saudi national. The content of some of those letters defies description.

I met Khaled al-Maeena at a conference in Saudi Arabia in February 2014. His wisdom on the Saudi condition is spectacular, his warmth and humour infectious, his knowledge of world cricket delightful.

He recounted an exchange between him and the author of one such letter, who had wanted to pour boiling oil into his eyes and wrote unspeakable things about Khaled's mother. A volunteer army had been recruited to deal with the hate mail. They suggested binning it. But Khaled insisted on engaging.

The New York Times recorded the story in an article published in March 2002, but it can never do justice to the mesmeric way in which Khaled brings this troubling tale to life. He corresponded with one hate-mailer in Montana, whose opening letter had started:

"I hate you all. The Koran is the book of Satan, the devil, the teachings of evil, the book that is used to justify murder. Anyone who worships Islam is the devil's child..."

Khaled continued to engage, to paint pictures of simple facts and truths and not to let his own upset with the prejudices of others ever turn to anger or hatred. After a lengthy correspondence, just before Christmas 2001, this note arrived from the Montana man, as reported in the *NYT*:

"The lesson I have learned is that making others feel bad does not, in the end, make one feel better about themselves . . . if my father read what I wrote, I would not be able to type any letters, as he would have broken my fingers.

"I have never seen nor have I read the Koran. Where I live, it would be hard to find such a book. Anyway, I'm sure the Holy Koran is a good book full of words of goodness, love and peace. I hope you will find it in your hearts to forgive me for my outburst of false emotions. May we all be blessed so that we may one day live in peace, if not for us, then for our children. If any of you ever come to Montana, I would welcome you in my home so that I may gain a greater understanding of Islam. God bless you, everyone."

Recounting this tale over dinner in Saudi Arabia over a decade later, Khaled revealed that, after the death of one correspondent, the correspondent's son had written to Khaled and offered more context. Up until Khaled's intervention, the man had been full of hate and prejudice, a white supremacist and member of the Ku Klux Klan. Yet Khaled's notes had transformed him: his spewings of hate had become more tranquil expressions of peace, by which he abided until his dying day.

At the time of writing, Khaled is working with his daughter in Saudi Arabia, building and connecting networks of women who play street basketball. These networks have already touched hundreds of thousands of Saudi women – thoughtful and inspiring proof that there is always a better way.

* * *

Google employs a Captain of Moonshots. His name is Astro Teller (though his birth name is Eric). "Moonshots," Google tells us, "live in that place between audacious projects and pure science fiction." In other words, it's all about taking huge, imaginative leaps forward – shooting for the moon. Astro/Eric challenges prevailing wisdom by asking why we cannot replace all the effort expended on the wrong problems with the bravery to change the very question itself.

It is a powerful point, perfectly expressed. We badly need a calculated resurgence of curiosity and imagination in a stagnating world that is now in almost constant crisis. PR is currently doing little more than reinforcing the status quo – stifling curiosity and imagination, and therefore progress. In a society that is increasingly fearful of failure, PR is there to maintain the guardrails, rather than loosen them. This is another manifestation of illegitimate control.

The right question is why do we fail to question the big picture, or ask questions only in increments? Where can we seek solutions that stretch into possible, not probable, futures? We fail ourselves by living with the expected and accepting the inevitable.

As Astro/Eric noted in one newspaper feature: "We need to keep pace with these challenges and then pull ahead of them, and incremental thinking isn't going to get us there. The only way we can do this is by shifting our focus away from mere 10 percent improvements — the traditional solutions — towards 10x gains: the moonshots."

The easy and most recognised path is the one that shuns the moonshots – or at least consciously refuses to recognise the infinite opportunities they present. We can happily seek continued solace in the incremental, self-applaud our limited progress, and tacitly accept the increasingly vacant promises of swaying leaders who themselves should be shifting in tune with the profound changes in society around them. In this way, we will remain unsurprised and mostly unbothered when leaders state the obvious as though they are preaching from the Book of Revelation – bankers saying that "we should stop selling products that are not in the interests of our customers" – and we will remain comfortable in our indifferent disbelief in the same leaders' apparent commitment to change. We will have begun to absorb and believe the spin.

The big issues maybe seem, well, just too much to chew, so it's tempting to stay in our comfort zones, from which we're unable to confront the bigger challenges facing us. We can leave it all to the next generation to figure it out. Except we can't. Because time is running out.

The powerful question is who, if not us, will be the change? And, if we fail, where will others succeed?

Citizens need to be the agents of transformation, the guardians of transition. Right now, we wilfully accept pragmatism and *realpolitik* mapped as journeys of change, but these are hardly the defiant acts of moonshot re-imagination that society should crave. Nor do they ever lead beyond the short-term horizon. Our extended curiosity is mostly confined to the occasional comment pages of the liberal media and the dining rooms of the chattering classes. This is why the new model of Public Leadership needs to be activist, driving change, and citizen-centric.

With the 2013 horsemeat scandal in the UK we saw the obvious labelling issues, as well as the immediate humour, but not the institutional dysfunction of food processing; the economic subjugation of the British poor; the crisis of consumption and the determination to always deal with supply over demand; even the corruption of re-constituted capitalism itself. PR was used to remedy the crisis but not, as it should have been, to question the very behavioural nature of business itself. How did it end up there?

The important, fundamental questions therefore surround the functioning of the capitalist model and the continued struggle within, together with the communications protocols that support and protect it. Why are we always dealing with supply, for instance, when we should be thinking equally (if not more so) about demand? Why advantage the producer over the citizen consumer? Needs, not wants, should surely prevail. Unfortunately, PR is hard-wired to promote wants over needs.

The indefensible defence of unpaid internships falls into the same category as the horsemeat scandal. Both are manifestations of modern economic slavery – the former articulated by apologist government Ministers as though explaining that at least the tobacco and cotton industries thrived while the workers were enslaved. The horsemeat issue was consistently positioned as a trust issue – but trust is as much an issue of power. The power imbalance that breeds distrust urgently needs to be addressed.

The critical question, as Tony Judt pointed out, is why or how we can choose to make our decisions in such a moral vacuum, evaluated only by principles of economics and authority. They are not enough.

In our reality, the easy solution is ready-meal pragmatism, but we must stretch ourselves to seek out the future-thinkers, to help us reimagine and inspire. Otherwise, we are citizens lost. Progressives need to think beyond what PR creates, to ask different questions and to explore the reimagined moonscape of possibilities. They should insist on a more open contract between citizens and state (and the corporations and body politics within) – an explicit statement of citizen values and citizen trust.

Answers to the right questions should be sourced from the *polis* and the wisdom of citizen crowds – on both micro and macro levels, in business and in government. We need to focus on the vital: to strip away tittle-tattle questions around pointless bureaucracies, meaningless fame and petty point scorers. We need to reappraise what we really mean by "common good", by "equality" and "social justice". If we are to change the current circumstances of profound imbalances and tense insecurities, we first need to search and find the bravery within to challenge and change the very questions themselves.

* * *

Empowered citizens want to believe and actively participate in the possibilities of tomorrow – to embrace change and address pivotal issues around climate, wellbeing and social justice. We have become mired in the tired language and unoriginal thinking of today, imprisoned by institutional hierarchies that fear the very liberating change that a digitally-enabled democracy will bring. More of the same will only lead to increased fragility, not change, and until we find a way out of the current stasis, we can never address the critical issues of trust. In the prevailing environment, any possible restoration of trust feels distant.

We are enslaved. We feel comfortable with the power we know. We are passive acceptors, often paralysed by our own fear of future, and so anchor ourselves in a failing past. We do not drive to change things, either through apathy, or because we (wrongly) believe that we cannot change things, or that only those with "power" and "authority" can precipitate the change we crave. We create our own, misplaced mystique around authority. The consequence is a gridlock of progress and an entrapment of enlightened citizen values within a probable future and not one of real possibilities. We cede the magic of our imagination to an incremental world of "status quo plus". We need to be the change – in Public Relations, for sure, but also in a much bigger world beyond.

We also too readily accept legacy institutions and benign power structures: the United Nations or Parliament, the civil service or a multinational employer. Radical thought is required: we need new bankers before we need new banks – and we need those same bankers to start thinking as citizens first and as bankers second. We are otherwise complicit in the acceptance of leadership norms and are then surprised at the frustrating lack of societal progress this engenders. Yet if we can intellectually grasp the increasing redistribution of influence (top to bottom; west to east; north to south), then surely we can understand the need for a parallel redistribution of leadership and authority? What we lack is the engineering skills to make this happen, the operators to sit alongside the prophets to make it real.

The traditional gatekeepers — managers, executives, producers and broadcasters – are controllers, if not owners, of the modern means of production. Few of them are real leaders. This era of vertical quasi-leadership is fast eroding, philosophically, but those in charge are understandably clinging onto control (because they can, while they can). Few are challenging them in peaceful dissent because the new channels that this book advocates remain in their relative infancy. Organisations similarly recognise the need for more profound change but remain comforted by the historical structures that cocoon them. They, too, are ultimately fearful of the shift to a possible, not probable, future. Why rock the boat (especially when you are sitting on the inside)? Courage is absent.

Those who seek only incremental change (the incrementalists) will not help us on the big issues ahead – for example, on climate change. The facts confirm a tectonic shift that demands urgent and radical action, but the response is at best tentative and full of platitudes: launching a recycling initiative, reducing water consumption, introducing Plans A, B or C. There is nothing wrong with doing the right things – but we need bigger change, and just speaking radical words without a corresponding shift in behaviour is not going to save the planet from its own meltdown. Business' approach to carbon reduction has to be fundamental and values-led, not merely compliant. Governments need to start addressing issues of reduced demand, not alternative supply.

The incrementalists will not meet the critical challenges of diversity and gender balance. We hear endlessly compassionate words about the need for greater access and greater opportunity in the workplace and in politics. These tick the boxes of responsibility and action, but they ignore the more fundamental truth – that a failure to aggressively address the access and gender issues is a denial of a pool of the future talent, future leadership and future authority that will make the world a better place. Homosocial reproduction flies in the face of citizen inclusion. It conspires to support the traditional authorities of power, not to liberate the new ones.

The incrementalists will not manifestly change leadership within corporations. A few more frequent Town

Hall meetings, a CEO blog post and the occasional webinar do not create a fully engaged workplace. They are instead, as Cliff Oswick notes, a futile mass-representation of implicit authority and might even be seen as pacifiers for the employed masses. They fail to feed the growing hunger of employee activism, which will in time hold corporations to account to do the right thing. Instead, let networks of Citizen Supervisory Boards and Employee Investment Funds and Social Impact Partnerships help re-orientate corporations and shape a new, sustainable capitalism.

Our failing society urgently needs a new and constant regenerative dialogue that seeks the active involvement of the citizen crowd, and not just the crowd's implicit acceptance of the status quo. Corporate monologue should not be tolerated as leadership.

The real change agents are those who are determined to change the legacy by asking bigger questions, putting citizens before capital and re-thinking organisations through activism and social movement. They are those who embody and live ethics rather than speak or learn them; those who properly embrace diversity; those who move beyond compliance; those who insist that all leaders can answer the five questions on trust; those who are prepared to think the unthinkable, even if it means that they, the current "controllers", now need to relinquish control; those who are prepared to accept that local might trump global; and those who understand that real shifts can never occur while in constant pursuit of short-term (shareholder) goals.

Leadership can be co-produced and consent made explicit. The legitimate power of the new will replace trust bestowed from above with trust and leadership properly earned from within, where the real wisdom of the crowd prevails and where capitalism itself is reimagined with collaborative citizenship at its heart – far beyond the sound bites of a Big Society.

* * *

In 2006, John and Helen Taylor drove a Volkswagen Golf across 25 countries on four continents in 78 days, consuming only 26 tanks of fuel. They covered 29,000 kilometres and achieved fuel efficiency of 4.5 litres per hundred kilometres. Their global fuel economy challenge was sponsored by Shell, one of my clients at the time. The message was simple (*drive better, consume less*). But it was not very progressive. Looking back, such a campaign seems naïve given both the scale of today's energy crisis and the march of technology.

I worked with Shell for seven years. Frustratingly, the company, rich in genius engineering skills, did not always seem to be able to translate great thinking into Progressive Communication. Huge opportunities may have been lost.

The Shell Eco-marathon is a brilliant concept that launched nearly 30 years ago. It brings together students and engineers to design vehicles that can travel furthest on just one litre of fuel. The Eco-marathon has now been extended to Asia and the US as well as Europe. An opportunity exists to build an incredible network that connects NGOs and policymakers, students and graduates, scientists and futurologists in a progressive global community to tackle energy efficiency, and yet the Eco-marathon remains one of Shell's best-kept secrets.

Similarly, Shell's "Scenarios" team has been engaged with addressing the world's toughest questions since the 1970s. They do ask bigger questions: "*What might the world look like in 2100?*" But look on the web for Shell Scenarios and you will find a mostly inward-facing function. It is listed far beneath the public face of Sustainability Reporting.

* * *

Celine Schillinger, a crowd contributor on the social dance floor, was France's *La Tribune* Woman of the Year in 2013. She is a disruptive thinker while still maintaining her day job at pharmaceutical giant Sanofi Pasteur in Lyon. I met her in the final stages of writing this book and was instantly in her thrall. As you will have read, she demonstrates an authoritative and compelling passion about the social re-engineering of businesses and organisations, without ever descending into corporate-speak, news-speak or data-speak. Every organisation desperately needs a Celine.

Celine is also a member of Change Agents Worldwide, which sounds very James Bond, but which is in fact an open, collaborative, networked community committed to working with forward-thinking companies and leaders. "Organisational inertia," they say, "can only be unlocked through disruptive change." That is, anger and impatience can both be virtuous.

Revolutionaries such as Celine will lead future corporate campaigns. They will be activist, co-produced, citizen-centric and society-first. They will place collaborative and communitarian thinking at the heart of what they do and speak to the new, social democracy of corporations and brands. They will not be PR campaigns as we know them and will be led by Change Agents from within the corporation. The company that speaks from within – thus rejecting the need for external agency – will be celebrated as more authentic and legitimate.

* * *

Emma Thwaites was introduced to me during the crowd-funding and research for this book by one of its supporters, the brilliant Emer Coleman. The imaginations of both were sparked by a piece I had written earlier about how, "in an age of data, PR is almost creationist in its thinking."

Emer and Emma agree. Emer is a former open data and digital guru within UK government; Emma manages communications for the Open Data Institute.

"In my very simple world," wrote Emma in a delightful and inspiring stream-of-consciousness email, "the whole idea of PR is formulaic and out-dated. I cannot fathom my kids (twins, aged seven, since you asked) even imagining the idea of it."

Has data killed PR?

"I would say that data is in the process of blowing PR's cover. Not even data – but the interpretation and use of data to develop knowledge and insight (not something most 'PR professionals' [*her inverted commas, not mine*] are comfortable with."

Emma continued: "from where I am sitting, I see that people now formulate their own networks of interaction; they create connections that they relate to and trust outside of formal institutions (brands, products, governments, services etc.) to deal with day-to-day issues and increasingly even solve huge, seemingly intractable problems. Zooinverse.com is just one example.

"These people make their voices heard, despite the voracious 'PR' efforts of hundreds of individuals, while political institutions ignore the intense political leanings of our young people. Research shows that young people are more, not less, politically engaged – a point also raised by Peter Mair in his treatise on *Ruling The Void*:

The Hollowing of Western Democracy. 'The evidence of withdrawal is somewhat disputed.'"

Herein lies a truth. The appetite for engagement is real. The issues are immediate and urgent. But young people understandably have little desire to channel their efforts through moribund institutions or knackered institutional authority. We live in revolutionary times.

Emma's kids – and mine, now 19 and 17 – will design their lives using data-driven tools and products. Current apps stand only on the threshold of what is possible. Where a generation of 40- and 50-something leaders sees only data headaches, the next generation sees data solutions. They understand that data will connect them, that they are not just spokes at the end of an old-fashioned hub, and that this will engender greater trust.

"Social" will move from being the connective tissue that binds us, to the essence of business conduct. We have only just begun to understand the micro-segmentation of communities, information and power, using data. The Internet of Things is now becoming reality, as is the creative, collaborative economy.

PR is not dentistry. It is not, as Emma points out, a profession, and never has been. And the next generation shows us the future.

* * *

Some global organisations are instinctively grasping this new way of being. HSBC is one of them, in no small measure due to the passion and vision of Pierre Goad, its Global Director of Comms. "You may be the CEO," he told me as part of my research, "but nobody reads your emails anyway." Now is the time, says Goad, when those in authority need to "shut up and listen," starting with listening properly to employees.

HSBC NOW is a weekly TV programme and Twitter stream that aims to unite the bank's 259,000 employees worldwide, using social media. HSBC NOW YouTube channels help tell the stories of HSBC workers. The website notes: "these are our stories: the passions that drive us, the challenges we set ourselves and our lives inside and outside work. Stories about ordinary people doing extraordinary things."

Each programme is presented by staff across the world and produced in three content hubs in London, New York and Hong Kong. The description sounds like the usual corporate-speak – but the intent is more ambitious.

Zappos is an American online shoe and clothing shop, historically feted by new economic and new business thinkers. In July 2009, the company announced it would be acquired by Amazon in an all-stock deal worth about $1.2 billion.

Zappos was always best-known for its unique company culture. "Positive office culture assures you of passionate employees, outstanding performance and the ability to attract the best talent," wrote CEO Tony Hsieh in an article for *The Guardian*. Once a year the company produces and shares a "Culture Book". "If you were to visit the Zappos office," reads one review, "you're likely to find a nap room, a petting zoo, a makeshift bowling alley, employees doing karaoke, or a popcorn machine dressed up as a robot. If you happen to visit on 'Bald & Blue Day' you'd find employees shaving each other's heads."

Agora Drinks is a beverage company that puts its online community at the forefront of decision-making for the brand, from what they produce to the packaging and even what they do with the profit. The idea is to create a company which reflects a community with ideas and values.

Every time an important decision needs to be made, Agora provides the community with all the information; decisions are then made through a voting process. The community also has a say on who to hire and how to finance the business. Agora says it is influenced by the idea that creative capitalism can be a counter-balance to the amoral behaviour some corporate giants engage in to gain profit.

Agora's goal for 2025 is clear: to return "the power over the food and beverage industry back to the people, and spread the idea of democracy in business across the world."

This is a radicalised, consumer-facing version of what we have learned from companies like India's HCL Technologies – crowdsourced corporate decision-making, beyond employees alone. It can be done.

* * *

All this contrasts starkly with Barclays Bank, which is determined to share its journey towards being, well, better. Since (relatively) new CEO Antony Jenkins took over from Bob Diamond in August 2012, the institution has been on an employee, corporate and customer charm-offensive. It *wants* to show us that it is listening. But is it really?

The Barclays "Your Bank" initiative invites members of the public, including non-Barclays customers, to help influence new products, digital banking tools, and in-branch experiences. Its online hub provides a space for submitting and sharing ideas to help to improve Barclays banking services, accessibility and tools. Barclays claims to be listening.

The PR blurb will tell you that action on ideas have included opening eight new Barclays Essential branches inside Asda stores, open seven days a week; two-way texting that helps you confirm if your purchase is genuine or not; and community projects such as teaching people over 65 years old to use the internet. But I went on the website and it seemed that there were only two settings for the "conversation": "registered" and "acknowledged". Hardly a human face.

Stephen Doherty is the Global Director of Communications for Barclays. I have known him for many years and would consider him absolutely one of the best – and most determined – professionals in the sector. If anyone can crack it, Stephen can. The question is whether Barclays want to be cracked.

* * *

In January 2013, music retailer HMV, having been struggling for at least two years, finally called in called in the administrators. This immediately placed 4,500 jobs at risk. Furious HMV employees took over the company's official Twitter account to publicly air their feelings. The employees managed to post several tweets before the company was able to regain (nominal) control, and deleted the posts. But not before sackings had been conducted live on Twitter.

"There are over 60 of us being fired at once! Mass execution of loyal employees who love the brand. #hmvXFactorFiring"

"Sorry we've been quiet for so long," posted another. "Under contract, we've been unable to say a word, or – more importantly – tell the truth."

"Just overheard ▮▮ ▮▮▮▮▮ ▮▮▮▮ (he's staying, folks) ask 'How do I shut down Twitter?'"

* * *

Guido Barilla, CEO of family-owned Italian pasta brand Barilla, went on record (on radio) with the suggestion that Barilla is for traditional families and that gay people can eat another pasta if they are not happy with his message.

Furious Twitter users, gay and straight, shared the hashtag #boicottabarilla, or "boycott Barilla."

Guido Barilla's subsequent official apology read: "with reference to remarks made yesterday to an Italian radio program, I apologise if my words have generated controversy or misunderstanding, or if they hurt someone's sensitivity... in the interview I simply wished to underline the central role the woman plays within the family."

In the old days, today's news was tomorrow's fish and chip wrapper; nowadays everyone has instant and continual access to exactly what was said – Google never forgets (unless the European Union tells it to do so).

* * *

Arriving at the Gare du Nord in Paris late on the evening of 11th June 2014, I struggled to find a cab to my hotel. That is because all the taxi drivers were on strike. Having left London two hours before, taxi drivers there were blockading the streets in protest. Uber was the object of their ire. Similar occasions of industrial unrest popped up in Berlin and other world cities on the same day.

Uber is a Google-funded start-up and transportation network company based in San Francisco, California.

At heart, Uber is a free app that, in its own words, "connects drivers with passengers at the touch of a button." When accessed, the app shows all the Uber-accredited cars in a user's vicinity. Users just tap on a car which is close by to hail a ride. At the end of the ride the fare is decided/measured by the app depending on the length and time of the journey.

Since starting business in London, Uber has caused upset for London taxi/black cab drivers, who believe that the company is not acting under the right regulations, and the registered Uber cars should be classed as taxis rather than mini cabs, as they charge on a metered basis. The legal challenge is that it should not matter that the meter is not physically located within the cab.

Uber now operates in 32 countries and has been hit with legal action, protests and bans of various kinds in Brussels, Paris, Berlin, Houston, Portland, New Orleans, Seattle, Miami, New York, San Francisco, Chicago, Washington DC, Vancouver and Toronto. Trade organisations of vested interests do not like the threat posed by disruptive technology. But we live in revolutionary times. It is no longer a question of "whether" but of "when". For London black cab drivers, read PR industry dinosaurs: a change is going to come.

As Uber's EMEA Head of Public Policy as gone on record saying, traditional intermediation is no longer needed. The current protests simply represent "a last, desperate throw of the dice."

* * *

The only agency we need is change. Conventional approaches to communications no longer work in effecting real behaviour change – whether it is influencing brand choice or social responsibility. This is partly due to the failures of the conventional communications model itself, but more about the significant changes in consumer and citizen behaviour over the past decade.

I have spent much of the past ten years thinking about the future of comms and its relationship with the future of business and indeed of our planet. I am sure that we will never resolve the global energy crisis, or those of food, water and population, if we do not fundamentally change the way we communicate.

In other words, what will drive change in the future is not what drove change in the past.

* * *

PR people, true to Edward Bernays' original vision, want us to believe in a manicured reality and forever-happy endings. It is a form of imposed hierarchy, of control. But real life does not operate like this. Like democracy, it is messy around the edges – full of contradictions, fractured relationships and unresolved conflicts. In an age of radical transparency, albeit sometimes unexpected or enforced, and new social democracy, with its own sprinkling of chaos, the conclusion of this book was always going to be more messy than happy.

There is no single conclusion to this book, by the way. We have considered some lists along the way – intended as practical navigation tools on trust, leadership, business and communications, for many of the themes and memes discussed. But if you are looking for what ad agency M&C Saatchi refers to as a "brutal simplicity of thought," you will not find it here. I think that is an anachronism in a world that is actually rich in chaos and complexity.

The ending to this book is not only messy but also under constant review.

Communications professionals will, like CEOs and Public Leaders, need to think and behave like social activists – as real agents of change.

Agency in its truest form has every right to survive and thrive. As an authentic agency of change, communications can become a catalyst for finding a better, more purposeful and values-rich way for business and brands to be, based on their actions, not their words. But agency as it is currently interpreted sees PR selling bureaucracy, not advice; too often, a bureaucracy of arms-and-legs support is monetised by large consultancies (the current model), when instead hyper-connected, global strategists and consultants with deep expertise in specialist areas (the future model) should be championed.

As we learned from Professor John Kotter, hierarchies (current model) may be needed for management and control, but it is within networks (future model) that the big changes happen. If the organisation does not facilitate the change, employees are likely to find an organisation that does. Or, in the words of one memorable blog post from Jemima Gibbons, "I don't want to work for your shitty agency anymore."

Trying to maintain organisations or behaviours that are top-down is untenable. As Cliff Oswick points out: "change is inevitable. It is now only a matter of time."

* * *

I enjoyed eight and a half amazing years at Edelman. My resignation was not a decision I took lightly. It had been 25 years since my lifelong friend and business partner Jackie Cooper and I co-founded Jackie Cooper PR, and 27 years, almost to the day, since I launched my first company. As I wrote in a final blog for colleagues, it really was time to step off the merry-go-round for a while: to think and to write.

As an advocate of Public Engagement, I was proud to have helped engineer the shift towards what was then a radical new philosophy, organising principle and operating framework that, if properly embedded within Edelman, would, I believed, undoubtedly solidify the firm's leading position within both the PR and wider communications industries. I was confident then that "PE" was the system that would future-proof Edelman and help maintain its status as a thought-leader in the industry and would therefore become a model that many – including those from beyond PR – would surely need to follow. The principles and behaviours that we codified – classified then as bottom-up, social, open, values-led, action-driven – were as important to me personally as they were an accurate reflection of the direction of global trends in autumn 2012. It was clear to me then that change was never going to be this slow again.

Regarding change, I was right. About the shift from PR to PE, I was wrong. It is clear to me now, that simply is not enough.

* * *

The BBC's much-loved Business (now Economics) Editor, Robert Peston, launched a blistering tirade against the Public Relations industry in the 2014 British Journalism Review Charles Wheeler Lecture, in tones far more aggressive than the *FT* article in April 2014 that quoted one business leader saying that "PR adds little value to my business ... except corporate-speak."

"As a journalist I have never been in any doubt that PRs are the enemy. Pretty much my first action when I joined the *FT* in 1991 as head of financial services was to tell the team that they would be in serious trouble if I heard them talking on the phone to a corporate PR rather than a chief executive or chairman. My view has never changed.

"I think the best explanation of why our mission as hacks is always to try to get around the PR, to sideline him or her, was made by Harry Frankfurt in his essay 'On Bullshit,' when he wrote:

'The fact about himself that the bullshitter hides ... is that the truth-values of his statements are of no central interest to him; ... [the bullshitter] is neither on the side of the true, nor on the side of the false. His eye is not on the facts at all, as the eyes of the honest man and of the liar are, except insofar as they may be pertinent to his interest with getting away with what he says.'

"Or to put it another way, many PRs can be seen both as more pernicious than the individual who consciously speaks the truth or the person who consciously lies – in that the liar knows that he is a liar, but many professional bullshitters have lost the capacity to see the difference between fact and fiction. I should point out that PRs aren't the only bullshitters; but if they are not paid to bullshit, to present their clients in the best possible light, what are they being paid to do?"

And, as Peston pointed out, some of his best friends are in PR and many of us know that at least one of them claims to be the source for some of his best stories. No matter.

Peston's Charles Wheeler lecture was quite a wide-ranging affair – touching upon the encroachment of online culture, readers dictating content, the dangers of native content, why the BBC licence fee is generally a good thing and so on. But on PR, Peston is, I think, somewhat wide off the mark. PR is just a cheap and easy target.

"When I worked on the *Sunday Telegraph* a decade ago," he excitedly explained, "the fax machine was strategically placed above the waste paper basket so that press releases went straight into what we called the round filing cabinet. Now newspapers are filled with reports based on spurious PR generated surveys and polls, simply to save time and money."

Most of us with backgrounds in PR have listened to this line for years. It is almost as though journalists, like the ad men alongside them, believe that somehow they are of a higher intellectual order than the bullshit-merchants that Peston describes. Maybe some are, but plenty are not. The PR industry is their shadow.

Peston is right to call bullshit on bullshit. But reading the full text of Peston's lecture, it made me think that, in many ways, he was not very different from a taxi driver scared of the disruption that Uber is bringing.

* * *

I owe a huge debt of gratitude to Jackie Cooper, with whom, over the course of a quarter of a century, I scaled the most incredible of heights and fought through the most despairing of lows in business. I have always been inspired and amazed by Jackie in equal measure, if occasionally a little tetchy. No one will ever really know how exceptionally lucky I have been to have shared such deep friendship alongside such peerless business brilliance. I defy anyone to have a sharper instinct in business or higher levels of pure emotional intelligence. More importantly, our friendship also taught me so much about belief and trust – the truth of what it really means and how it really holds.

I have never been particularly motivated by money, but rather led by a love of thought and ideas and an obsessional excellence in execution, winning and panache; by principled and ethical behaviour in business, as in life; and, fundamentally, by an unshakeable belief in citizen democracy and the collective good. This is as important in the workplace as it is in the outside world.

As I wrote on my Edelman farewell blog, I have learned so much since starting out in business in 1985, not least through my own (many) failings. My only leadership mantras, such as they are, are: "Be Fair"; "Do Good"; "No Mediocrity"; "No Fear"; and "No Assholes". At Jericho, we have refined this to "no bullshit, no bureaucracy and no gits."

Like capitalism itself should be, business for me has always been about Profit with Purpose, a force for transformative good, where everyone has a real voice in shaping the future. This belief in a better way of being formed the bedrock of *Citizen Renaissance* and values, both personal and professional, have always provided the vital lifeblood of my thinking and my work for any organisation that I have been charged with leading. Such values must not only energise, but also inspire. They must stare back at us in the mirror every morning – individually and collectively – helping us understand what it is we seek and how it is we want to be.

I will always be guided by my intrinsic values, and by a sense of natural justice and optimism. These are the principles that my late father, a quiet challenger of illegitimate authority who proudly called himself a liberal with a small "l", gifted me – and the ones that I will forever champion and cherish.

When we each look in the mirror every morning, we know where our truths lie.

* * *

Wise Crowd Contributor:

Publishing Is Dead

Dan Kieran
The day I realised publishing was dead I was sitting on a battered, grey beach in Bognor Regis. I was on my lunch hour while

working for minimum wage clearing out the rat-infested basement of an accountant in a seaside town. Even the King it is named after hated. After ten years my career as a writer seemed over and I was back doing the same kind of work I was doing before I'd started my quest to become a published author. In the previous decade I estimate I'd sold somewhere in the region of half a million copies of the ten books that had my name on them all over the world. My books were published in ten languages and one of them got to number five on the *Sunday Times* Bestseller List. The books had led to some freelance travel journalism, but that day I realised journalism was dead too.

The reason for my despair was simple. I suddenly realised I'd spent a decade building an audience for my work but had no idea who any of the people who bought my books were. I had no data. I had no means of connecting with whatever audience I had created. The gatekeepers I'd used to build my career – agents, publishers, newspapers, magazines, radio stations and bookshops – had no interest in collecting my data and no interest in me. For them I was just a content provider that they could monetise. Not only did they not care about me, they didn't care about my audience. They actually had a vested interest in keeping us apart! It was then that I realised someone had to build a more sustainable, authentic way for authors to connect with the people who give them their livelihood – their readers – and for the communication between the two parties to be BOTH ways.

Of course for some authors publishing is very much alive and kicking. My friend and co-founder at Unbound, John Mitchinson, likens it to agribusiness. Publishers have worked out what crops give them the greatest yields and stick to them. Celebrity memoir, TV tie in, genre fiction, humour. If you're not the kind of author that fits into those categories – or are not already established as an author brand in your own right – publishing is not very interested in you. Sadly for those of us who love books, this means bookshops are becoming very predictable and homogenised – so much so that last year Sainsbury's won Book Retailer of the Year at the publishing industry's annual awards ceremony.

I was reminded of the agribusiness analogy while travelling through the Sussex Downs a few weeks ago. I was driving at dawn from South Harting to Chichester. Sure enough there were the fields of agribusiness, lifeless and drenched with pesticides that prevent anything other than the specific crop planted from getting through. Just like a traditional publisher. Those fields had a kind of beauty: there was a lot of expertise, a lot of science that had gone in to extracting just as much as could be extracted from the ground. But there was no ecosystem at work and there was no room for unexpected growth. They were monotonous. Relentless. They were predictable and dull.

Next to the fields it was a very different picture, of course. Alongside the perimeter of the endless rows of wheat and barley were eruptions of colour as poppies and other wildflowers bloomed out from beneath hedgerows that themselves were teeming with life. A chaotic, wild life at the margins. Not the kind of structured, predictable order of the fields but one where the ecosystem itself was deciding what would or wouldn't thrive. No one was in charge of those hedgerows, and there life was ebullient. As I looked wider across the horizon I spotted other oases of wildlife between the fields. Trees, plants, colour all living and thriving. Islands of variety in a world of beige. Those islands of colour offered a wonderful scene of promise, and I realised John's analogy had a wider application.

All the established businesses that rely on a gatekeeper model, with their bureaucratic pesticides that block the light from the very enterprises they are supposed to support, reminded me of the endless fields of wheat. And the new disruptive enterprises – like Unbound, the one I run – are finding new ways to thrive at their edges. We may seem wild and untamed. We may even seem rather frightening, but the gatekeepers will have to make way for a new colourful world where people are fed up with passively consuming crops that someone else has chosen for them. We want variety. We want a choice that's an actual choice, not the illusion of choice where each direction is being manipulated. We actually want to decide what it is we buy, and because of the nature of the web we can find what we want and choose the people or company that can give is to us. And don't try and con us or treat us like idiots. Now we have the power to find out if we're being duped.

Back on the beach in Bognor I got a call from my friend John, who was kindly paying me to help him with something he was working on. I mentioned to him an idea that our mutual friend Justin Pollard and I had talked about in a pub. He had loads of ideas that made it even more tempting to try and build a new kind of company. I, for one, had nothing to lose.

That was five years ago. The three of us built a website that brings authors and readers together. It's called Unbound. We published the book you're holding in your hands and the names of the people who supported Robert by pledging and deciding it SHOULD be published are printed in the back of this book. They didn't just buy this book. They *made* this book. Without them it wouldn't exist. I met Robert last year and immediately knew I'd found a kindred spirit. When I read the first draft of this book I cheered him on with every page. He's right. Everything is changing. It's exhilarating. Not many people get to live in times of such dramatic change. If you embrace it you can enjoy it.

* * *

"We are all naked now," entrepreneur Mo Ibrahim said at the BAFTA launch of Richard Branson's B-Team. "So we might as well look good."

The Wall Street Journal's Peggy Noonan, writing after the death of Osama Bin Laden, sees it slightly differently: we live in a time of disbelief. "Here is the fact of the age. People believe nothing. They believe everything is spin and lies. When people believe nothing, they believe everything."

These are our times.

* * *

In March 2014, the US arms manufacturer Armalite found itself in unlikely conflict with the Italian art establishment, and the Italian government itself.

As the publishers Phaidon noted on their blog: "the row between US gun manufacturer Armalite and the Italian government intensified over the weekend when Italy's culture minister Dario Franceshini called for the company to withdraw an advert that depicts the latest version of its popular single shot bolt-action rifle, the AR-50A1, draped across Michelangelo's David."

Yes, that's right: The potent symbol of Renaissance art, of city-state strength, of (literally) David versus Goliath, had been used by a global arms manufacturer in its advertising. David is seen carrying a huge $3,000 bolt-action rifle, alongside the slogan "The AR-50A1: a work of art."

The legal challenge was about an infringement of copyright (held by the Italian government), rather than an infringement of civility and common sense. More evidence on both fronts, perhaps, of a world gone wrong.

Scan the web and you can find any number of mocked-up images of Michaelangelo's masterpiece. The obese David certainly offers pause for provocative thought.

A decapitated version of the David adorned the front cover of my first book *Citizen Renaissance* (we did have copyright permission for its use). It was a deliberate choice – a protest against the erosion of citizen values in the second half of the 20th century and yet an optimistic thought that, once reattached, David could stand proud and symbolic once again.

I use the image frequently in my presentations on leadership and trust. This is partly because, to me, David is still the ultimate symbol of citizen strength, right down to the bulging vein in the hand that carries the slingshot – but, more importantly, because David stands absolutely naked. There is nothing to hide, no awkwardness or pretence. Just as every Public Leader of tomorrow should stand naked, too.

The Wise Crowd Contributors

Lucy Adams *is the Founder of Disruptive HR and former HR Director of the BBC.*

Tom Fletcher *is the British ambassador to Lebanon. He was Private Secretary for Foreign Affairs to PM Gordon Brown and Foreign Policy Adviser to PM David Cameron. He* *was awarded a CMG for services to the Prime Minister in 2011.*

Dan Kieran *is a writer and the co-founder and CEO of Unbound, the world's first crowd funding publisher. He is the author of 11 books including* The Idle Traveller *("a brilliant insight...deeply alluring... all beautifully told" -* The Telegraph*). In 2011 Dan co-founded the award-winning platform Unbound. Dan has lectured on business, creativity, writing and how to have ideas at UCA and UCL. He is also a travel journalist for* The Guardian, The Times, The Telegraph, The Observer *and* Die Zeit *in Germany.*

Neal Lawson *is Chair of the good society pressure group Compass and a partner at Jericho Chambers.*

Cliff Oswick *is Professor of Organisation Theory and Deputy Dean at Cass Business School, City University London. He has published over 140 academic articles and contributions to edited volumes. His current research interests are around employee-instigated processes of change and non-hierarchical forms of organising.*

George Pitcher *is a journalist, author, Public Relations pioneer and an Anglican priest. He is currently Editor-in-Chief of* International Business Times UK, *a Contributing Editor at* Newsweek Europe *and head of its editorial panel. He co-founded Jericho Chambers, a radical development of consultancy expertise, with Robert Phillips in June 2013. Previously, he was appointed Secretary for Public Affairs to the Archbishop of Canterbury in October 2010 and left the post a year later. George founded Issues Management consultancy Luther Pendragon and was Industrial Editor of* The Observer *between 1988 and 1991, during which his com-*

mentary on the high summer of Thatcherite utility privati-sation led to the Industrial Society (the precursor to the Work Foundation) voting him National Newspaper Indus-trial Journalist of the Year in 1991.

Recognised with the 2013 French Women's Award by the business daily La Tribune, **Celine Schillinger** *directs stakeholder engagement at Sanofi Pasteur. With over 20 years of multi-industry experience in Asia-Pacific and in Europe, she is a Charter Member of Change Agents World-wide. Celine is passionate about leading collaborative pro-jects at the service of business and organisational transfor-mation. Celine's community engagement initiative against Dengue was rewarded by the 2014 Shorty Awards for Best Use of Social Media for Healthcare. In her free time, she enjoys tweeting, blogging and rowing on the nearby river Saône.*

Paul Westbury *is the Chief Executive Officer of Buro Happold, a 1,500 person global engineering consultancy that specialises in delivering smart solutions for buildings and cities. He has more than 20 years' experience in global design and engineering and has led the delivery of a number of major construction projects including London's 2012 Olympic Stadium and Arsenal's Emirates Stadium.*

Jim Woods *is CEO of The Crowd, which helps organi-sations succeed by solving society's biggest challenges. By developing crowd-based formats it helps the latest develop-ments in strategy to enter the mainstream, where organisa-tions can learn from each other. Its monthly gatherings have been attended by 12,000 people since 2008.*

... and over 250 others

This book was crowd-funded via Unbound. Over 250 people came together to make it happen. This is their story, as much as it is mine.

THANKS

None of this would have been possible without...

Over 250 wonderful supporters – many of who have been constant sources of warmth and encouragement and many of whom I only met through crowd-funding the book; Professor Cliff Oswick for his original insistence that I write it all down; Jim Woods for opening my eyes to crowds; Christian Seiresen for the early work and research on case studies; all the interviewees and Wise Crowd Contributors; Gabriel Phillips for his diligent footnoting and fact-checking; Jane Phillips for her invaluable legal advice and the occasional foray into editorial comment; George Pitcher, Christine Armstrong, Jules Peck, Neal Lawson and Alaric Mostyn for their wisdom and advice as critical friends; Dan Kieran for being an inspirational publisher who shares the belief; Isobel Frankish, Phil O'Connor and Miranda Ward at Unbound for their brilliant editing. And, above all, to Venetia, Gabriel and Gideon for their incredible patience, tolerance, love and support – and for the many missed or distracted weekends and endless conversations about what the book's title should eventually be.

I think that's it... any omissions are entirely unintentional.

BIBLIOGRAPHY

"$21,900 Swarovski-Encrusted Vacuum Cleaner by Hyla U.S." *Bornrich RSS*. 03 October 2012. Web. http://bit.ly/1vDYKP5

"2014 EDELMAN TRUST BAROMETER." *Edelman*. Web. http://bit.ly/1vDYM9C

"Change Agents Worldwide." *Change Agents Worldwide*.Web. http://bit.ly/1vDYM9z

"HSBC NOW." *YouTube*.Web. http://bit.ly/1vDYM9A

"*Independent* on Sunday's Happy List 2014." *The Independent*. Independent Digital News and Media. Web. http://ind.pn/1Af7cs9

"Italy V ArmaLite over Use of Michelangelo's David." *Phaidon*. Web. http://bit.ly/1vDYKPa

"JOIN TODAY!" *The Alliance of Trustworthy Business Experts*. Web. http://bit.ly/1vDYKP8

"Meaningful Brands." *Havas Media*. 11 June 2013. Web. http://bit.ly/1vDYKP9

"Pope Francis." *Wikipedia*. Wikimedia Foundation. Web. http://bit.ly/1vDYM9G

"Public Value." *Wikipedia*. Wikimedia Foundation. Web. http://bit.ly/1vDYM9F

"Red Bull Media House." *Red Bull Media House*. Web. http://win.gs/1vDYKPc

"Run the Business." *Agora Puts You in the Shoes of the CEO*. Web. http://bit.ly/1vDYKPd

"Servant Leadership." *Wikipedia*. Wikimedia Foundation. Web. http://bit.ly/1vDYM9J

"Social Democratic Party: Thirty Years on." *The Guardian*. Guardian News and Media, 22 March 2011. Web. http://bit.ly/1vDYM9K

"The CEO and Society", The Crowd. 7 April 2014. Keynote: http://bit.ly/1IAwneP. Panel: http://bit.ly/1siSHPY. Audience Q&A: http://bit.ly/1DaTpc9.

Ahlam, Shabiya Ali. "Promoting Radical Evolutionary Authentic Leadership". *DailyFT*, 4 July, 2013. Web. http://bit.ly/1vOkuwR

Alexander, Douglas. "The Decency of David Miliband." *The Independent*. Independent Digital News and Media, 31 Mar. 2013. Web. http://ind.pn/1vDYKPg

Annie Hall. Dir. Woody Allen. MGM/United Artists Entertainment, 1977. Film.

Arup, Ove. "The Key Speech." *Arup*. Web. http://bit.ly/1vDYM9N

Bader, Christine. *The Evolution of a Corporate Idealist: When Girl Meets Oil*. Bibliomotion, 2014. Print.

Bafta launch B-Team, live stream. Web.

Bajo, Claudia Sanchez and Bruno Roelants. *Capital and the Debt Trap: Learning from Cooperatives in the Global Crisis*. London: Palgrave Macmillan, 2011. Print.

Beckford, Martin. "Archbishop of Canterbury: Gordon Brown's Recovery Plan like 'addict Returning to Drug'" *The Telegraph*. Telegraph Media Group, 18 Dec. 2008. Web. http://bit.ly/1vDYM9O

Bennett, Asa. "Godfrey Bloom's 15 Best Quotes From 'Guinea A Minute'"*The Huffington Post UK*. 18 October 2013. Web. http://huff.to/1vDYKPh

Bernays, Edward, introduction by Mark Crispin Miller. *Propaganda*. New York: Ig Publishing, 2004. Print.

Bishop, Matthew, and Michael Green. *The Road from Ruin*. London: A. & C. Black, 2011. Print.

Bollier, David. "Power-Curve Society: The Future of Innovation, Opportunity and Social Equity in the Emerging Networked Economy". The Aspen Institute, 2013. Print.

Bower, Tom. *Branson: Behind the Mask*. Faber & Faber, 27 January 2014. Print.

Bowman, Betsy and Bob Stone. "Cooperativisation on the Mondragon Model as Alternative to Globalising Capitalism".Web. http://bit.ly/1vDYL5u

Butterworth, Trevor. "When Research Should Come with a Warning Label."*Harvard Business Review*. 6 March 2014. Web. http://bit.ly/1vDYM9R

Callanan, Neil. "Prisoners Turn Painters as London Building Boom Adds Jobs."*Bloomberg.com*. Bloomberg, 25 June 2014. http://bloom.bg/1vDYL5y

Cameron, Kim. "Leadership Through Organisational Forgiveness." *Michigan Ross School of Business*. Michigan Ross. Web. http://bit.ly/1vDYMq4

Campbell, Alistair. KPMG tax summit. Berlin. October 2013, private film observed by the author

Carroll, Dave. "United Breaks Guitars". *Youtube,* 6 July 2009. Web. http://youtu.be/5YGc4zOqozo

Carswell, Douglas. *The End of Politics and the Birth of IDemocracy*. London: Biteback, 2012. Print.

Castells, Manuel. *Networks of Outrage and Hope: Social Movements in the Internet Age*. Cambridge, UK: Polity Press, 2012. Print.

CEO of Samsonite luggage speaking on the BBC Radio 4 *Today* programme, 14 March 2014.

Colvin, Geoffrey. "Failing to build a culture of trust". CNN Money, 31 May 2006.Web. http://cnnmon.ie/1vOkuwP

Colvin, Geoffrey. *Talent Is Overrated: What Really Separates World-class Performers from Everybody Else*. New York: Portfolio, 2008. Print.

Conversation between McDonalds executives and George Pitcher as told to author by George Pitcher.

Cookson, Robert. "Rothschild buys into peer-to-peer lending." *Financial Times*, 9 December, 2012. Web. http://on.ft.com/SQtLAH

Costa, Ken. "Ken Costa: We've Had the Fall, Now It's Time for the Resurrection." *The Evening Standard*. 17 April 2014. Web. http://bit.ly/1vDYMqa

Coyle, Diane. "The Road from Ruin." *The Enlightened Economist*. 1 February 2011. Web. http://bit.ly/1vDYL5D

Craven, Simon. Interview. 19 March 2014 and various email correspondence.

Crowd Sessions including Dan Kieran, Paul Dorman, Jon Alexander, Fran Findlater, Dan Kieran, Jemima Gibbons, Alaric Mostyn. One: 9 April 2014. Two: 19 May 2014.

Cyriac, Joseph, Ruth De Backer, and Justin Sanders. *Preparing for Bigger, Bolder Shareholder Activists*. Rep.: McKinsey & Company, 2014. Print.

Davidson, A. "How millennial are you?", *Business Life,* pp.18-21. 1 May 2014. Article.

Davis, Nick. Polis trust 2013 conference, *Flat Earth News*. 2013.

Day, Michael. "'I would never use homosexual couples in my adverts': Barilla pasta boss's anti-gay comments spark boycott call". *Independent*. 26 September 2013. Web. http://ind.pn/1GjO5zp

Democracy at Work. Mondragon Cooperative Corporation. Web. http://bit.ly/1vDYMqb

Denning, Steve. "Is The Creative Economy Also In Trouble?" *Forbes*. Forbes Magazine, 9 May 2014. Web. http://onforb.es/1vDYMqc

Denning, Steve. "Why Most Of What We Know About Management Is Plain, Flat, Dead Wrong." Scrum Alliance, 20 February 2014. Web. http://shar.es/1WCs0B

Dilley, Philip. Interview. 25 June 2014.

Dylan, Bob. *Another Side of Bob Dylan*. Columbia, 1964. CD.

Edelman, Richard. "Richard Edelman on How Leaders Can Regain the Public's Trust." Interview. *McKinsey & Company*. April 2014. Web. http://bit.ly/1vDYMqd

Egan, Timothy. "The Corporate Daddy: Walmart, Starbucks, and the Fight Against Inequality". *The New York Times*. 19 June 2014. Web. http://nyti.ms/1vOkuwQ

Email correspondence between the author, Jim Woods, and interview subjects. "The CEO & Society". *The Crowd*. April 2014. Roundtable.

Fairbanking Foundation report, November 2013. Report. https://www.fairbanking.org.uk

Felber, Christian. *Die Gemeinwohl-Ökonomie: Das Wirtschaftsmodell Der Zukunft*. Wien: Deuticke, 2010. Print.

Fernandez-Armesto, Felipe. "It's Time We All Suffered for the Sake of Our Art."*The Evening Standard*. 19 September 2008. Web. http://bit.ly/1vDYL5J

Fletcher, Tom. "A Post Not Called 'Is Diplomacy Dead Too?'" *NAKED DIPLOMAT*. 21 March 2014. Web. http://bit.ly/1vDYL5L

Ford, Jonathan. "'Branson:Behind the Mask' by Tom Bower – FT.com."*Financial Times*. 5 February 2014. Web. http://on.ft.com/1vDYMqi

Forest, L, William. *If Aristotle Ran the Catholic Church: The Present Leadership Problem of the Church*. 1st Books Library. 2004.

Frankel, David, and Humayun Tai. "Giving US Energy Efficiency a Jolt."*McKinsey & Company*. December 2013. Web. http://bit.ly/1vOkvRm

Friedman, Milton. "The Social Responsibility of Business is to Increase its Profits." *The New York Times Magazine*, 13 September 1970.

Global Economic Symposium 2012, Willem Kok.

Goad, Pierre. Interview with the author. 9 May 2014.

Godin, Seth. "Deconstructing Generosity." *Seth's Blog*. 26 April 2014. Web. http://bit.ly/1vDYL5M

Goffee, Rob, and Gareth Jones. "Creating the Best Workplace on Earth." *Harvard Business Review*. May 2013. Web.http://bit.ly/1vDYMqk

Gombita, Judy. "Declaring Piffle on Those "traditional PR" Publicity Arguments." *PR Conversations*. 11 Dec. 2013. Web. http://bit.ly/1vDYL5N

Gratton, Lynda. *The Shift: The future of work is already here*. London: HarperCollins Business, 2011. Print.

Gratton, Lynda. *The Key: How Corporations Succeed by Solving the World's Toughest Problems*. London: McGraw-Hill Professional. May 2014. Print.

Grey, Rob. *Great Brand Blunders: The Worst Marketing and Social Media Meltdowns of All Time and How to Avoid Your Own*. London: Crimson Publishing Company, 2014. Print.

Halfon, Rob. "The Left are winning the internet battle. It's time to fight back". *Conservative Home*, 11 March 2012. Web. http://bit.ly/1vDYMql

Hallam, Jed. *The Social Media Manifesto*. London: Palgrave Macmillan, 2012. Print.

Heffer, Simon. "My Word Was My Bond": Ethics and the City." St James' Church Piccadilly, London. 26 September 2013. Lecture.

Heffernan, Margaret. *Willful Blindness*. New York: Walker & Company, 2012. Print.

Hickman, Leo. "Jeremy Grantham, Environmental Philanthropist: 'We're Trying to Buy Time for the World to Wake Up'" *The Guardian*. Guardian News and Media, 12 April 2013. Web.http://bit.ly/1vDYLm0

Hobsbawm, Julia. *Where the Truth Lies: Trust and Morality in PR and Journalism*. London: Atlantic Books Ltd., 2010. Print.

Hollender, Jeffrey. "Lessons we can all learn from Zappos CEO Tony Hsieh". *The Guardian*. Guardian News and Media, 14 March 2013. Web. http://bit.ly/KCee6j

Hutton, Will. *The State We're in*. London: Vintage, 1996. Print.

Ignatieff, Michael. "Free Polarised Politics from Its Intellectual Vacuum." *Financial Times*. 9 January 2014. Web. http://on.ft.com/1uksss4

Jackson, Tim. "An economic reality check", Oct. 2010. Video. http://bit.ly/1vOkuNa

Jacobs, Emma. "Publicity Is Free with No PRs." *Financial Times*. 7 April 2014. Web. http://on.ft.com/1vDYMGE

Johnson, Luke. "Why My Alma Mater Oxford Will Struggle" *Financial Times,* 4 March 2014. Web. http://on.ft.com/1vDYLm3

Johnson, Miles. "Mondragon: Collective approach pays big dividends". *Financial Times*, 27 March 2012. Web. http://on.ft.com/1vOkuNb

Joseph, Sebastian. "Carlsberg Shifts Spend from TV to Social Content." *Marketing Jobs & Marketing News*. 5 February 2014. Web. http://bit.ly/1vDYLm5

Judt, Tony. *Ill Fares the Land*. New York: Penguin, 2010. Print.

Judt, Tony and Timothy Synder. *Thinking the Twentieth Century.* London: Vintage, 2013. Print.

Kahneman, Daniel. *Thinking, Fast and Slow.* London: Penguin Books, 2012. Print.

Kelly, Joe. "The Grim PReaper?" *The Comms Dept.*, 30 Mar. 2014. Web. http://bit.ly/1vDYLm6

Kieran, Dan. Interview with the author.

Kotter, John P. "Hierarchy and Network: Two Structures, One Organization." *Harvard Business Review,* 23 May 2011. Web. http://bit.ly/1vDYMGI

Kotter, John P. "Management Is (Still) Not Leadership." Web log post. *Harvard Business Review,* 9 January 2013. Web. http://bit.ly/1vDYLm7

Krugman, Paul. "Milton Friedman, Unperson." *The New York Times,* 11 August 2013. Web. http://nyti.ms/1vDYLm8

Lacy, Peter, and Rob Hayward. "Why Green Is The New Gold." *Accenture.* February 2014. Web. http://bit.ly/1GcWypP

Lafuente, José Luis. "The MONDRAGON Cooperative Experience: Humanity at Work". Management Exchange, 11 May 2012. Web. http://bit.ly/1vDYMGJ

Lamb, Natasha and Danielle Fugere. "Exxon Mobil's commitment to carbon asset risk is just the beginning". *The Guardian.* Guardian News and Media, 24 March 2014. Web. http://bit.ly/166eAxi

Lambie-Nairn, Martin. "Why Small Is Intensely Powerful." *Why Small Is Intensely Powerful.* 25 March 2014. Web. http://bit.ly/1vDYMGK

Lecture at Circle for European Communicators, Potsdam 2012. Guy Sorman

Leggett, Jeremy K. *The Energy of Nations: Risk Blindness and the Road to Renaissance.* N.p.: n.p., n.d. Print.

Levine, Rick, Christopher Locke, Doc Searls and David Weinberger. *NY: The Cluetrain Manifesto*: Basic Books, Tenth Anniversary Edition 2009. Print.

Lewis, Patrick. Interview. 7 April 2014.

Limehouse Declaration. Shirley Williams, David Owen, Bill Rodgers and Roy Jenkins. 25 January 1981.

Lloyd, Bruce, Dr. "Power, Responsibility, and Wisdom: Exploring the Issues at the Core of Ethical Decision Making and Leadership." *WABC Coaches Inc.* N.p., n.d. Web. 11 July 2014. http://bit.ly/1vDYLm9

Machiavelli, Niccolò, W. K. Marriott, Nelle Fuller, and Thomas Hobbes. *The Prince*. Chicago: Encyclopædia Britannica, 1955. Print.

Mackey, John, and Rajendra Sisodia. *Conscious Capitalism: Liberating the Heroic Spirit of Business*. Boston, MA: Harvard Business Review, 2013. Print.

Mair, Peter. *Ruling the Void: The Hollowing of Western Democracy*. London: Verso, 2013. Print.

Makower, Joel. "How GE and Apple Shareholders Became Tools for Climate Deniers." *GreenBiz.com*. 3 March 2014. Web. http://bit.ly/1vDVtiM

Marcus, Lucy P. "Trust Must Be Earned." *Linkedin*. N.p., 11 January 2013. Web. http://linkd.in/1vDYLmb

Mason, Paul. *Why It's Kicking off Everywhere: The New Global Revolutions*. London: Verso, 2012. Print.

McEwan, Ross. "RBS: Ross McEwan Speech in Full." *BBC News*. BBC, 27 February 2014. Web. http://bbc.in/1vDYMGL

McInnes, Will. *Culture Shock: A Handbook for 21st Century Business*. West Sussex: John Wiley & Sons Ltd, 2012. Print.

Mill, John Stuart, and W. J. Ashley. *Principles of Political Economy, with Some of Their Applications to Social Philosophy*. New York: A.M. Kelley, 1965. Print.

Miños, Daniel Chaves. "Porto Alegre, Brazil: A new, sustainable and replicable model of participatory and democratic governance?". The Hague, April 2002. Available at http://bit.ly/1vOkvRo

Monbiot, George. "How Have These Corporations Colonised Our Public Life?"*The Guardian*. Guardian News and Media, 8 April 2014. Web.http://bit.ly/1vDYLmd

Monbiot, George. "The Spark of Hope." *George Monbiot*. Blog post.Web. 1 April 2013. Web. http://bit.ly/1vDYMGM

Moore, Mark Harrison. *Creating Public Value*. Bridgewater, NJ: Replica, 1997. Print.

Moore, Ronald D. "Redemption Part 2." *Star Trek: The Next Generation*. 23 September 1991. Television.

Morozov, Evgeny. "The Snowden Saga Heralds a Radical Shift in Capitalism – FT.com." *Financial Times*. N.p., 26 December 2013. Web. 8 July 2014. http://on.ft.com/1vDYLme

Morris, Tom. *If Aristotle Ran General Motors: the New Soul of Business*. New York: Henry Holt & Company Inc, 1998. Print.

National Intelligence Council. *Global Trends 2030 Alternative Worlds*. Washington, DC: NIC, 2012. *Public Intelligence*. December 2012. Web. http://bit.ly/1vDYLmg

Norman, Jesse. *The Big Society: The Anatomy of the New Politics*. Buckingham: U of Buckingham, 2010. Print.

O'Neill, Onora. Onora O'Neill: *What we don't understand about trust*. June 2013. Video file. http://bit.ly/1vOkvRp

Oswick, Cliff. Interview. 29 April 2014 and various conversations.

Packard, Vance. *The Hidden Persuaders*. New York: D. McKay Co., 1957.

Pagano, Margareta. "Peer-to-peer lending boom could make banks obsolete". *The Independent*, 17 December, 2012. Web. http://ind.pn/1vOkuNe

Palmer, Paul. Interview. 23 May 2013.

Peacock, Matt. Interview. 18 October 2013, 19 February 2014 and various email correspondence.

Peck, Jules. "Project Sunlight and the Journey to Intrinsic Values". *Huffington Post*, 2 November 2014. Web. http://huff.to/1vDYLmj

Peck, Jules. "There Has To Be a Better Way to Run Business and Economics."*Jericho Chambers*, 23 April. 2014. Web. http://bit.ly/1vDYLmi

Peston, Robert. "Charles Wheeler Lecture."*University of Westminster*. Web. http://bit.ly/1vDYLCw

Phillips, Robert. "Brand PR: A Failure to Modernise." *Campaign News & Jobs*. 7 November 2013. Web. http://bit.ly/1vDYMGR

Phillips, Robert. "People Let down by Government Turning to Social Networks." Interview. *Russia Today,* 8 February. 2012. Web. http://bit.ly/1vDYLCx

Piketty, Thomas, and Arthur Goldhammer. *Capital in the Twenty-first Century*. Harvard University Press. 2014. Print.

Pitcher, George. "I Love Mike Love Dearly, but He's Got It Wrong." *Jericho Chambers*. 25 March 2014. Web. http://bit.ly/1vDYLCy

Polman, Paul. "2012 Annual Awards Dinner – Paul Polman, Unilever CEO." *YouTube*, 24 May 2012. Web. http://bit.ly/1vDYLCz

Polman, Paul. "Business, Society, and the Future of Capitalism." *McKinsey & Company*. May 2014. Web. http://bit.ly/1vDYMGT

Porter, Michael E., and Mark R. Kramer. "Creating Shared Value." *Harvard Business Review*. January 2011. Web. http://bit.ly/1vDYMX6

Raines, Bonnie. "Democracy Needs Whistleblowers. That's Why I Broke into the FBI in 1971." *Theguardian.com*. Guardian News and Media, 7 January 2014. Web. http://bit.ly/1vDYLCD

Rentoul, John. "Douglas Carswell: Dangerous and Wrong."*Blogsindependentcouk,* 23 February 2013. Web. http://ind.pn/1vDYLCE

Romer, Paul. (2009, July). "Paul Romer: Why the world needs charter cities". Video file. http://bit.ly/1vOkuNf

Roose, Kevin. "Nuns Who Won't Stop Nudging." *The New York Times*, 12 November 2011. Web. http://nyti.ms/Mm5imI

Rushdie, Salman. "Whither Moral Courage?" *The New York Times,* 27 April 2013. Web. http://nyti.ms/1871J7P

Sachs, Jeffrey. "Self-interest, without Morals, Leads to Capitalism's Self-destruction." *The AList*. 18 Jan. 2012. Web. http://on.ft.com/1vDYMX8

Sacks, Jonathan. "Thought for the Day." Interview. *BBC Radio 4,* 12 Dec. 2008. Radio.

Said, Edward W. *Orientalism*. New York: Vintage, 1979. Print.

Sainsbury, D. "The Enabling State". *Royal Society of The Arts Journal* [online], Spring 2013, 42-45.

Sandel Reith lectures. *BBC Radio 4,* July 2009. Radio. http://bbc.in/1GoQSJb

Sandel, Michael J. *What Money Can't Buy: The Moral Limits of Markets*. New York: Farrar, Straus and Giroux, 2012. Print.

Schillinger, Celine. "We Need Social." *We Need Social.* Web. http://bit.ly/1vDYLCF

Sender, Henny. "Unilever Learns How to Tap Pakistan's Consumption Boom."*Financial Times,* 26 December 2013. Web. http://on.ft.com/1vDYMX9

Sheldrake, Philip. *The Business of Influence: Reframing Marketing and PR for the Digital Age.* West Sussex: John Wiley & Sons Ltd, 2011. Print.

Sherwin, Adam. "'We're All Being Fired! Exciting!': HMV Staff Take to Official Twitter Account to Liveblog Their Own 'mass Execution'" *The Independent.* Independent Digital News and Media, 31 January 2013. Web. http://ind.pn/1vDYLCI

Shirky, Clay. "The Disruptive Power of Collaboration: An Interview with Clay Shirky." Interview. *McKinsey & Company.* March 2014. Web. http://bit.ly/1vDYMXb

Steare, Roger. *Ethicability: (n) how to decide what's right and find the courage to do it.* England: Roger Steare Consulting Limited, 2008. Print.

Stevens, Philip. "Nothing Can Dent the Divine Right of Bankers." *Financial Times,* 16 January 2014. Web. http://on.ft.com/1vDYMXc

Stevenson, Seth. "Patagonia's Founder is America's Most Unlikely Business Guru". *The Wall Street Journal,* 26 April 2012. Web. http://on.wsj.com/1vDVtiP

Strauss, Josh, Philip Oltermann, and Phil Maynard. "Manuel Castells: How Modern Political Movements Straddle Urban Space and Cyberspace." *Theguardian.com.* Guardian News and Media, 25 March 2013. Web. http://bit.ly/1vDYMXe

Sudhaman, Arun. Interview. June 2013.

Sutton, Robert. *The No Asshole Rule: Building a Civilised Workplace and surviving One That Isn't.* London: Piatkus, 2007. Print

Symcox, Jonathan. "Archbishop of Canterbury Slams 'rotten' Banks and Warns They Will Not Change Overnight." *Mirror.* 5 December 2013. Web. http://bit.ly/1vDYLCM

Teer, Phil. "Paul Mason on post-capitalism at FutureFest". *Creativy Consumerism Conflict.* 7 October 2013. Blog. http://bit.ly/1B80C82

Teller, Astro. "Google X Head on Moonshots: 10X Is Easier Than 10 Percent." Interview. *Wired*. 2 November 2013. http://wrd.cm/1vOkvRv

Terazono, Emiko. "Syngenta Unveils Seven-year Plan to Boost Yields." *Financial Times,* 19 September 2013. Web. http://on.ft.com/1IzQxpt

The Bottom Line. 11 February 2010. Television and Radio.

The Style Council. *Walls Come Tumbling Down!* Polydor, 1985. CD.

Thwaites, Emma. Interview with the author.

Thwaites, Emma. Email to the author. 28 May

Topping, Alexandra. "Trayvon Martin Petition Site Change.org Comes to UK."*The Guardian*. Guardian News and Media, 14 May 2012. Web. http://bit.ly/1yPxLGr

Trivett, Vincent. "25 US Mega Corporations: Where They Rank If They Were Countries." *Business Insider*. Business Insider, Inc, 27 June 2011. Web. http://read.bi/1e52TX9

Turner, Adair. "Speech by Adair Turner, Chairman, FSA The City Banquet, The Mansion House, London." *Financial Standards Authority*. 22 September 2009. Web. http://bit.ly/1yzQbqy

UK Companies Act 2006.

United Nations Global Compact: Accenture CEO Study on Sustainability, 2013.

United Nations Intergovernmental Panel on Climate Change Fifth Assessment Report (AR5).

Uniting Corporate Purpose And Personal Values To Serve Society. *Five Principles of a Purpose Driven Business*. Web. http://bit.ly/1vOkvRu

Vallance, Charles. Interview with author. 15 January 2014.

Vallance, Charles and David Hopper. *The Branded Gentry: How New Era of Entrepreneurs Made Their Names*. London: Elliott and Thompson Limited, 2013.

Verfüth, Eva-Maria. "More generous than you would think", interview with Giovanni Allegretti. *D + C: Development and Cooperation Magazine, Vol. 40*. 2013.

Victor, Philip. "Starbucks Wasting More Than 6 Million Gallons of Water a Day."*ABC News*. ABC News Network, 6 October 2008. Web. http://abcn.ws/1GjeNrU

Vogel, Martin. "The Co-op, Revolution and Public Leadership." *Vogel Wakefield*. 14 March 2014. Web. http://bit.ly/1uleIhB

Wallis, Stewart. "The Four Horsemen of Economics." *Yale Global Online,* 28 September 2011. Web. http://bit.ly/12thBWh

Watson, Tom. "Brand publicity and strategic communications are two different professions, says Bournemouth University's Prof Tom Watson". *PR Moment*, 21 February 2013. Web. http://bit.ly/1vOkvRw

Wauters, Robin. "Uber's Head of Public Policy EMEA Weighs into Disruption Debate." *Techeu,* 20 June 2014. Web. http://bit.ly/1vOp1iG

Wheatley, Martin. "Ethics and Economics." *Financial Conduct Authority*. 4 March 2014. Web. http://bit.ly/1vOp1iH

Willson-Rymer, Darcy. Interview with author. 30 August 2013.

Wojciechowicz, Dagmara. Interview with author. 4 March 2014.

Wolf, Martin. "A More Equal Society Will Not Hinder Growth – FT.com."*Financial Times*. 25 April 2014. Web. http://on.ft.com/1vE0fwL

Wolff, Michael. "Remember When Trust Actually Meant Something?" *USA Today*. Gannett, 6 January 2013. Web.http://usat.ly/1vOoYUa

Wood, Shawn Paul. "PR Is Dead! Long Live PR!" *PRNewser,* 20 March 2014. Web. http://bit.ly/1vOoYUb

Wright, Marc. "HSBC Exchanges Top down for Listening." *Simply-communicate*. N.p., Web. http://bit.ly/1vOoYUc

SUBSCRIBERS

Unbound is a new kind of publishing house. Our books are funded directly by readers. This was a very popular idea during the late eighteenth and early nineteenth centuries. Now we have revived it for the internet age. It allows authors to write the books they really want to write and readers to support the writing they would most like to see published.

The names listed below are of readers who have pledged their support and made this book happen. If you'd like to join them, visit: www.unbound.co.uk.

Adam Grodecki
Adam Parker
Alan Simpson
Alaric Mostyn
Alex Griffiths
Alex Waite
Alexis Wilson
Allie Wharf
Amanda Fone
Amanda Little
Amanda Mackenzie

Andrew Smith
Anja Schlicht
Anna Perkins
Ant Babajee
Arteveveldehogeschool Mediatheek
Arthur Sheriff
Ash Donaldson
Austin Brailey
Beth King
Beth Lewis
Brandon Brewer
Brian Lott
Caroline Warnes
Catherine Ackroyd
Catherine Stewart
Celine Schillinger
Charlie Dawson
Charlotte West
Chris Green
Chris Owen
Chris Rumfitt
Christian Seiersen
Christine Armstrong
Christine Jewell
Christopher Sampson
Claire Macaulay Martin
Cliff Oswick
Clyde McKendrick
Dagmara Wojciechowicz
Dan Kieran
Dan Slee
Daniel Courtouke
Daniela Jumanca
Darcy Willson-Rymer

Dario Mezzaqui
Darren Baguley
Darryl Sparey
David Chin
David Hughes
David Lea-Wilson
David Norris
David Sylvester
David Weinberger
Debbie Walters
Despo Ptohopoulos
Donald Steel
Dorothy Crenshaw
Eamon Clarkin
Eamonn Carey
Eb Adeyeri
Ed Cartwright
Eddie Coates-Madden
Emercoleman
Emma Coles
Emma Gannon
Erin Dente
Fiona Cierach
Fiorenza Lipparini
Fran Valmana
Frankie Farrell
Gary Harley
Gary Phillips
Gavin Griffiths
George Pitcher
Geraldine O'Neill
Gilly Jolliffe
Glenn Manoff
Grainne Byrne

Harender Branch
Henry Chevallier Guild
Herbert Heitmann
Hilary Gallo
Ian Maynard
Ian Walls
Igor Andronov
Inge Wallage
Ingmar de Gooijer
Isobel Frankish
Jack O'Dwyer
James Harkness
James Taylor
Jan Altink
Jason Korman
Jason MacKenzie
Jemima Gibbons
Jennifer Attias
Jeremy Cohen
Jim Hawker
Jim Woods
Jimmy Leach
Joe Kelly
Johannes Hvidsten
John Frewin
John Lloyd
John Peyton Cooke
John Urpeth
John Warehand
Jon Akass
Jon Alexander
Jon Dawson
Jorge Garzon
Joseph McKeating

Joseph Piper
Jules Peck
Julia Hobsbawm
Julie Winterton
Justin Pollard
Justine Roberts
Kandú Tapia
Karan Chadda
Karin Sebelin
Karren Harker
Katie Marlow
Katja Gehrmann-Weide
Kellan Palmer
Kelly-Anne Smith
Kinan Suchaovanich
Kristina Eriksson
Kristjan Kristjansson
Lee Nugent
Leon Halperin
Liam Faulkner
Liam Spinage
Lorraine Finnigan
Louise Leadbetter
Lynda Gratton
Malin Nilsson
Marcus Dyer
Marianne Hewlett
Marilyn Fancher
Marilynn Morgan Hill
Mark Borkowski
Mark Carbery
Mark Comerford
Mark Jones
Mark Wakefield

Mark Young
Marsha Iverson
Marshall Manson
Martin Vogel
Martina Stansbie
Matt Appleby
Matt Churchill
Matt Silver
Meg McAllister
Michael Lamb
Mick Howarth
Mike Love
Nadia Gabbie
Naomi Healy
Nathalie Masse
Neal Lawson
Neil Maedel
Neil Major
Neville Hobson
Nick Allen
Nick Blackburn
Nick Keppel-Palmer
Nicola Green
Nicole Gorfer
Nigel Rushman
Nikolaus Bourboulis
Oliver Hutt
Olivier Fleurot
Pål Karlsen
Paul Cheng
Paul Doran
Paul Durman
Paul Epstein
Paul Lockstone

Paul Wooding
Paul Zernitz
Pauline Godfrey
Pedro Pires
Peter Chadlington
Peter Gerdemann
Peter Hunt
Peter Paul van de Wijs
Peter Vander Auwera
Philippe Borremans
Pierre Finot
Prakash Mirpuri
Préface
PRmoment.com
Rachel Miller
Regina Urich
Rhys Fowler
Ric Hayman
Rich Teplitsky
Richard Bagnall
Richard Lander
Richard Martin
Rickard Andersson
Rob Gray
Robert M. Burnside
Robert Phillips
Robi Zocher
Robin Hamman
Rod Banner
Roxanne Wilson
Sally Atkinson
Sally Pain
Sam Whitaker
Sara Evans

Sara Galbraith
Sarah Feazey
Sarah Liang
Sarah Miles
Shao Wang
Sheila Hockin
Shweta Kulkarni Van Biesen
Simon Craven
Simon Hargreaves
Sinead Whooley
Sonia Afzal
Spencer Hyman
Stefan Stern
Stefano Maggi
Steffen Moller
Stephanie Forrest
Stephanie Mar
Stephanie Speck
Stephen Waddington
Steve Earl
Steve Falla
Steve Smith
Steven Spenser
Stuart McBride
Susan Phillips
Susan Simmonds
Susanne Kahle
Sylvain Perron
Tim Rich
Tina Groves
Tom Hashemi
Tom Murphy
Tony Wood
Val Millar

Venetia Rose
Veronica Benini
Victoria Daly
Vijay Solanki
Vilhelm Laursen
Warren Beckett
Will Spratt
Will Brown
Will Roberts
ZM
Zina & Stephen Sackur

INDEX

INDEX